DATE DUE

JAN 2 1 1995		
NOV 0 9 1995		
MAY 1 1 2004		
APR 2 5 2006		
GAYLORD		PRINTED IN U.S.A.

ECOPOLITICS

ECOPOLITICS
BUILDING A GREEN SOCIETY

DANIEL A. COLEMAN

RUTGERS UNIVERSITY PRESS

New Brunswick, New Jersey

Library of Congress Cataloging-in-Publication Data

Coleman, Daniel A., 1952–
   Ecopolitics : building a green society / by Daniel A. Coleman.
     p. cm.
   Includes bibliographical references.
   ISBN 0-8135-2054-1 (cloth) — ISBN 0-8135-2055-X (pbk.)
   1. Green movement. 2. Environmental policy—Social aspects.
   I. Title.
   GE195.C65 1993
   363.7'05—dc20

93-6029
CIP

British Cataloging-in-Publication information available

To my son, Elijah Coleman

CONTENTS

ECOPOLITICS

INTRODUCTION

A work on environmental politics in the United States can claim many starting points. Perhaps the earliest is the 1854 publication of *Walden*, by Henry Thoreau, which advocates forcefully for the importance of the experience of nature and wilderness. The conservation movement, the precursor of contemporary environmentalism, took form in 1892 with the founding of the Sierra Club. The environment as a political issue came of age in 1962 with the publication of Rachel Carson's *Silent Spring*, which described the devastating impact of industrial pollution on the natural world. Finally, many cite 1970, the year of the first Earth Day, which led to the Clean Air Act, the Clean Water Act, and the founding of the Environmental Protection Agency (EPA), as the galvanizing moment for environmentalism as a force to be reckoned with. From that point, the environment became an unavoidable concern for modern society.

Rather than these historic milestones, I prefer to set the stage for this work in 1989, which was perhaps an unprecedented year for the environment. The year began with *Time* magazine announcing that its prestigious " . . . of the year" award would go for the first time ever to a celestial body: Planet Earth. A few weeks later the first self-proclaimed "environmental president" took office. George Bush, of course, had swamped the Michael Dukakis campaign in the polluted waters of Boston Harbor. President Bush went on to appoint, for the first time, a professional environmentalist, William Reilly, then head of the World Wildlife Fund, to be administrator of the EPA.

In March, things turned sour, though the focus remained on the Earth. The *Exxon Valdez* spilled its millions of gallons of oil, which spread across the Gulf of Alaska, fouling beaches and killing vast numbers of wildlife. Fingers pointed everywhere while images of oil-mired marine fowl and toothbrush-wielding cleaning crews filled the evening news.

It was in this light that the American public began to learn of the coming twentieth-anniversary celebration of Earth Day. The first Earth Day, held in 1970, was an outpouring of national concern about the environment. This time, organizers were planning a massive international event to focus global attention on the Earth and to usher in what they declared would be "The Decade of the Environment."

They succeeded: by the time the April 22, 1990, event finally arrived, everyone and her brother had taken up the cause of environmentalism. Perhaps the biggest event in the United States since the

1976 bicentennial, Earth Day was celebrated by millions of people and supported by organizations ranging from 4-H clubs to the federal government, from local natural food stores to McDonald's. Rock 'n' roll, endless speeches, and widespread efforts at tree-planting and recycling marked the day.

Earth Day also spawned a number of books on the environment. Particularly popular were guides for personal action, including:

> *The Green Lifestyle Handbook: 1001 Ways You Can Heal the Earth,* by Jeremy Rifkin
>
> *Our Earth Ourselves: The Action-oriented Guide to Help You Protect and Preserve Our Environment,* by Ruth Caplan
>
> *Shopping for a Better World,* by the Council on Economic Priorities
>
> *50 Simple Things You Can Do to Save the Earth,* by the Earthworks Group

The last book proved to be a blockbuster best-seller. My reflections on its title helped to crystallize many years of research and activism and to catalyze the project that became *Ecopolitics: Building a Green Society.*

The title and thrust of *50 Simple Things* have some obvious implications. The first implication, of course, is that the planet needs saving. If there was any consensus on the twentieth anniversary of Earth Day, this was surely it. The second implication is that saving the planet depends on things that individuals can do. According to the title, there are a limited number of such things and they are simple to do. This is supported by a glance through the table of contents, which reveals chapters on such daily activities as recycling, saving water, and efficient gas-pumping techniques.

Viewed in this manner, *50 Simple Things* was born to succeed. Faced with a crisis, what could be better than to be able to resolve it through simple actions undertaken by individuals, primarily in their own homes and through changes in their day-to-day lifestyles?

Unfortunately, it's not quite that easy. Don't get me wrong: *50 Simple Things* and the other Earth Day best-sellers make an important contribution to developing environmental awareness. But those who want to apply more than Band-Aids to the bleeding Earth must look further. The conventional Earth Day approach of simple solutions to vast problems overlooks a number of important considerations.

The first Earth Day, in 1970, raised many of the same issues as its 1990 counterpart, spurring increased environmental awareness in the intervening years. Why then have most environmental problems worsened since that time? Indeed, the "simple things" approach entirely overlooks the question of why our society does such damage to the environment in the first place. An understanding of how we got where we are today is an important aspect of developing workable solutions.

Additionally, why have so many efforts aimed at environmental protection and at reversing environmental damage failed? Many programs involving government regulation, policy making, and enforcement are particularly noteworthy failures. For example, in the 1970s, the Superfund program identified over one thousand toxic-waste sites for cleanup. By 1990, fewer than one hundred of these "priority" sites had been completely cleaned. Although billions of dollars have been spent on environmental restoration and protection, the programs by and large have dealt only with symptoms, failing to attack the problem at its roots.

This volume, then, attempts to address the environmental crisis through an examination of its roots, seeking an understanding of its political, economic, and social underpinnings on which to build a program for change. My hope is that it will be as accessible as the various "save the Earth" guidebooks but that it will challenge the thinking of those who are concerned for the Earth, leading to more effective action and wiser stewardship.

Part One begins a search for the roots of the environmental crisis, examining how the three problem areas most commonly identified by conventional wisdom, while important, can be misconstrued or exaggerated, obscuring other fundamental concerns. Chapter 1 addresses the relationship between population growth and the environment. Rapidly increasing population is often made out to be the number-one cause of environmental destruction. This perspective overlooks the fact that much environmental damage, in particular atmospheric pollution and toxic-waste production, is caused by industrial nations whose populations are stable. In the world's less-developed nations, environmental and population problems develop in tandem, sharing a common source in poverty. As we search for solutions, it is important to remember the long history of both population stability and environmental stewardship based in once-sustainable communities in cultures around the world.

Chapter 2 takes a brief look at the history of society's relationship to technology, asking whether it is correct to view technology as responsible for our environmental woes or if, in fact, the environmental impact of technology is determined by the more fundamental values of society that guide technological development. Chapter 3 explores the responsibility of consumers for the current environmental crises and the extent to which our society provides citizens with the power to function as effective stewards of the earth. Through the analysis in these first chapters of the conventional view of our environmental predicament, three underlying elements are revealed: community, values, and power. These factors form the basis for Parts Two and Three.

Part Two continues the discussion of roots, offering an alternative to the conventional perspective, looking at the systemic and historic roots of the present crises, and examining three factors not covered in the lifestyle-oriented books. Chapter 4 examines the failure of movements for participatory democracy and the antiecological effect of concentrated power. Chapter 5 discusses how the narrow instrumental values of profit-centered capitalism, which dominates the global economy, undermine our ability to care for the Earth. Chapter 6 looks at the devastating social and ecological impact of treating land and labor as commodities. In each chapter an alternative is offered: participatory democracy to counter the impact of concentrated power; the development of broad, life-affirming values to counter the constricted values of capitalism; and cooperation and community to heal the alienation and fragmentation in contemporary society and in its relationship to the earth.

Finally, Part Three offers a philosophy and strategy rooted in personal and social responsibility to effectively channel concern for the environment in a way that will make a difference. What is sought is not just a program for protecting the Earth but a broad-based movement committed to a transformation to an ecological society. Chapter 7 discusses the formation of healthy, sustaining values on which to base environmental organizing. Chapter 8 develops an understanding of community and cooperation in an ecological context. Chapter 9 offers a conception of active citizenship as the foundation of a participatory, grassroots democratic society.

Chapter 10 ties these strands together with a discussion of Green politics as an approach that embodies the sense of "think globally, act locally." Green politics combines an understanding of the global and national dimensions of modern society with a grassroots approach based on local organizing and activism. The Green movement combines a commitment to a transformation to an ecological society over the long term with a transitional program aimed at more immediate short-term gains. While the Green movement as currently constituted may not be the formation that ultimately achieves an ecological society, it nonetheless provides an important model and point of departure for anyone concerned for the Earth. The discussion of Green politics draws on my own experience in both local and national organizing. Many of the problems, opportunities, and internal debates of the Green movement are presented from firsthand experience as the discussion moves from theory to practice. This chapter is not intended as advocacy for the Green movement but rather to provide an explanation of an approach to ecological politics that the Green movement is struggling to actualize.

Finally, Chapter 11 brings the principles of ecological politics into practice through the example of organizing for a sustainable energy policy. Out of the myriad issues that could be discussed, energy is selected both because of its direct relevance to all readers and because of its association with numerous environmental problems, including oil spills, global warming, and nuclear waste. The book closes with an afterword discussing time and how to cope with the sense of urgency that surrounds the environmental crises.

Throughout, I draw liberally on the thinking of a number of environmental and social theorists whose works provide additional resources for the reader. There are many people doing excellent work on the environment and related issues whose writing is either not widely available, not well known, or not written for a general audience. My hope is that the reader will appreciate the many references to those works and the citations in the notes as an introduction to a rich body of thought on politics and ecology.

The reader should be forewarned that this work will not describe how to pursue an "environmentally correct" lifestyle. There are plenty of books, such as those listed above, that provide that information. *Ecopolitics* also will not provide a laundry list of environmental problems and policy solutions. The reader's "favorite" environmental crisis may be addressed only in passing if at all. That discussion is available from others, with Worldwatch's annual *State of the World* report providing the most accessible and up-to-date source. Unfortunately, in spite of all the good information available on ecological living and environmentally sound policy, the destruction of the natural world continues. Provided here is an approach to environmental politics based on citizenship, participatory democracy, and community-based activism that will enable those concerned for the Earth to make a difference.

In this work, I refer to a variety of past societies and groups: the Iroquois, the Populists of the 1890s, or the peasant society of preindustrial Europe, to name a few. Although some environmentalists idealize and seek to emulate past societies, that is not the intention here. Anthropology and history hold much that is of value to the search for an ecologically harmonious way of life. Thus, we can appreciate the Iroquois' commitment to future generations, the democratic spirit of the Populists, or feudal Europe's preservation of much of nature in the form of common land. Yet these examples provide only a small part of the solution to the puzzle of ecological living in our own time. That solution also depends extensively on contemporary understandings of nature, society, and politics.

Ecopolitics will refer to a concept of a sustainable community that recognizes the interrelatedness of human society with its natural environs. That which is sustainable is often considered to be static, precluding change. But nature itself is dynamic and continually changing, sometimes slowly and imperceptibly and sometimes quite dramatically. For example, the coral reef is often celebrated as a mature and stable ecosystem, marked by a diversity of life-forms. Yet, once every couple hundred years or so it is likely to be ravaged by a tropical storm and must be reestablished. An ecological society will appreciate the dynamic balance between change and stability in the natural world and in human affairs. Many environmentalists see their goal as minimizing or even eliminating human impact on the Earth. This perspective overlooks the fact that any species—a worm, an ant, an elephant—has a profound influence on the world around it. Human activity has already, over many millennia, shaped and reshaped the world we live in. At the heart of an ecological way of life will be the ability of human society to temper its impact on the natural world with an appreciation of the mystery and complexity of life that surrounds and includes us.

The subject of this book is, broadly speaking, the interplay between politics and ecology. The term "politics" is not used in the conventional twentieth-century American sense of two parties jockeying for power. Rather it harks back to a politics that is part of the day-to-day life of citizens, as understood in the Greek origin of the term in the *polis* (city-state) of ancient Athens. It conveys the sense of an active citizenry engaged in a community-based process of democratic self-government. This image of a community of citizens evokes the sense of home contained linguistically in the term "ecology" through its Greek root *oikos* (house). Thus, the goal of this book is to present ecopolitics as a way of life: an ecological way of life based on a renewal of citizenship and community and an understanding of the Earth as our home.

The first stages of writing this book coincided with the stationing of American and international troops in Saudi Arabia to guard the oil fields from Iraqi armies. That conflict, of course, led to great loss of life as well as vast economic and environmental cost. The tragic irony is that if efforts begun in the 1970s to develop alternative fuels and energy efficiency had been maintained and increased, the tone of this crisis would have been quite different if, in fact, it had occurred at all.

We find in thinking about the environment that those systems and policies which hurt the Earth (for example, the oil economy) are usually implicated in a variety of other economic, political, and social problems as well. Ultimately, the crusade to save the planet must bring us home to find a better way of living for ourselves, our communities, and our species, based on the understanding that our political life as citizens and the natural ecology on which we depend are intimately bound together.

I

THE SEARCH FOR ROOTS

CONVENTIONAL WISDOM

Chapter *1*

THE SPECTER OF
POPULATION GROWTH

*Be fruitful, and multiply, and replenish the
earth, and subdue it.*—Genesis 1:28

This first of many commands found in the Bible ties population
growth directly to the mastering of the Earth. But today, unfortunately, to subdue the Earth seems to be to destroy it. In the
minds of many, the link is direct: it is the burgeoning human
population that imperils the global environment. The prolifera-
tion of human beings seems to threaten not just our own species but the entire ecosphere with extinction. While it is
certainly true that a rapidly increasing global population and
unprecedented environmental destruction are both characteristics of the modern era, it is not as clear that one is fundamentally the cause of the other. Each, while affecting the other,
may be seen as more directly resulting from the development,
structures, and organization of modern society. A look at both
the nature of population growth and the actual sources of environmental damage can clarify this relationship.

The War against Population Growth

Although 1968 is remembered by most as the year of the
assassinations of Martin Luther King, Jr., and Robert Kennedy,
the year when Chicago police rioted with antiwar demonstra-
tors outside the Democratic national convention, and the year
of the election of Richard Nixon to the presidency, it was also

the beginning of the latest round of the population wars. That year, Paul Ehrlich published *The Population Bomb,* placing the threat of global population growth firmly in the popular consciousness. Like Saint Paul en route to Damascus, Ehrlich received his prophetic vision on the road:

> I have understood the population problem intellectually for a long time. I came to understand it emotionally one stinking hot night in Delhi a few years ago. My wife and daughter and I were returning to our hotel in an ancient taxi. The seats were hopping with fleas. The only functional gear was third. As we crawled through the city, we entered the crowded slum area. The temperature was well over 100 degrees F.; the air was a haze of dust and smoke. The streets seemed alive with people. People eating, people washing, people sleeping. People visiting, arguing and screaming. People thrusting their hands through the taxi window begging. People defecating and urinating. People clinging to busses. People herding animals. People, people, people. As we moved slowly through the mob, hand horn squawking, the dust, noise, heat and cooking fires gave the scene a hellish aspect. Would we ever get to our hotel? All three of us were, frankly, frightened. It seemed that anything could happen—but, of course, nothing did. Old India hands will laugh at our reaction. We were just some over-privileged tourists, unaccustomed to the sights and sounds of India. Perhaps, but since that night I've known the feel of over-population.[1]

So well did Ehrlich capture the imagination and fears of the American public that *The Population Bomb* went through thirteen printings in two years.

Population growth had, of course, been an issue in the nineteenth century, with Thomas Malthus's predictions of a geometrically increasing population rapidly outstripping arithmetically increasing food supplies. Like Ehrlich, Malthus was moved by the sight of teeming masses, although in his case it was the specter of the impoverished people of industrializing England.

Analogous to Malthus's bias in stigmatizing the English lower classes, Ehrlich's statement has a clear implication of cultural chauvinism, if only in his choosing to describe a crowded street in Delhi rather than a similar scene in, say, ethnically heterogeneous Manhattan (where taxi rides are no great joy either). The result is that Ehrlich, a biologist by training, rather unscientifically introduces his argument with an appeal to our emotions in the form of the discomfort an American audience feels with Third World crowds and poverty. Such an appeal to bias in regard to the population problem is not uncommon. On the cover of its issue previewing the 1992 "Earth Summit" in Rio, the *Economist* called population "The Question Rio Forgets."[2] The accompanying photograph is not of the teeming millions of London, the *Economist*'s home city, but instead depicts a group of hungry-looking, brown-faced Third World children.

For Ehrlich, population growth is not just one problem among many for twentieth-century humanity. In fact, it threatens a catastrophe of vast scale in the history of the planet. Ehrlich calls the population bomb the most significant event of the past "million millennia," as he describes a burgeoning mass of humanity threatening the Earth with thermonuclear bombs and DDT.[3] Ehrlich never explains how such threats are attributable to population growth. If "mankind" threatens the planet with catastrophic weapons, would "Spaceship Earth" be less threatened if those weapons were wielded by fewer people? For example, if our nuclear arsenal were deployed by one billion rather than five billion humans, would the planet be any safer? For Ehrlich, what humans do and how we live is of secondary importance. Primarily, it is the numbers that count.

Nonetheless, population had become an issue, for its threat of starvation and poverty, for its threat to the environment, and for the threat to First World high-consumption lifestyles seen in the hungry eyes of our dark-skinned neighbors in the Southern Hemisphere. Or, as Ehrlich's description of his trip to the Delhi hotel metaphorically asks, will we privileged tourists arrive safely at our luxury accommodations?

Fear of population growth has stayed with us over the years. Ehrlich was joined a few years later by the Club of Rome, which published its controversial *Limits to Growth,* warning that at the then-current level of growth, the population limit of the planet would be reached sometime in the twenty-first century.[4] In 1989, in its "Planet of the Year" issue, *Time* magazine tied population growth directly to environmental destruction, reporting that "exponential growth in the human population . . . could doom the earth as a human habitat."[5] *Scientific American* later that year agreed, asserting that "the exponential growth of population and its attendant assault on the environment is so recent that it is difficult for people to appreciate how much damage is being done."[6] Note that both *Time* and *Scientific American* raise the Malthusian specter of "exponential growth" in population. This is a red herring. While population is some areas has increased dramatically, an actual exponential increase has not been maintained.

Certainly Paul Ehrlich deserves much credit for bringing a critical issue to popular awareness, and one might be inclined to forgive him the bias and hyperbole of his early works. But unfortunately he has stayed true over the years not only to his convictions but to his doomsday rhetoric as well.[7] In 1990, he and his wife Anne published *The Population Explosion*, maintaining that the population bomb described twenty years earlier had finally detonated. The book jacket explains that overpopulation is our number-one problem, overshadowing global warming, rain forest destruction, famine, and air and water pollution.

Today, the images of population pressure are familiar. One writer in the *Time* "Planet of the Year" issue described the "swarms of settlers, slashing and burning huge swaths through the forest" in Brazil's previously "unspoiled showcase."[8] Another *Time* article described a barrio in Mexico City in which two bathrooms serve a hundred people as "the odor of grease and sewage permeates the air. Flies buzz relentlessly."[9] Again, as in the initial quote from Ehrlich, we know "the feel of overpopulation."

In spite of Paul Ehrlich and his followers, the link between population growth and the environment remains as controversial as Malthus's conclusions were in the last century. When one looks at the actual sources of major pollutants and the forces driving such problems as deforestation and species loss, the focus on population growth begins to appear as a way for Western society to avoid responsibility for its own environmental legacy both at home and around the globe. While Third World peoples have confronted and must continue to confront the issue of population growth for their own sake, we in the industrial nations, while supporting them in those efforts, must take a hard look at the pressures our own wasteful and extravagant way of life places on the rest of the world.

Which Population Hurts the Earth?

While most of the population explosion is taking place in the developing nations, most environmental damage, particularly that with global ramifications, is caused by industrial nations whose populations are today fairly stable. Thus we find, for example, that ozone-killing chlorofluorocarbons are emitted from the air conditioners, Styrofoam production, and aerosols of the industrial nations. Unfortunately, much of the environmental impact of the activity of the developed nations is felt in the impoverished nations of the Third World. Toxic garbage leaves industrial ports and travels on barges around the world seeking a burial site, most likely in a cash-hungry Third World nation. Toxic pesticides, banned for use in the industrial nations, are still sold in developing nations. As recently as 1991, the chief economist of the World Bank maintained that Third World nations are "underpolluted" and should accept the transfer of toxic waste from industrial nations.

Much of the damage genuinely rooted in the Third World is the result of First World economic development programs that export environmentally destructive policies. Historically, global economic institutions such as the World Bank and the International Monetary Fund (IMF) have offered developing nations incentive programs that encourage environmentally destructive chemical-dependent agriculture and monocropping aimed at export rather than self-sufficiency.[10] Additionally, the pressures on Third World nations to compete in the global economy and to escape their notorious burden of international debt lead to large-scale agriculture based on an ever-decreasing number of jobs rather than small-scale family farming oriented toward self-reliance. Giant agribusinesses farm vast tracts of land that were previously forested or subject to diverse use by a self-reliant population. Those uprooted and displaced from traditional ways of life are forced to settle on marginally productive land in hopes of eking out a living. Consequently, forests fall, species are lost, deserts spread, and atmospheric carbon dioxide increases, leading to global warming. When the global dynamics of environmental degradation are considered, it is clear that Third World population could stabilize tomorrow with negligible effect on environmental problems such as global warming, ozone destruction, and toxic-waste production and with only a moderate effect on the problems associated with deforestation.

In spite of this, while today it is First World automobiles that release the pollutants which contribute to acid rain, the finger remains pointed at the Third World: what if justice prevails and those billions of people reach Western levels of prosperity? Won't all those additional cars, refrigerators, and electric power plants deliver the final blow to the global environment?

The answer here lies in pointing the finger back at ourselves and remembering the ancient adage "Physician, heal thyself." A focus on potential Third World drivers neatly distracts us from the fact that we're already choking on our own exhausts. For example, a study projected that by the year 2010 deteriorating air quality will contribute to 100,000 deaths per year in Los Angeles alone.[11]

As the industrial nations introduced toxic pollution to the world, they are now both uniquely positioned for creating and in dire need of establishing a healthy basis for human sustenance and well-being. It is up to the industrial nations to turn their wealth and knowledge to the task of developing a sustainable economy based on nonpolluting technology. Simultaneously, international agencies must establish programs to promote such an economy worldwide. These programs would include in their mission the empowerment of people around the world to determine and attain a desirable level of population. It is possible for social and economic justice to arrive hand-in-hand with population stability and a healthy environment.

Population and Poverty

Still, it must be recognized that, in much of the world, burgeoning population is taking its toll on the environment. The slash-and-burn practices of those seeking to enlarge their arable land area lead to soil erosion, desertification, and increased atmospheric carbon dioxide. Large populations can foul the water with their wastes and the air with their exhausts. The destruction of rain forests by expanding tropical societies threatens numerous species with extinction. But even as much of the environmental damage in the developing nations is exported by the West either directly or through international market pressures, so too Third World population growth results from the intrusive nature of the global economy that disrupts previously stable societies and prevents them from achieving a new balance. In many ways, both population growth and environmental destruction are symptoms of the same basic disease. For the Third World, that disease is the modern experience of poverty and dependency by previously self-reliant people. The poverty in question is not the seeming poverty of those "primitive" peoples with a vibrant culture and sustainable lifestyle who nonetheless lack the technological amenities of industrial society. Rather, it is the poverty of people who have been deprived of the economic means required to sustain themselves.

A major factor in the population explosion is the disruption of the pattern of demographic transition by global market relations. Demographic transition is a four-stage theory of population that particularly applies to the industrialization of Europe and North America from the eighteenth through the twentieth centuries.[12] Stage 1 is a preindustrial society with a stable population due to the combination of a high birthrate and a high death rate. In stage 2, industrialization brings an improved standard of living with the opportunity for improved hygiene and medical care leading to a decrease in mortality and therefore, since the birthrate remains high, to an increase in population. However, stage 3 requires a further improvement in living standards, which leads finally to a reduction in birthrates. The fourth stage entails a once again stable population based on low birth and death rates. Developing nations have experienced stage 2, but since neocolonialism deprives them of the wealth from their own industrialization, stage 3 is reached only slowly if at all. Thus, population growth continues unabated. To reach the last stage, neocolonialism and self-serving international aid programs must give way to an economy aimed at the needs of the local populace, lifting them out of poverty.

An example of the impact of economics on population is

found in the effect of British colonialism on the population of the Parsees in India. In 1881, the Parsees were the fastest-growing segment of the Indian population. At that time, they were chosen by the British as their agents in India. With the success of the East India Company and of the British Empire, their status and economic condition rapidly improved. The result was that by 1961, while the general population of India continued to grow, the Parsee population was declining.[13]

Poverty's impact on population growth is associated with psychological, cultural, and social forces. On an individual level, poverty can lead to an emphasis on reproduction as a source of self-esteem. Thus teenagers may have children as a way of demonstrating competency and adulthood. Society's denial of security, status, and opportunity, particularly for Third World women, often makes large families the only source of dignity, meaning, and hope for the future.[14] Poverty also denies millions access to birth-control devices and health care that could lead to fewer and healthier babies. To end the population crisis, we must end poverty.[15] From this perspective, Ehrlich's "feel of over-population" (that is, heat, stench, fleas, and run-down taxis) may be more accurately viewed as the "feel of poverty."

Efforts at population control are undermined by the paternalistic point of view of Western society. The West looks at the burgeoning population of the Third World and sees only the need to limit reproduction. The Third World looks at the same conditions but sees the need for food, shelter, work, and a successful economy. Yet for the West it is population growth that is seen as preventing the achievement of these social and economic goals. The West blames the victims, viewing the impoverished people of the world as reaping the results of their own reproductive excesses. For the West, the task of taking historic responsibility for colonialism (and neocolonialism) and of rectifying the resulting economic imbalance is not one readily accepted. But imposing our standard of family size on other people without our standard of educational, economic, and political opportunity is futile, cruel, and absurd.

To draw an analogy, like environmental damage, world hunger has often been attributed to overpopulation. However, those analyzing global agricultural and food distribution practices have found this to be more of a political than a population problem.[16] Vegetarians know that a meat diet consumes many times more protein in raising the animals than is actually produced by them. Moving from the top of the food chain to a vegetarian diet has been suggested as one way to end world hunger. Additionally, much of the Third World grows food for export rather than for local consumption. Global agribusiness and export-oriented agriculture lead to monocropping and to the loss of well-adapted, high-yield native vegetable species that could nourish the indigenous populations. The profits from the labors of peasant farmers, rather than ensuring their own sustenance, go to distant corporations. Thus, the roots of world hunger are found in a variety of political, economic, historic, and cultural factors, all of which would not be in any way directly remedied by a reduction in population.

Like hunger, population growth is itself rooted in global power relations, both economic and political, particularly as they affect the social and cultural lives of poor people. In the modern world, population growth and its associated environmental stresses derive from such factors as concentration of land ownership, colonial patterns of taxation and cash-cropping, aid programs that undermine traditionally well-adapted systems, and profiteering. The same economic and political forces that lead to industrial pollution in the developed nations destabilize the cultures and economies of the developing world, leading to population increases and consequent pressures on the environment.

Whether a complex pattern of political, economic, and cultural factors is seen as underlying the contemporary population explosion, or the cause is viewed simply as poverty, the solution remains the same: developing the economic self-sufficiency and political capacity of the world's underclass. To diminish Third World impacts on the environment will require a program of ecologically sustainable economic development for those impoverished peoples. Family planning will be an important part of a successful program, but only one part among many. Even more vital is the political and economic empowerment of the poor peoples of the world who are experiencing high rates of population growth. This must be placed in the context of a culture that values people for who they are, for their efforts and accomplishments, not merely for their material property or reproductive capacity. Although population growth can greatly exacerbate environmental problems, increasing population and environmental destruction develop in tandem, the result of common historic forces. They can be resolved only by a willingness to go to the social, political, and economic roots of the problem.

Population and Community

It is instructive to look back at the history of Third World and even Western nations, to see how various cultures functioned over the centuries in relation to both population growth and the natural environment. What we find is that, prior to the modern era, many societies maintained through their indigenous culture the mechanisms both for a stable population and for a healthy relationship to their natural environs.

European family planning practices were well established and quite successful prior to the modern era. Studies of England, Italy, and the Netherlands ranging from the sixteenth to the nineteenth centuries reveal a cultural ethos of population stability. Methods included chastity, rhythm birth control, coitus interruptus (withdrawal), and coitus reservatus (male restraint of ejaculation). These various methods were part of the socialization process of men as well as women. Skillfulness in birth-control techniques was often an important component of self-esteem.[17] Cultural traditions and mores, such as the socially expected age of marriage or the ability of a widow to remarry, limited population growth while also varying over time to adapt to the reproductive requirements of society.

Contemporary anthropological studies from around the world also reveal an astonishing array of indigenous population control practices.[18] The Dani of Indonesia practice four to six years of sexual abstinence after the birth of a child, without any apparent distress. Taboos in New Guinea require sexual abstinence during the growing season to ensure a successful yam harvest. The Burmese population has been limited by a strictly ascetic form of Buddhism that represses sexual desire and pleasure. The Yoruba in Nigeria typically are sexually abstinent until approximately six months after the cessation of lactation, a period of about three years. The marketing of infant formula in

Nigeria undermines this age-old system. Thus, around the world and historically, societies have struggled successfully to keep their numbers in balance with available resources, making the means for population control an intrinsic feature of their cultures.[19]

This historic stability was shattered at the onset of a modern era characterized by the dominance of capitalist economics, rapid technological innovation, and the intrusion of European civilization throughout the world.[20] These developments undermined traditional peasant communities and drove landless workers to industrial centers in search of jobs or to marginal lands in search of an elusive subsistence. The ability to limit population was bound up in the traditions, culture, knowledge, and practices of self-reliant communities. Such communities, even at a subsistence level, valued a quality of life that led to a limiting of family size. Traditional practices maintained a birthrate that generally matched the mortality rate. When conditions would support an increase in population, say through climate change or the introduction of new foods or improved agricultural techniques, these customs would slowly evolve, allowing population to grow.[21] Throughout the modern era, beginning in western Europe and spreading around the planet, this heritage was uprooted by the pressures the expanding market economy placed on traditional ways of life. Regardless of one's view of the cause and consequences of population growth, the destruction of self-reliant communities, with their traditional ethos of population control, removed an important social capacity to respond to such changes.

The loss of these traditional cultures also represents the loss of a historically successful way of living in relation to the Earth. A small-scale, self-reliant, locally oriented way of life with an emphasis on indigenous culture and community also encourages stewardship of the natural world. Anthropologists have used the term *ecological equilibrium* to describe a society in which the population level is maintained in harmony with the natural environment through cultural forms that value the stability and sustainability of the human community.[22] Societies in ecological equilibrium understand the carrying capacity of their ecological setting and maintain a way of life that simultaneously preserves both environment and community. Thus, for premodern societies, population control and ecological sensitivity are two aspects of a sustainable way of life.

When a people's well-being relies on a local water supply, local soil fertility, and local food supplies, these natural resources tend to be carefully protected. When such a community does engage in environmentally destructive practices, the impact tends to be local.[23] The activity of community-based enterprise does not have the global ramifications of the operations of multinational corporations. But just as modern society has undermined traditional family planning, it has eroded an age-old record of human care for the natural environment, similarly based in sustainable communities committed to ecological equilibrium.

Our contemporary environmental and population problems will be solved together through a renewed understanding of ecological equilibrium in a contemporary context. An understanding of community and its attendant values of self-reliance, cooperation, stability, and stewardship will prove to be fundamental in developing the vision of an ecologically wise culture and in establishing an environmentally responsible society. As the industrialized nations seek a sustainable and self-reliant way of life for themselves, they will remove the pressures of the global economy from the rest of the world. This, coupled with international aid programs geared toward self-reliant, ecologically sustainable development, will empower the developing nations to tackle their own economic and population problems in an environmentally sensitive manner.

Chapter 2

DOES TECHNOLOGY HARM THE EARTH? CAN TECHNOLOGY SAVE IT?

The explanation of our present difficulties as mainly due to over-population applies only to local concentrations. For immediate ecological improvements, power control, mass-production control, rubbish control, and pollution control are more imperative than birth control.
—*Lewis Mumford,* The Pentagon of Power

With this statement, the social critic Lewis Mumford neatly turns our attention from population to technology.[1] To many, technology is seen as the driving force in the environmental crisis. To others, it is the potential source of salvation. Such a focus on technology is nothing new. Like concern about population, concern about the effects of technology is rooted in the early nineteenth century, when the upheavals of the industrial revolution were changing the way of life for western Europeans. These early concerns were not expressed by environmentalists, but came instead from working people who resented the new machines that deprived them of independent work and drove them into the factories. They were angry at the loss of control over their time, their tools, and their products. Their self-worth as well as their economic well-being was threatened.

Between 1811 and 1816, workers in England rioted and broke machinery in protest against industrialization and the factory system. They signed their leaflets "Ned Ludd" or "General Ludd," a name thought to be derived from a Leicester youth named Ludlam, who, when ordered to square his needles, instead rebelliously took up a hammer and broke them. Today, those who question technological innovation, whether scientifically or merely in a knee-jerk manner, tend to be dismissed with the pejorative label of "Luddite."

While British workers were smashing looms, across the channel the German writer Johann Wolfgang von Goethe recounted the fable of the sorcerer's apprentice. This tale, well known to Americans from Walt Disney's animated feature *Fantasia,* depicts a magician's apprentice who uses a simple spell to bring a broom and bucket to life to do his chores for him. The tools quickly grow beyond the apprentice's control until they finally threaten to drown him. He is saved only by the return of the stern and powerful sorcerer.

This story presents an apt image for an analysis of our modern relationship with technology. On the one hand, it tells of technology out of control, endangering the uninitiated. On the other, it reassures us that the master of technology will save us in the end. It is more hopeful than the story of Frankenstein's monster, (written at about the same time), which conveys the message that there can be no safety until the dangerous creation is destroyed. Much like the broom of the sorcerer's apprentice, which seems to have a mind of its own, technology somehow seems to follow its own rules, beyond the comprehension of the mere human beings who hope to benefit from it.

Arguably the leading environmentalist in the United States, Barry Commoner is one who, throughout a diverse and important body of work, has focused extensively on science and technology as both cause and cure of the environmental crises. Although Commoner is not one who has overlooked the political dimension, even running as Citizens party candidate for president in 1980 and registering in California's nascent Green party in 1991, he nonetheless believes that changes in technology since the Second World War are a root cause of modern environmental woes, accounting for over 80 percent of total output of pollutants.[2] His condemnation of technology is quite severe, as he insists that "ecological failure is apparently a necessary consequence of the nature of modern technology"[3] and calls for a comprehensive transformation of the present systems of production.[4]

While Commoner maintains faith in the possibility of a "comprehensive transformation" of present systems, there are those who proudly wear the Luddite label. Earth First! activists often argue that since technology is the problem, let's get rid of it. This view is exemplified by their bumpersticker slogan "Back to the Pleistocene," which explicitly calls for a return to a pretechnological era. In the book *Eco-defense*, a handbook for Earth First! activists, the publisher is listed as Ned Ludd Press, a direct homage to their nineteenth-century forebears. If Commoner calls on the wise sorcerer to transform our technology, these radical environmentalists prefer to destroy Frankenstein's monster.

Is Technology the Solution?

Today, genuine Luddites are still a rare breed. The conventional understanding is that if it is technology that got us into this mess, then certainly the way out is through better technology. Most environmental scientists call not for the comprehensive transformation advocated by Commoner but for a piecemeal reform of technology to rectify particular problems. This approach was exemplified in a special issue of *Scientific American* dedicated to "Managing Planet Earth," which maintained that "many of the adverse effects of industrialization have been brought under control by further applications of technology."[5] President Richard Nixon, in a State of the Union message, proposed to solve the environmental crisis by mobilizing the energy "of the same reservoir of inventive genius that created those problems in the first place."[6] Like Nixon, those with faith in the march of progress generally hold that any problem created by technology can be solved by further applications thereof.

A case in point is the expectation that it is only a matter of time before the problem of radioactive nuclear waste is solved. In the 1950s, the United States, followed shortly by other nations, embarked on an ambitious program to develop nuclear power. Launched by President Dwight D. Eisenhower as the

Atoms for Peace program, it included the now-notorious promise of electricity "too cheap to meter."

Omitted from this rosy picture was the problem of radioactive waste, the unfortunate by-product of nuclear power. Plutonium in particular, perhaps the deadliest poison known, must be safely stored for tens of thousands of years. The unwieldy reactor cores, when their active life of thirty years or so is over, are themselves highly contaminated and require complicated dismantling, transport, and long-term safe storage.

Decades after Atoms for Peace, the waste continues to pile up. The nuclear industry and its attendant scientists persevere in assuring the public about the problem of radioactive-waste disposal. However, the successful outcome they optimistically predict continues to elude them. Nonetheless, faith in the technological solution accompanies the enthusiastic call for a new generation of "safe" nuclear power plants.

Those who are more measured in their embrace of technology generally look toward the adopting of environmentally benign methods. Barry Commoner, for example, believes that scientific analysis can develop technology that is consistent with environmental well-being.[7] Commoner quite properly advocates organic agriculture, the use of photovoltaic cells for generating electricity, and strategies for replacing petrochemicals, all of which employ immediately available, environmentally favorable technologies. Vice President Al Gore follows Commoner's example, calling for the United States to boost its economy by taking the lead in developing environmentally safe technology.

While the proposals of Commoner and Gore have much to commend them and will be an important part of a program for ecological renewal, their point of view leaves out a critical consideration. If both benign and destructive technologies are available, it is important to understand the factors that have caused destructive technology to proliferate in the past. Why, for example, does petrochemical-based agriculture proliferate while organic agriculture remains a fringe activity? We must examine the qualities of modern society, not just of modern science, that have led repeatedly to the development and acceptance of environmentally damaging technology. Only then can we be sure that we can chart a successful course to adopt healthy technologies in the future. Only by looking back at the history of technology to see how we got where we are today, can we understand our options for moving forward.

Preindustrial Technics

The ancient Greeks made no distinction between technology and art. They, along with other preindustrial societies, viewed *techne,* or technics, as an integral part of a life-centered culture.[8] Preindustrial societies were generally characterized by what Lewis Mumford termed "poly-technics," a diverse application of technology embedded in the cultural and ethical sensibilities of the community.

While today our faith in a benevolent technology insists that if something can be created, it should be created, earlier societies sought to understand the impact of new technologies on their way of life and on the Earth. A strict traditionalism that seems quaint to us today often served to protect the stability of the community and to maintain a way of life that was in harmony with the Earth. The point of this comparison is not to romanticize a lost way of life. Rather it is to make it clear that our modern faith in technology as a universal good is a recent development and not necessarily always a healthy one.

Prior to the industrial era, technics developed within the context of social relations and political structures, all of which were understood holistically.[9] Preindustrial technics, like the community itself, was closely related to the natural ecology of the immediate locale.[10] Anthropological literature is filled with descriptions of primitive societies in a state of ecological equilibrium, balancing population with the carrying capacity of the natural environs through an ecologically sustainable way of life. Such societies maintained a commitment to a technology suitable to cultural and ecological stability and showed little interest in technological innovation, preferring instead to focus on leisure pursuits such as arts, crafts, and a dynamic community life.[11] The sensitivity that is sought today by supporters of organic gardening or "appropriate technology" was an integral part of the life of preindustrial people. Their organically rooted technics persisted until the dawn of the modern era, at which time the development of technics was still constrained by "a richly communal social matrix, a deep respect for diversity, and a strong emphasis on quality, skill, and artfulness."[12] Many preindustrial societies maintained a way of life, often for centuries, with stable social forms and minimal destructive impact on the environment. Where environmental damage did occur, for example as a result of excessive logging to produce building material, fuel, or farmland, the impact was local and limited in scope.

Since the beginning of the scientific revolution during the time of Bacon, Descartes, Galileo, and Newton, the organic sensibility of technics has been eroded and lost. The modern era brought with it a fundamental change in world-view, in humanity's conception of itself, in its relation to nature, and in its understanding and use of technology.

The Scientific Revolution

Many volumes have been written about the origins and development of the scientific and industrial revolutions. The scientific revolution from the outset explicitly pitted humanity against nature. René Descartes described the goal of scientific inquiry as being quite simply to "make ourselves masters and possessors of nature."[13]

Francis Bacon criticized the ancient Greeks for a "wisdom [that] abounds in words but is barren of works."[14] In its search for such works, much of the philosophy, theory, and experimentation of the Renaissance defied the common-sense approach of the Middle Ages. This change in orientation is exemplified by Galileo's experiments with gravity.[15] Throughout the Middle Ages, the belief was held that heavy objects would reach the ground faster than light ones. They were thought to be returning home to the dense center of the earth and were excited and in a hurry to get there. Galileo's assertion that heavy and light objects fell at the same speed introduced a new idea: that material objects had no purpose or any properties other than those tangible ones that could be concretely measured by science. By abandoning the question of why the phenomenon occurs, Galileo finds the scientific breakthrough in the more instrumental search for how it occurs. This, perhaps, is the cornerstone of the modern era.

This change in orientation is justifiably termed a revolution, representing a way of viewing the world that is completely at odds with that of most people through the vast majority of human history. Certainly the attributing of purpose to falling objects is foreign to our modern understanding (although a number of contemporary environmental thinkers are engaged in an endeavor to assign a purpose and value to other life-forms and even to the inorganic components of the planet).

Major changes in scientific perspective like that found at the beginning of the modern era are generally viewed as paradigm shifts, as defined by Thomas Kuhn. In *The Structure of Scientific Revolutions*, Kuhn described the history of science as a succession of paradigms, a paradigm being a coherent scientific tradition or an accepted model or pattern.[16] A change in paradigms begins with a buildup of contradictions to the currently accepted paradigm. In Kuhn's theory, a scientific revolution takes the form of a paradigm shift, which occurs when the contradictions grow so great that the dominant paradigm is overturned and a new one takes its place. Thus, classical physics is replaced by Newtonian physics, which in its turn is replaced by relativity theory. Kuhn's model applies here in that the scientific revolution was not a gradual evolution in human knowledge but rather was an abrupt change. However, its origins lie beyond the scope of the scientific discipline in a paradigm shift with social and economic underpinnings. The scientific revolution cannot be properly understood without considering the economic and social context that nurtured and sustained it.

In effect, science and technology had historically been held in check by an ethic that shunned accumulation and embedded economics and technics in a holistic understanding of community, including the natural environment.[17] Economic activity and the technology that supported it had been geared toward the sustenance of the community and the maintenance of its way of life. It was the birth of modern capitalism in the late Middle Ages and the development of the market economy that unleashed technical development as it loosed the forces of acquisitiveness, materialism, and self-interest. The rise of capitalism, with its imperative toward growth and its removal of economic activity from the restricting confines of the community, released the forces of science and technology in service to an expanding economy.[18] Personal profiteering, previously considered a sin, became the greatest goal. No longer carefully developed in a broad ethical context, technological innovation, geared toward the improved efficiency of the productive apparatus, became an end in itself. Capitalism ended the relatively stable social relations of the feudal period and ushered in an era whose paramount goal was the accumulation of wealth. This new materialistic orientation was not narrowly limited to the development of organic technics into mechanical technology or to the shift of one scientific paradigm to another. The pervasiveness of this change is now a matter of cliché: turn on the television and, regardless of the program, you will likely be watching an extended advertisement for a life of acquisition of wealth and artifacts and for the apparent power and status that accompany conspicuous accumulation and the trappings of the high-tech lifestyle.

As technology was applied to the process of production, the human world-view became increasingly organized in mechanical terms. Social organization adapted to the mechanistic order of the workplace until even the human person came to be understood through the metaphor of the machine.[19] The extent of this can be seen in the writings of Buckminster Fuller, inventor of the geodesic dome and a firm believer in bettering the human condition through technology. Fuller wrote what is perhaps the ultimate high-tech definition of humanity as soulless machine. An excerpt is enough to give a sense of his page-long description of the human person as an amalgamation of mechanical systems.

> Man? A self-balancing, 28-jointed adapter-base biped, an electro-chemical reduction plant, integral with the segregated stowages of special energy extracts in storage batteries, for subsequent actuation of thousands of hydraulic and pneumatic pumps, with motors attached; 62,000 miles of capillaries, millions of warning-signal, railroad and conveyer systems; crushers and cranes . . . et cetera.[20]

Fuller would probably consider "woman" as well as "man" to be little more than an "adapter-base biped." He was writing shortly before recent efforts to free language from its sexist heritage. Nonetheless, it is instructive to remember that the scientific revolution we are discussing dovetailed neatly with the murder of vast numbers of women during the late Middle Ages for the alleged practice of witchcraft. Some feminist scholars have interpreted the persecution of women as necessary for the destruction of the "old organic worldview," rooted as it was in home and community, as modern society took form with a subordination of women and nature that went hand in hand.[21] In this interpretation, the violent ascendancy of an abstract patriarchal world-view over an immanent nature-based spirituality helped open the door to a modern era in which the defiling of the earth followed close on the heels of the debasement of women. In this light, Fuller's use of the male pronoun may be unfortunately appropriate.

Today, though few might fully embrace Fuller's stark definition, the ascendancy of technology is virtually complete. The ultimate technological credo was aptly expressed by the mathematician John von Neumann, who proclaimed that "technological possibilities are irresistible to man. If man can go to the moon, he will. If he can control the climate, he will."[22] It is perhaps not too cynical to add, "If he can destroy the planet, he will."

This widespread acceptance of the scientific paradigm would lead one to expect that each technological advance would be understood and received as an improvement in the lot of humanity. On the contrary, the developers of new technology have often had to go to great lengths to gain public acceptance of their products. Mass marketing of everything from cameras to nuclear power plants is well known. The marketing of infant formula to Africans who lacked the clean water or the knowledge to utilize it properly contrasts with economists' claims of production driven by consumer demand.

When marketing alone is not enough, outright conspiracies are found within the parameters of "business as usual." Particularly notorious is the history of the automobile and oil industries creating holding companies to buy up and destroy trolley systems in the 1930s and 1940s in order to promote gas-powered transportation.[23] While it is usually the opponents of technology who find themselves stigmatized, Lewis Mumford turns the table on technology's advocates in cases like this, labeling them "counter-Luddites" and "craft-wreckers."

At the Crossroads

To advocate merely the obvious, albeit essential, point that science must develop technology in harmony with nature is to overlook the social, political, and particularly the economic structures that drive the development of technology.[24] The economic transformations at the end of the Middle Ages, accompanying the rise of capitalism, nurtured the scientific revolution and loosened cultural constraints on the development of technology.[25] Continuing through the industrial era, these economic forces have driven the pace of technological innovation, the choice of technology employed, and the manner in which technology is extended through the global economy. The growth imperative of capitalism requires the expansion of markets and the development of forms of technology that provide better economies of scale and easier centralized control.[26] Technology has grown beyond the scope of community control, its application no longer directly subject to considerations of social and ecological preservation. Where modern technology has damaged the Earth, it has been a technology driven by the instrumental world-view and materialistic values of the capitalist economy. If technology is to restore the Earth, it will be a technology reconceived within broader values that fundamentally respect both nature and the human community.

The mechanical world-view has pervaded our consciousness and even our sense of self. In this context, it is clear that no mere technological solution will be adequate to the current crises. If our current technology derives from the world-view of modern science as it serves the expansion and control requirements of capitalism, what is needed is a new world-view in a new social order.[27] In the search for an ecological society, we are at a crossroads in which, as Morris Berman describes it,

> one fork retains all the assumptions of the Industrial Revolution and would lead us to salvation through science in technology; in short, it holds that the very paradigm that got us into trouble can somehow get us

out. . . . The other fork leads to a future that is as yet somewhat obscure. Its advocates are an amorphous mass of Luddites, ecologists, regional separatists, steady-state economists . . . [whose] goal is the preservation (or resuscitation) of such things as the natural environment, regional culture, archaic modes of thought, organic community structures, and highly decentralized political autonomy.[28]

In this chapter, I have only touched on the historic processes that have placed us today on Berman's first fork. I have sought to show that technology, like population stability, develops within a social and political framework. Of course we need nonpolluting technology. But we will not have it without understanding the greater forces that underlie the development of technology. Technological choices are not made in isolation, but rather arise out of the cultural and social systems that form the dominant world-view. It is in this broader perspective, and in our response to it, that an ecologically harmonious future will be found.

The history of technology can be viewed as driven or contained by the values prevalent in society at any given time. Precapitalist society generally valued life in a broad sense that entailed the preservation of the community and its natural environment. This broad matrix of values limited the development of technology. Capitalism, with it preeminent valuing of profit and its attendant values of efficiency, materialism, and economic growth, has driven technological development in service to these values, to the detriment of the Earth. An extensive reform of technology does not begin with technology itself. Rather, it requires a reenvisioning of a broad and life-affirming set of social values on which the development of an ecologically sustainable technology can be based.

Chapter 3

CONSUMER CHOICE: WE'RE ALL TO BLAME

*I decided to ask him a blunt question: "What do
you think is the cause of the present ecological
crisis?" His answer was very emphatic: "Human
beings! People are responsible for the ecological
crisis! . . . They overpopulate the earth, they
pollute the planet, they devour its resources, they
are greedy. That's why corporations exist—to
give people the things they want."*
—*Murray Bookchin,* Remaking Society

Thus Murray Bookchin describes a 1987 encounter with someone he identifies only as a "California Green."[1] Encapsulated in
the Green's emotional statement is one of the most common
beliefs about the environmental crisis, the belief that we are all,
generally and equally, responsible for the deteriorating condition of the Earth. As the promotional brochure for Earth Day
1990 put it, "Our species got itself into this mess, and we must
get ourselves out of it."

As a consequence of the rise in environmental consciousness
since the twentieth anniversary of Earth Day, Americans are
approaching life a bit differently. We understand our responsibility as consumers to choose environmentally benign products
and to think about such things as packaging, disposable products, and recycling. We know that it is us regular folk who are
responsible for the Earth's ills. As *Time* magazine, in its 1989
"Planet of the Year" issue, told us, "No attempt to protect the

environment will be successful in the long run unless ordinary people—the California housewife, the Mexican peasant, the Soviet factory worker, the Chinese farmer—are willing to adjust their life styles."[2]

The idea that we are all responsible for the environmental crisis rings true to Americans' folk wisdom and sense of individual responsibility. A post–Earth Day TV commercial depicted a group of children collecting trash in plastic bags while the superimposed image of a stern Native American looked on in mute approval. Certainly these children did not leave all that trash on the lovely mountain landscape. Yet somehow they happily took responsibility for cleaning it up. This image is probably an affront to a traditional Native American sense of responsibility and care for the natural environment, which would not condone such littering in the first place. Nonetheless, it rings true to the more limited environmental vision of the average American.

The ease of Americans' acceptance of this "we're all responsible" perspective is what led to the success of the rash of lifestyle-oriented books published around and since Earth Day 1990. The titles of some of these books are listed in the Introduction. With their help, it is possible for solitary consumers to examine virtually every aspect of their lives and come up with ecologically responsible alternatives. The possibilities offered by the titles of these books range from fifty ways to help the planet for the modest environmentalist to over a thousand activities for the truly ambitious. Beginning in 1991, Earthworks published a "Simple Things You Can Do to Save the Earth" calendar, which provides a "tip a day" for ecological living. Adding only a single small square of paper each day to the recycling bin, one can learn valuable lessons in green living.

Time magazine is not alone, of course, in its focus on the responsibility of ordinary citizens. Across the magazine spectrum, *New Age Journal,* in its 1990 "Definitive Guide to New Age Living," declared that "this revolution must take place within each of us, and through the small actions we take in our everyday lives. . . . Global change can be a matter of individuals simply changing their minds."[3] This New Age belief in the power of "individuals simply changing their minds" was exemplified in the 1980s by the popularity of the legend of the hundredth monkey. According to the story, popularized in a 1982 book by human-potential guru Ken Keyes, Jr.,

> There were these Japanese scientists in the '50s who left potatoes out every day for these wild monkeys on Koshima Island and then watched what they did. One of these monkeys learned to wash the potatoes and began teaching this to the others. Then, when a certain number had learned, maybe a hundred—scientists call this a "critical mass"—an amazing thing happened. Suddenly, all the monkeys knew how to wash potatoes, even monkeys on other islands hundreds of miles away! Scientists consider this to be conclusive proof of a telepathic "group mind."[4]

New Age enthusiasts consider this to be conclusive proof that if enough people share a good idea it will become a reality. The implied message is that each of us may be the hundredth monkey, that person whose adopting of the environmentally correct lifestyle sets humanity on a new course.

In fact, the hundredth monkey phenomenon has been debunked by a number of researchers.[5] First of all, the monkey troop on Koshima grew during the period of study from twenty in 1952 to fifty-nine by 1962. Thus, there was never a "hundredth" monkey at all. Similarly, the number of potato-washing monkeys grew from seventeen of thirty noninfant monkeys in 1958 to thirty-six of forty-nine in 1962. The increase in potato washers was exactly equal to the increase in population and is thus readily attributable to normal learning behavior without any mysterious or miraculous forces involved. Potatoes, which are not native to the Japanese islands, were introduced on a number of islands simultaneously. Potato washing on the other islands can be attributed to the cleverness of the monkeys without requiring any paranormal communication processes across the islands. In sum, the position of Ken Keyes, and the work of Lyall Watson from which he draws, is based on a complete misinterpretation of the facts. If anything, the popularity of the hundredth-monkey story proves, not the power of a group mind, but the power of wishful thinking.

The popularity of such stories is an indication of the extreme passivity and disempowerment of people in contemporary society, who, unaccustomed to effective, organized action, instead turn hopefully to the putative power of good thoughts. At the same time, the story of the hundredth monkey resonates with the Christian emphasis on salvation through faith. Just as faith in an afterlife facilitates the acceptance of all sorts of hardship on earth, so does faith in the power of a group mind lead to acceptance of socially and environmentally destructive practices. The mystification represented by the hundredth-monkey story obscures the social and political dimensions of human behavior. Acceptance of such myths is reinforced by an educational system that teaches us, by and large, to view knowledge as something we receive uncritically from others. Critical thinking and a healthy skepticism are important aspects of effective environmentalism.

Ken Keyes, Jr.'s, book *The Hundredth Monkey* sold over a million copies to people wanting to stop the nuclear arms race. Of course, even with the end of the Soviet Union and the cold war's ever-present nuclear threat, nuclear weapons continue to roll off the production lines. With arms, as with the environment, it is not enough for a million people to have the right idea; they must also know how to express the idea through action. If rational thinking and organized, directed action are part of what separates humanity from the apes, then a handful of humans working together is vastly more important than one hundred monkeys with the same wish.

Prominent environmentalists have joined *Time* and *New Age* in jumping on the lifestyle bandwagon. For example, Jeremy Rifkin is the editor of a valuable source book, *The Green Lifestyle Handbook: 1001 Ways You Can Heal the Earth*, in which, in an introductory essay, he contrasts the "green lifestyle" of the 1990s with the "rank consumerism of the 1980s." Rifkin sees green consumers leading the way to a new era. He believes that merely by adopting the green lifestyle "we establish a cultural framework that promotes and reinforces a new approach to science, technology, economics, and politics."[6] Of course, in the context of Rifkin's lifework and many important contributions to environmentalism, this is a minor lapse. Nonetheless, it demonstrates the seductive quality that the lifestyle issue holds even for leading environmentalists.

This principle of consumer responsibility is so widely accepted that it is likely to come up whenever environmental problems are in the public eye, and from the most unlikely sources. After the *Exxon Valdez* accident, the controversial environmental group Greenpeace ran ads with a large picture of Joseph Hazelwood, captain of the *Valdez*. The headline told readers that "it wasn't his driving that caused the Alaskan oil spill. It was yours." The ad went on to explain that "it would be easy to blame the *Valdez* oil spill on one man. Or one company. Or even one industry. Too easy. Because the truth is, the spill was caused by a nation drunk on oil." Of course, this perspective completely overlooks the fact that it was Exxon that chose to use single-hulled ships, that failed to manage the drinking habits of its ship captain, that has worked and lobbied persistently to maintain America's need for a large supply of petroleum, and that pressed to open up the Alaskan oil fields in the first place against the protests of environmentalists.

This ad, remember, came from Greenpeace, renowned for disrupting the nuclear tests of the French government and the activities of Japanese whaling fleets. Greenpeace's record of radical action, personal risk taking, international success, and inspirational leadership is outstanding over the last quarter century. The focus on generalized blame in this ad is so foreign to their programmatic emphases that one can only conclude that Greenpeace too was momentarily caught up in the popularity of consumer-oriented environmentalism.

Citizens engaged in grassroots environmental battles must also fight the onus of consumer choice. For example, those fighting waste dumps are regularly told that they create the waste and so they should live with it. So deeply ingrained is this sense of individual choice and responsibility that even those who oppose a policy wind up feeling responsible for its outcome. For example, members of a Green organization in Charlotte, North Carolina, responded to a proposed nearby landfill for low-level radioactive waste by discussing to what extent their use of electricity made them responsible for nuclear waste. They apparently overlooked the fact that none of them had chosen nuclear energy as their preferred power source. They were also forgetting that environmentalists had actively and consistently opposed nuclear power, citing problems disposing of radioactive waste as one of the reasons for their opposition.

Who Chooses?

One problem with the reasoning of those who would have us all share the blame is that consumers do not make choices about production. This was brought home to me on a trip to the supermarket in search of peanut butter. I discovered that my childhood favorite, Peter Pan, was now available only in plastic containers. The production of plastic creates extremely hazardous chemical wastes. As a responsible green consumer, of course, I'd rather not support that, preferring to choose reusable/recyclable glass jars.

Murray Bookchin's California Green told him that corporations exist "to give people the things they want." But is this really the case? Have people indicated that they prefer plastic to glass for storing peanut butter? While I don't claim to be a careful monitor of the supermarket shelves, I can't remember a time when the Peter Pan product stood side by side in both glass and plastic containers, sized, priced, and labeled the same, allowing consumers to indicate their preference on the basis of container alone. In fact, such decisions are not made by consumers, but rather by manufacturers seeking to cut production costs. In many cases, the manufacturers will use the new packaging as the basis of a marketing campaign, perhaps touting the advantage of unbreakable jars. There has certainly never been an ad from industry explaining that although new packaging may be less expensive and more convenient, it is more damaging to the environment and thus more costly to society; such an ad would offer consumers a fully informed choice. Of course, it will be argued that manufacturers carefully test-market new packaging to ensure consumer acceptance. The crucial point is that it is the manufacturer who determines the package design and materials. Consumer acceptance is a secondary and passive activity at best.

The mistaken nature of the theory of consumer choice as the determining factor in these matters is obvious to anyone visiting a conventional supermarket. Is milk available in glass as well as plastic containers? Are natural, fully biodegradable cleaning products available? Is meat from free-ranging, hormone-free and antibiotic-free animals available? How about organically grown produce?

In effect, our sense of individual responsibility is exploited in the crafting of the myth that we're all responsible by those making production decisions. If everyone contributes equally to the problem, then we cannot hold any specific institutions or people accountable.[7] If we're all to blame, then any individual or organization actually making decisions that hurt the Earth is off the hook. When it comes to pollution or the creation of toxic chemicals, the problems originate in production decisions that take into account only cost, not environmental impacts. The well-known global environmental problems have their origin in production decisions made by specific managers in positions of corporate power, whose guiding principles are cost reduction and profit maximization.

The failure to distinguish between individuals and institutions leads concerned citizens to ignore government complicity in and responsibility for environmental destruction.[8] For example, rather than enumerating the environmental failures of the federal government, the 1990 Earth Day prospectus read as if the government had done no more damage to the environment than the typical consumer. To the contrary, the government is responsible for numerous critical environmental problems. The extent of the federal government's contribution to pollution was confirmed in a study by *Newsday* that found "a huge catalog of leaching landfills, leaking underground tanks, radioactive waste piles, and lab disposal pits at U.S. facilities. It is a record of widespread environmental neglect . . . revealing a government that has broken the same pollution laws it enforces on others."[9]

Of course, the common counterargument to this is that the American people elected their government and certainly it is doing their will. Consider, however, that in the mid 1980s the Reagan administration lowered the automobile fuel-efficiency goal adopted during the 1970s energy crisis. This action was not the result of citizens writing to the government calling for less-efficient cars; it was the automobile manufacturers and the oil companies that lobbied, as they always do, for the lower standard. Even in the wake of the Persian Gulf war, they would not moderate their position.

The extent of radioactive contamination in nuclear weapons facilities is already notorious, even though the final figures are not yet in. It may be argued that citizens supported the nuclear weapons program throughout the cold war period and thereby accepted responsibility for the ecological consequences. However, citizens did not have the opportunity to knowingly acquiesce to the contamination, since for years information about it was kept secret. Had it been known, it would have added a strong argument against weapons programs.

There is a flip side to the "consumer choice/we're all responsible" fallacy. This is the notion that anonymous, perhaps inevitable, forces lead to environmental ills, that perhaps no one is responsible. *Time,* again in the "Planet of the Year" issue, provides us with an example of this viewpoint: "Starting at the dawn of the Industrial Revolution, smokestacks have disgorged noxious gases into the atmosphere, factories have dumped toxic wastes into rivers and streams, automobiles have guzzled irreplaceable fossil fuels and fouled the air . . . forests have been denuded, lakes poisoned with pesticides, underground aquifers pumped dry."[10] Note that there are no actors or decision makers in this description. In fact, there are not even any people. However, each of the destructive situations described by *Time* was caused by industries whose managers made decisions about what to produce and how to produce it. These decision makers are educated and well paid, perhaps pillars of their communities, seeking to increase the prosperity of their firm and by implication the prosperity of society. Such decision making, often the result of careful cost-benefit analyses, is an indictment not of consumers but of our system of economic decision making and accountability.

The notion that we're all responsible places the grandmother driving to church on an equal footing with Exxon. An effective response to the environmental crisis must ask where the decision making occurs that leads to the pollution. Most of those decisions are made by industry and government. The choice left to the consumer is often little more than a selection from among environmentally destructive alternatives.

From Consumer to Citizen

Superficially, there may appear to be a paradox in a book espousing citizen activism criticizing the idea that people's choices make a difference. The point of this chapter is that the environmental crisis has more to do with decisions made in the corporate boardroom, in the manufacturing plant, and in Congress than it does with those made in the supermarket. Yes, this book is ultimately aimed, like the lifestyle books, at what we can do. However, it is aimed at what we can do as active citizens rather than as passive consumers, and what we can do by organizing and working together rather than in our separate, atomized lives. The aim is not to do away with our feeling of responsibility but to enhance it with an understanding of the means to an effective, empowered sense of citizenship.

A recent example will help to illustrate the difference between individual responsibility and organized activism. In the late 1980s, a tuna boycott spread, bringing to public awareness the number of dolphins ensnared and killed in the nets of tuna fishers. This boycott achieved such prominence that the issue was raised supportively in a hit film of 1989, *Lethal Weapon II.* In 1990, the major tuna packers announced that they would use only tuna caught by methods that do not endanger dolphins. This was a great victory for environmentally conscious consumers, although it has since been challenged by international tuna interests.[11]

A short time later, an ad appeared from the Council on Economic Priorities, publishers of *Shopping for a Better World.* The ad proclaimed to the reader that "you changed the fate of the wild dolphin population. You made visionary product choices. You made a difference."[12] It then solicited the reader to "make a difference in so many other ways" by using *Shopping for a Better World,* which in its subtitle is called a "quick & easy guide to socially responsible supermarket shopping."

This appealing promotion notwithstanding, changing the way modern consumer goods are produced and distributed is neither quick nor easy. The crucial point is that while *Shopping for a Better World* is a reference tool for individual purchasing decisions, the tuna policy was changed because of a widespread, well-organized, clearly targeted boycott. Too often, when con-

II

THE SEARCH FOR ROOTS

AN ALTERNATIVE VIEW

Chapter 4

THE STRUGGLE FOR DEMOCRACY: CONCENTRATION OF POWER

As much as the idea that we're all to blame for the environmental crisis is a fallacy, it nonetheless strikes a chord in reminding us of the desire of people to take responsibility for the world and society that they live in. To fulfill that responsibility requires an avenue through which to express and actualize it. In the Western world, particularly in the United States, that avenue is understood to be the process of democratic government. Although the modern Western democratic tradition is usually traced back to the signing of the Magna Carta by England's King John in the thirteenth century, the founding of the American republic is generally viewed as the blossoming of the democratic era.

Yet, paralleling the increase in environmental damage over the last two hundred years is a failed struggle for more participatory forms of democracy and against the increased concentration of economic and political power. This conflict persisted side by side with successful efforts to expand voting rights to include African Americans and women. Unfortunately, the rights they won were exercised in a setting where decision making was increasingly removed from the day-to-day lives of the American people. The history told in this chapter is not that of the expansion of the right to vote for representatives in government, important as that is. Rather, it is about the struggle over the process of government itself, over whether power would be wielded by citizens or by elites. This conflict is rooted in the earliest days of the American republic, when many Americans struggled to achieve a genuinely participatory democracy that would distribute power equitably among the people. The failure of that effort set the tone for developments over the following two centuries and for difficulties citizens have in protecting the environment today.

The Failed Revolution

"America, the land par excellence of democracy"—Alexis de Tocqueville

Alexis de Tocqueville's love affair with American democracy is well known to students of American history. He wrote over seven hundred pages (in a recent translation), primarily of praise, in his famous work of the 1830s, *Democracy in America*.[1] In the early nineteenth century, most of Europe was under aristocratic rule, though some nations were struggling with the uneasy transition from monarchy to democracy. By contrast, the newly created U.S. government looked very good indeed. The United States happily embraced the role of "land par excellence of democracy," to the extent that eighty years later it was able to enter World War I in Europe with the claim that its mission was to "make the world safe for democracy." Forgotten, and generally left untaught in our history books, is the failure of the struggle for participatory democracy in the United States in the 1780s and the fact that the American system of government is the legacy of a concerted effort to rein in the democratic forces unleashed by the Revolution.

In the seventeenth and eighteenth centuries, colonial America was very much part of a trend across western Europe and particularly in England away from the ancient traditions of aristocracy, patronage, and hereditary privilege and toward more open social forms. The English colonies were at the forefront of this transformation, due in part to the character of those who would stake out a life in such unfamiliar lands, in part to their distance from the locus of aristocratic power, and in part to the exigencies of life in the New World. The American Revolution itself, perhaps more accurately called the War of Independence, removed certain constraints on the rate and extent of change but did not entail any of the fundamental social and political changes or the general upheaval associated with the French Revolution that soon followed. Many of the leaders of the war effort sought only to remove the yoke of British rule without disturbing the political and economic status quo within the colonies. At the end of the war in 1783, the final form of the government of the new nation was far from certain. American opinion ran the gamut from monarchists who would install George Washington as king to fiercely independent yeoman farmers who we might think of today as anarchists. In between, most Americans wanted some form of stable democratic government, but even that allowed much room for debate as to the form and authority of the national government.

Because of the abuses of the English governors, most Americans had a distrust of centralized government. In England itself, as early as 1723, radical Whig political writers were asserting that concentrated power led inevitably to abuse.[2] In 1775, at the dawn of the American Revolution, the political theorist James Burgh wrote that "the people can never be too jealous of their liberties. Power is of an elastic nature, ever extending itself and encroaching on the liberties of the subjects."[3] During the revolutionary period, such fears led twelve of the thirteen states to alter the structures of their governments to make them more democratic. Many abolished property requirements for voting. Most limited the power of the governor, providing no veto and limiting terms to a single year. The Articles of Confederation that gave form to the new national government were also designed to limit centralized power. For example, delegates to Congress were elected annually, recallable by the state legislatures, and could serve only three years out of six. Thus, in the early years of the new nation, the democratic ideal was understood to include a limiting of the power of the state and national governments.

There was much dissatisfaction with the new national government, however, particularly from those concerned about the repayment of war debts and the honoring of contractual agreements. The large population of subsistence farmers resisted the higher taxes that would allow the national government to repay its debts. These farmers lived in communities based on a high degree of mutual aid, in which contracts were viewed in the context of broad social relations and debts were easily forgiven or repaid in trade. Bankers and suppliers in the cities demanded much stricter enforcement of contracts than the rural population was accustomed to, insisting on a legalistic interpretation of contractual debt and on repayment in cash. Wealthy Americans were eager for the young nation to repay its debts, both to them and to the Europeans whose continued credit was important to economic development and international trade. Critics of the Articles of Confederation were unabashed in their advocacy of economic privilege. According to a minority address to the Pennsylvania Council of Censors, the government "retains too much power in the hand of the people who do not know how to use it, so well as gentlemen of fortune . . . and it gives no advantage to the rich over the poor."[4] A typical expression of this bias against the less-privileged classes was that of the *New York Daily Advertiser,* which in 1786 complained that "of all the evils which attend the republican form of government, there are none that seem to have more pernicious effects than the *insolence* which liberty implants into the lower orders of society."[5]

In 1787, a convention was called for the purpose of revising and presumably improving the Articles of Confederation, which specified that any changes required the approval of all thirteen states to take effect. However, rather than mere revisions, the outcome of that convention was a completely new Constitution, one that proclaimed its own adoption if nine states approved, and one that served the interests of economic elites rather than the common people.

The Founding Fathers, as the framers of the Constitution are popularly known, are generally regarded as political geniuses who created an innovative and superior form of government. While features of the new government, such as separation of powers and checks and balances, have much to commend them, the framers were also representing a definite segment of the population, one with clear interests. While the majority of citizens at that time were struggling farmers or part of a growing middle class, the convention was dominated by the wealthy and powerful. Most of the fifty-five men at the constitutional convention were men of wealth, with fully forty of them holding government bonds. Edmund Randolph, for example, owned seven thousand acres of land, two hundred slaves, and considerable public securities. In desiring to protect these interests, most of the framers had a direct economic stake in establishing a strong federal government. The resulting Constitution was carefully crafted to serve the economic needs of its authors. As well as the repayment of debts and the enforcement of contracts mentioned above, the framers of the Constitution wanted federal regulation of interstate commerce. Most importantly, the Constitution places a fundamental right of private property beyond the reach of government and safe from any interference from popular majorities.[6] While democracy may have been an important value to the framers, it was nonetheless second to property.

The Constitution's treatment of contracts is typical of its tendency to favor those with property and power. Article 1, Section 10 forbids the states from passing any "law impairing the obligation of contract." While this sounds evenhanded, contracts generally favor the more powerful of the parties involved: landlord over tenant, employer over employee, and so forth. Moreover, those with greater wealth and power are likely to have more contracts with greater value than are the less privileged. While today we take the enforcement of contracts by government as a matter of course, things were different then. In the agrarian communities of eighteenth-century America, contractual agreements were informal and were understood to be secondary to the community's commitment to the continued livelihood of its citizens. Forgiveness, flexibility, and payment in trade rather than cash were hallmarks of that society. This stood in sharp contrast to the practices of the bankers and suppliers from the cities, who would readily seize a farmer's land or crops if a cash payment was not made on time. This debate about the enforcement of contracts remains pertinent today as vast numbers of family farms, facing overwhelming indebtedness, have gone into bankruptcy, leading to ever-more farmland in the control of ever-fewer hands. Of course, self-reliant agrarian communities emphasizing mutual aid were generally far better stewards of the earth than are the absentee owners and agribusinesses that have taken their place in the twentieth century.

The economic concerns of the Founding Fathers dovetailed neatly with an elitist sensibility as to how the new nation should be governed. John Jay, later to be the first chief justice of the Supreme Court, was a coauthor, with Alexander Hamilton and James Madison, of *The Federalist Papers*, which attempted to justify the new Constitution. Jay believed that the upper classes "were the better kind of people [and that] the people who own the country ought to govern it."[7] Hamilton agreed, asserting the political philosophy that "the people are turbulent and changing," seldom correct in their political opinions. He advocated a permanent body of representatives of the upper class to curb the democratic impulses of the people, and at the constitutional convention, he suggested a president and senate chosen for life. Although these proposals were not adopted, the constitutional provisions for election of the president by an electoral college and for the appointment of senators by state legislatures (the latter changed to direct election by the Seventeenth Amendment in 1913) went a long way toward removing the federal government from direct accountability to the people.

The eighty-five *Federalist Papers* of Madison, Hamilton, and Jay were published in New York, considered one of the key states for ensuring ratification. While much scholarship on the Constitution has made use of the records of the debate at the convention and the letters and diaries of the participants, the *Papers* themselves provide the best formal presentation of the political philosophy of the framers.

In the tenth and perhaps best known of the papers, James Madison argues for a government that protects against the passions of the majority, maintaining that "democracies have ever been spectacles of turbulence and contention; have ever been found incompatible with personal security or the rights of property."[8] Among the "ruling passions" that might sway a majority, Madison includes "a rage for paper money, for an abolition of debts, for an equal division of property, or for any other improper or wicked project."[9] In other words, Madison has singled out those concerns that might set the lower classes against the privileged. His defense of the structure of the proposed government is that it will prevent the majority of propertyless citizens from challenging the prerogatives of the propertied elite. The notion that democracy is in conflict with property rights is well expressed in the words of Madison.

The supporters of the Constitution, understanding that the idea of confederation was still a popular one, anticipated the Newspeak of George Orwell's *Nineteen Eighty-Four* by two hundred years and began calling themselves Federalists and their opponents Anti-Federalists. Of course, they were in fact opposed to a federated form of government. By labeling their opponents as "anti," they made it appear that the latter were obstructing positive change.

The opponents of the Constitution, these so-called Anti-Federalists, continued the tradition of distrust of centralized power. Among the issues of concern were presidential power, the nature of the Senate, standing armies, and taxation. The Anti-Federalists believed that freedom required strong local governments, since the history of national governments was one of aristocratic rule if not outright tyranny.[10] One Anti-Federalist, writing under the name "Rusticus," feared "a monstrous aristocracy [which would] swallow up the democratic rights of the union, and sacrifice the liberties of the people to the power and domination of a few."[11] The Virginian George Mason believed that the Constitution was setting up, at best, "a moderate aristocracy," which, at its worst, might lead to monarchy or "corrupt tyrannical aristocracy."[12]

The Federalist viewpoint was not widely popular. The Federalists were a majority in at best six or seven states, fewer than the nine needed for ratification, and thus they should have been defeated.[13] Their success in spite of this can be attributed in part to their control and exploitation of newspapers and publishing and to their use of what would today be called a disinformation campaign.

The importance of the financial power of the Federalists was evident in their access to and control of newspapers. Very few papers opposed ratification or even presented both sides impartially.[14] The papers often contained misinformation on events in distant states. News traveled slowly, and the correcting facts might be learned only much later, if ever. Pennsylvania newspapers claimed that Patrick Henry was working for ratification, when in fact Henry was leading the struggle in Virginia against ratification. Charleston readers were told that most New Yorkers favored ratification, even though Anti-Federalists formed a majority in New York's ratifying convention.[15]

The Federalists, because of better education and greater experience in government, were also able to use parliamentary procedures to their advantage. For example, in Pennsylvania a ratifying convention was called with only six weeks' notice, severely limiting the time for debate on the issues, a debate that might have gone against the Federalists. The Federalists were able to structure the ratification process so that the Constitution was in fact approved by only one-sixth of the adult male population.

Had the Anti-Federalist position won out, the result would likely have been a significantly more democratic form of government. The Anti-Federalists would have emphasized local government and held representatives accountable through shorter terms, rotation in office, and recall by the electorate.[16] Nonetheless, after fierce struggles in the thirteen states, the Constitution was ratified. No less prestigious a figure than President John Quincy Adams looked back at that era and noted in his diary that the Constitution was "calculated to increase the influence, power and wealth of those who already have any." Adams concluded mournfully that "it is hard to give up a system which I have always been taught to cherish."[17]

Jefferson's Radical Democracy

There was one man whose reputation and democratic vision might have changed the form of government that emerged from the constitutional convention. Unfortunately, Thomas Jefferson, beloved in the new nation as author of the Declaration of Independence, was in Paris serving as ambassador to France through the late 1780s. Alexis de Tocqueville regarded Jefferson as "the most powerful apostle of democracy there has ever been."[18] Although Jefferson's stature is ultimately diminished by his failure to disavow the practice of slavery, his commitment to the theory and practice of democratic government certainly merited de Tocqueville's praise. Jefferson, who certainly never heard of environmentalism, nonetheless connected democracy to nature, declaring that "every man and every body of men on earth, possesses the right of self-government: they receive it with their being from the hand of nature."[19]

Jefferson disagreed with Alexander Hamilton that government belonged to the "first class." He believed that democracy could succeed only by involving all citizens in self-government. As much as Alexander Hamilton's politics reflected a pessimistic view of humanity, so did Jefferson's democratic vision stem from an idealism as to the nature and potential of humankind.[20] Jefferson's humanitarianism was closely tied to his belief in the importance of education. To those who feared giving power to the "ignorant masses," Jefferson insisted that the remedy was to provide education to all citizens.[21] Ever committed to putting his principles into practice, Jefferson spent his later years busy with the founding and development of the University of Virginia.

Unlike the Federalists, who were by and large oriented toward the nation's urban centers, Jefferson maintained a pastoral vision in which the ownership and working of the land by all citizens was the foundation of democratic government. For him, a society that concentrated the ownership of property in a few hands was antithetical to democracy. Democracy depended on providing all citizens with access to land and education. Jefferson wrote to James Madison that "it is not too soon to provide by every possible means that as few as possible shall be without a little portion of land. The small land holders are the most precious part of the state."[22] In an early draft of the Virginia constitution, Jefferson included the provision that each adult was entitled to an appropriation of fifty acres.[23]

Once land ownership was universal, Jefferson believed that democracy could be maintained by administering government at a local level. Jefferson admired the town-meeting system of government practiced in New England and believed that a democratic government must be based in face-to-face assemblies of small communities he called wards. Wards and town meetings were in his view "the wisest invention ever devised by the wit of man for the perfect exercise of self-government"[24] and should be of a size that allowed all citizens to convene as a body for government decision making. Jefferson saw this as the basis for the involvement of all citizens in government activity, not just once a year at election time, but on a day-to-day basis. In his view, the active participation of the citizenry was the best safe-guard against tyranny. An activist citizen "will let the heart be torn out of his body sooner than his power be wrested from him by a Caesar or a Bonaparte."[25] For Thomas Jefferson, good government should not be entrusted to the few but must be exercised by all.[26]

Jefferson's emphasis on ward democracy was also part of his hope to keep alive the revolutionary spirit of 1776, a spirit to which he was firmly committed.[27] The Federalists' insistence on a strong central government had been fueled by an uprising of farmers in western Massachusetts in 1786. Shays's Rebellion, named after its leader Daniel Shays, protested lack of payment for war service, high taxes, and the seizing of cattle and land by creditors. The rebellion was violently repressed by the Massa-chusetts government under the leadership of such former revo-lutionaries as Samuel Adams. But Jefferson took a different view of Shays's Rebellion, writing to a friend that occasional rebel-lion is "a medicine necessary for the sound health of govern-ment."[28] Despite Jefferson's belief in healthy rebellions, the new government under the Constitution proved well able to subvert and suppress any such challenges to the state.

The strong central government instituted by the U.S. Consti-tution, with a powerful executive and senate, was quite at odds with Thomas Jefferson's vision of townships and wards filled with a robust spirit of self-government. The new government fulfilled the fears of the Anti-Federalists, institutionalizing the interests of a wealthy and powerful elite. Still, Jefferson and the Anti-Federalists represent what has been a continuing urge to genuine democracy in the American people. Although our his-tory books for the most part recount the stories of presidents, generals, and industrialists, emphasizing power and control, the currents of grassroots democracy run deep in our conscious-ness and traditions.

The Populist Era

Political heirs to Thomas Jefferson and the Anti-Federalists who gave strong expression to the American democratic im-pulse, the Populists, a mass movement primarily of southern and western farmers, are remembered for their struggle in the

1890s to assert democratic control over the excesses of corporate America.[29] The political struggles of the People's party, formed by the Populists in the 1890s, represented the peak of a movement that surfaced in the 1870s with the economic struggles of farmers across the South and Great Plains. Farmers at that time faced severe hardships in a system that required them to mortgage their crops in advance to obtain needed equipment and goods from monopolistic suppliers. These suppliers were able to dictate both a high price for manufactured goods needed by the farmers and a low price for crops. Farmers faced high rates of indebtedness. This often led to the loss of their land and homes, and they became tenants. Many could not even afford to pay rent, and, losing their independence, they became farm laborers.

In 1877, a group of farmers gathered in Texas to form the first Farmers' Alliance. The Alliance's purpose was to strengthen the economic lot of the farmers. The first and fundamental tool for this was the development of cooperatives. Alliance cooperatives bought bulk goods at lower cost from manufacturers and passed the savings on to members. Selling cooperatives were established to maintain higher prices for farm products. These farmers were engaged in pioneering efforts in cooperative enterprise, both in marketing and in purchasing. Over the next ten years, the Alliance spread across the South and into the West and Midwest. In Texas alone, membership leaped from 10,000 in 1884 to over 50,000 by the end of 1885, and to 250,000 by 1888.[30] The Alliance attracted members through its lecturing system, which eventually included 40,000 lecturers who traveled from county to county, recruiting, educating, and politicizing 2 million farm families in states across the South and West.[31] It was particularly successful in the South. Black farmers, disillusioned by the defeat of Reconstruction, formed Colored Farmers' Alliances, whose votes later would often contribute the margin of victory to Alliance-backed political candidates. The Alliance depended on thousands of independent newspapers to inform its members. Some of these papers had circulations of up to 100,000. Through newspapers and lecturers, the Farmers' Alliance created something lacking in most grassroots movements of the twentieth century: a broad membership with a high level of political awareness.

The potential success of the Alliance was limited by one crucial factor: to succeed, the cooperatives needed capital and credit. Unfortunately, loans were available only from the banks, which were allied both financially and ideologically with the system of centralized industrial capitalism that the Alliance was challenging.[32] Loans were not forthcoming. The problems of a statewide cooperative formed by the Texas Alliance are typical of these difficulties. The cooperative could raise only a small amount of cash from members, and with the banks refusing to issue loans, the effort failed.[33] Ultimately, the lack of credit threatened the Alliance with collapse.

As a result of their financial problems, the Alliance members became increasingly aware that their success was dependent on enacting a major reform of the system of national finance. This reform was proposed by the radical Alliance leader Charles Macune, who called for federal warehouses or "subtreasuries" in which farmers could store their crops and borrow up to 80 percent of the crops' value while awaiting sale. Since the subtreasury plan depended on action by the government, the Alliance went to work on the electoral level with great success, running candidates on the Democratic party ticket. In 1890, Kansan Alliance candidates won 96 of 125 seats in the state legislature. In Alabama, the Alliance claimed more than 75 of the 133 members of the state assembly. Unfortunately, the political effectiveness of the Alliance legislators was not proportional to their numbers, since the party machinery and committee chairmanships remained in the hands of conservatives. Once elected, many of the so-called Alliance Democrats turned to the politics of power and privilege, with no feeling of accountability to the Populists who elected them. They were often correctly accused of being little more than a front for conventional Democratic party interests. This fostered a feeling that the Alliance should abandon a strategy of "reform though the Democrats" and create a national third party.[34]

In 1890, the first convention of the People's party was held in Topeka, Kansas. By 1892, the party was ready to choose as its first presidential nominee the popular and highly respected southerner L. L. Polk. Unfortunately, Polk died suddenly, just before the convention, and the party nominated the less popular James Weaver of Iowa instead. Weaver received over a million votes in a losing effort that was nonetheless a significant achievement for a new party. Polk would likely have done even better. In their electoral efforts, the Populists faced opponents who controlled all the forces of the culture and the economy, from the banks to the universities. Impressive as they were for a grassroots organization, the independent newspapers and lecturers of the Alliance were little more than a weak David challenging a formidable Goliath.[35]

The opponents of populism employed a variety of tactics, such as co-opting populist rhetoric and gaining influence in the national committee of the new party. In South Carolina in 1892, for example, Governor Ben Tillman convinced the Democratic party to endorse the full Populist platform. The result was chaos for the Populists. Their leaders were outmaneuvered and forced to go along with Tillman, while the radical identity of the movement was lost. It was impossible for the Populists to portray themselves as a clear alternative when the Democrats endorsed the same platform.[36] Having disrupted his opposition, Tillman supported the presidential campaign of the Democrat Grover Cleveland, a friend of business and defender of the status quo.

Nationally, the Democrats advocated adoption of the silver standard by the U.S. Treasury to replace the prevailing use of gold as the basis for currency. The Alliance had been concerned about the availability of cash, an issue that, while rooted in the 1840s, had spawned the Greenback party of the 1870s. In the United States, currency was backed only by gold and issued in limited quantities. A larger monetary supply would mean more cash for crops and more funds available for credit. While some reformists called for expanding the monetary basis to include silver as well as gold (the silver standard), the Alliance wanted a currency supply based on the needs of the economy. Recall, in this regard, that in the *The Federalist Papers*, Madison warned against a potential "rage for paper money" arising from a propertyless majority. Indeed, the Populists represented just the sort of majority faction that Madison had feared. Their defeat demonstrates how well the Founding Fathers did their job in designing the Constitution.

The call for a fiat currency without a metal standard cut at the heart of the power of the economic elite. The Democrats' advocacy of a silver standard addressed the Alliance's need for an expanded monetary supply but fell far short of the fundamental reforms advocated by the Populists, such as the virtual nationalization of the banking system and democratization of fiscal policy-making embodied in the subtreasury plan. The silver issue would bring much of the Populist energy into the Democratic party, leaving their more radical demands isolated on the political fringe.

In 1896, those representing silver interests on the Populist national committee were able to schedule the Populist national convention one week after the Democratic convention. The Democrats nominated William Jennings Bryan, known for his fiery orations in support of silver. The Populists were in a bind. They lacked a candidate of their own with Bryan's national stature and feared a losing competition with the Democrats. Ultimately, after a chaotic convention, the People's party also endorsed the Bryan ticket. This placed the Populists in a no-win situation. If Bryan won, the People's party would be irrelevant, absorbed by the Democrats. If Bryan lost, the Populists would lose with him. The People's party never recovered from the 1896 debacle. The Farmers' Alliance had committed itself to the People's party in the quest for financial reform, but with the party ravaged by its national competition and then by association with the Democrats, the movement met its demise.

Although the period following the decline of the Populist movement is generally termed the "Progressive Era," it was in fact an era of conservatism. The McKinley campaign of 1896 represented the first coordinated effort of the industrial and financial leaders of American capitalism to dominate an election. Progressivism represents the triumph of Hamilton's vision of an elitist yet activist state working in partnership with the economically privileged. The political appointees of Theodore Roosevelt and Woodrow Wilson were friends of business, and under their administrations it was normal for industry to determine or even veto the regulatory processes that concerned it, defining the limits of political intervention.[37] There was an extensive consensus among business leaders and the major political parties, whether Democratic, Republican, or Progressive.[38] The failure of populism left America without a serious alternative to the status quo. This resulted in "a vacuum that permitted political capitalism to direct the growth of industrialism in

America, to shape its politics, to determine the ground rules for American civilization in the twentieth century, and to set the stage for what was to follow."[39]

Although there have been many other significant struggles for democracy in America since the 1890s, such as those of the labor movement, the women's suffrage movement, and the civil rights movement, their potential was restricted by the consolidation of power in the Progressive Era. The system of government was well designed so that votes did not necessarily translate into power. Thus, women, a majority of the population, can vote but have been unable to pass the Equal Rights Amendment or ensure reproductive rights. Thus, thirty years after the civil rights movement under the leadership of Martin Luther King, Jr., produced the Voting Rights Act, black Americans still struggle against racism and discrimination. And thus, environmentalists achieved the passage of clean-air, clean-water, and pollution-control regulations, all of which have been poorly enforced.

As the success of these later movements was limited by the failure of populism, so the Populists in their time were limited by the earlier defeat of the Anti-Federalists. The form of the U.S. government served its purpose, frustrating efforts toward democratization and allowing the further concentration of power.[40] Today, the political climate is one in which the biggest spender in a campaign for public office is four times more likely to win; the overwhelming majority of elected officials come from the wealthiest 5 percent of the population; and most U.S. senators are millionaires.[41] The Anti-Federalists would have predicted no less.

Power, Inc.

"The real difference between democracy and oligarchy is poverty and wealth. The rich are few and the poor are many.... Where the poor rule, that is a democracy."—Aristotle, Politics 1279–1280

Of course, the tendency to concentrate power is neither new nor uniquely American. After the relative decentralization of the Middle Ages, there was an increasing centralization of power.

The personal sovereignty of the king was identified with the nation itself and led ultimately to the impersonal sovereignty of the nation-state.[42] The powerful nation-state, the multinational corporation, and the contemporary calls for world government are the culmination of trends spanning the past several centuries.

In America, the fears of the Anti-Federalists and the dreams of the Federalists for the U.S. government were fulfilled. The structure of the government worked well to put the most unlikely tools in the service of the interests of property. By the 1890s, the Supreme Court had used the due process clause of the Fourteenth Amendment, supposedly passed to protect the rights of African Americans, to establish that corporations were "persons" subject to the protections of the Constitution. Of the Fourteenth Amendment cases brought before the Supreme Court between 1890 and 1910, 19 dealt with African Americans, and 288 dealt with corporations. In 1895, a New York banker toasted the Supreme Court, saying, "I give you gentlemen, the Supreme Court of the United States—guardian of the dollar, defender of private property, enemy of spoilation, sheet anchor of the Republic."[43] With the extension of the protection of the Fourteenth Amendment, the Constitution's favoring of business has gone beyond its original ensuring of the obligation of contract. The extension of rights to the corporation has protected its expanding power from challenge by its employees, by the communities in which it operates, and even by the national government.

The extent of this is exemplified by the history of the Seabrook nuclear power plant in New Hampshire. Through the late 1970s, massive demonstrations protested the construction of Seabrook. Thousands were arrested. The local communities and the state of Massachusetts refused to accept the proposed evacuation plans. That refusal, according to Nuclear Regulatory Commission (NRC) rules, should have prevented the plant from opening. To the contrary, thanks to intense industry lobbying and the cooperation of the Reagan and Bush administrations, the NRC changed its rules. It removed the requirement for local governmental approval of, and cooperation with, the evacuation plan. This paved the way for the opening of Seabrook in 1989, despite the years of opposition by the local citizenry and despite the threat to the densely populated areas and often-crowded swimming beaches in the vicinity.

Over fifty years ago, the German sociologist Max Weber asked, "How are freedom and democracy in the long run at all possible under the domination of highly developed capitalism?"[44] The American economist Robert Heilbroner considers questions such as Weber's to be ones "before which economics today comes to a disconcerted stop . . . questions that will remain on the agenda of society for a very long period to come." Freedom and democracy, to say nothing of environmental integrity, require that today's concentration of economic and political power be brought under social control. What is needed, according to Heilbroner, is "to subordinate corporate power within the larger social and political framework of society" so that "the great firm may become a responsive servant of the community."[45]

Today, this subordination remains a distant goal. The trend toward concentration of power continues at this writing, with international talks involving trade representatives from over one hundred nations seeking to revise the General Agreement on Tariffs and Trade (GATT). The proposed revision would provide an international panel with the power to review environmental, health, and safety standards and "harmonize" them across nations, ostensibly to promote free trade. GATT would create a central agency with veto power over regulations designed to protect local communities, states, and nations. Writing in the *Nation*, Daphne Wysham reports that GATT standards allow fifty times the current U.S. limit on cancer-causing residues on fruits and vegetables.[46] GATT could override the ban on the dangerous bovine growth hormone, as well as on the export of raw logs from the Pacific Northwest. Under GATT, environmental protection regulations are seen as unfair barriers to free trade. The North American Free Trade Agreement (NAFTA) was negotiated in a track somewhat parallel to GATT and threatens the same disregard for ecological and human well-being.

Particularly telling for purposes of this discussion is the case of Mexico's complaint against the U.S. Marine Mammal Protection Act, which bans the import of tuna caught by methods that kill dolphins.[47] This prohibition has been widely hailed as one of the great victories of environmental organizing. A GATT panel ruled in favor of Mexico's claim, declaring the tuna ban to be an unfair restraint of trade. The Bush administration agreed and pressured Congress to change the dolphin protection law. Although Congress held its ground in this instance, stronger GATT agreements in the future will limit the ability of nations to maintain such laws. This case clearly demonstrates how, even in the rare event that grassroots efforts are successful on the national level, they can be overridden by the increasing international concentration of corporate power.

Meanwhile, Wysham reports that the U.S. negotiating team for the GATT revisions has significant representation from firms such as Nestlé, Coca-Cola, and Kraft, all of which have much to gain by eliminating regulation. David Morris, director of the Institute for Local Self-reliance, is quoted as asking, "Why shouldn't community groups be allowed the same standing as corporations in determining international trade regulations?" Wysham responds, "Why indeed?"

The concentration of power in the corporate form and in the political structures that mirror and support it are deeply ingrained in our view of ourselves and the world around us. The modern multinational corporation itself is highly undemocratic, teaching passivity, subservience, and conformity.[48] Lewis Mumford linked the modern corporation, the nation-state, and their technological arsenal as aspects of a single "pentagon of power." The physical appearance of the U.S. Defense Department's Pentagon building is appropriate, with its squat walls keeping out information and its vast surrounding parking lots tying it to a wasteful economy. The pentagon of power is indifferent to broader human needs and social values: "It operates best in what is, historically speaking, an ecological, cultural, and personal lunar desert, swept only by solar winds."[49] Today, as ancient aquifers are depleted, as centuries of accumulation of topsoil are eroded, and as the rain forests are destroyed, a lunar desert could well be what lies ahead.[50] These images and the pentagon of power are, of course, not unique to the United States. They are well applied to the ecologically devastated nations of the former Soviet Union and in varying degrees to countries around the world.

Ironically, the perverse effects of concentrated power can make state and national government appear more environmentally sensitive than local government, even though the latter is more amenable to democratic participation. The reality is that local governments usually resist the economic costs associated with environmental protection rather than the programs themselves. The local tax bill, while a small fraction of state and federal taxes, is the one most responsive to local concerns and citizen activism. Local governments feel squeezed by state and federal regulations, environmental and otherwise, which mandate expensive, locally funded enforcement measures. In addition, much of the wealth of local communities is taken from them to fund state and federal programs that may offer little in return. Were citizens on the local level offered the choice between funding a B-2 bomber and protecting on their water supply, they would quickly choose the latter. Unfortunately, that choice is not available, and citizens concerned with rising taxes go after local tax policy, where their efforts are more likely to succeed.

It must also be recognized that, at all levels of government, politics is highly influenced by the very wealthy and by large corporations. Municipalities often temper their regulations to favor a single large corporation, usually not even locally owned, that is viewed as central to the their economy. In sum, the seeming resistance of some local governments to environmental regulation is an unfortunate expression of the dynamics of a society structured around the concentration of wealth and power.

The concentration of power and the erosion of democracy underlie the environmental crises in two ways. First, power as an end devalues human needs as well as ecological sensitivity. As one rises up the hierarchy, wielding ever more power, one is increasingly removed from the direct experience and understanding of the social and ecological dynamics of a particular locale. The decisions of the bureaucratic functionary or the captain of industry are no longer moored in the relationships that form the foundation of a just and sustainable society. The news today is rife with stories of distant corporations leaving behind a legacy of toxic pollution and impoverished workers in small communities.

The second way that the concentration of power underlies the environmental crisis is its tendency to render irrelevant the benevolent impulses of the people to protect and restore the environment. Concerned citizens continually find themselves hamstrung by bureaucratic complexities and government protection of the property prerogatives of distant owners. Citizen efforts are particularly subject to challenge on the basis of the Constitution's protection of interstate commerce. Thus, while citizens may wish to keep hazardous wastes out of their communities, government repeatedly denies them that authority. Disempowered, Jefferson's ward citizen who actively participates in the day-to-day affairs of government is replaced by the passively conscientious consumer who "votes" with his or her dollars but lacks any genuine political power. Of course, voting dollars do not make for a genuine democracy, since some people happen to have a lot more of them than others. Ultimately, a healthy environment depends on our developing new democratic forms and a reawakened sense of the citizenship on which they depend. Such a democratic citizenship will allow us to take meaningful responsibility for the host of problems for which we, as consumers, are blamed.

Chapter 5

THE NARROWING OF VALUES: "GROW OR DIE"

"It's business, not personal, Sonny!" as the
Godfather's consigliere says after the family
patriarch has been pumped full of bullets by his
Mafia rivals. Thus are all personal values reduced
to entrepreneurial ones.
—*Murray Bookchin,* The Progressive, *August 1989*

The Invisible Hand

Even as the modern era emerged with its emphasis on science and rationalism, the study of economics has nonetheless remained dependent on the mysterious benevolent force of the "invisible hand." This faith in the ultimate sanctity and justice of the free market has dominated our economy from the first formulation of the rules of capitalism by Adam Smith in the eighteenth century right up to the present. In *The Wealth of Nations*, published in 1776, Smith introduced the concept of the invisible hand: The businessman, "by directing . . . industry in such a manner as its produce may be of greatest value . . . intends only his own gain, and he is in this, as in many other cases, led by an invisible hand to promote an end which was not a part of his intention. . . . Pursuing his own interest he frequently promotes that of Society more effectually than when he really intends to promote it."[1] As Smith states clearly, the goal of the capitalist business person is "only his own gain." It is a given of our society that holders of capital should invest it with the maximum return in mind. Although many economists have analyzed and justified profit maximization as the foundation of economic activity, it is instructive to look at the approach taken by business schools that educate those making the day-to-day decisions that in aggregate define our economy.

Ezra Solomon and John J. Pringle are the authors of *An Introduction to Financial Management,* which is a basic text for business school students. In it they describe to their students the foundation of modern economics. The modern firm uses the decision criterion of profit maximization for economic efficiency, in which, quite simply, "actions that increase the firm's profit are undertaken and those that decrease profit are avoided."[2] In capitalist societies, anyone who's "ever met a payroll" (as a political candidate might proudly proclaim) knows the simple rule of profit maximization. For Solomon and Pringle, there is no question whose profit is being maximized. Although the invisible hand will supposedly ensure the benefit to society at large, profit maximization focuses on the needs of those investors who provide the capital on which a business depends.[3] Solomon and Pringle are quick to make the claim that profit maximization can serve a range of social values, insisting that it is a decision criterion rather than a goal.[4] They maintain that this decision criterion is consistent with social goals, such as producing desired goods and services and maintaining full employment.

This claim flies in the face of the actual history of capitalist economies. Certainly full employment has been an elusive goal. Only government intervention has kept industry from undermining social goals such as good health and a clean environment. Just as the twentieth century has been ravaged by the environmental excesses of industry, the nineteenth was notorious for its sweatshops and child labor. In both periods, social intervention in the form of government policy-making and community and labor activism was required.

To their credit, later in the text Solomon and Pringle moderate their faith in the benevolent consequences of profit maximization. In a discussion of "net present value," an analytic technique for financial decision making, they provide the example of a polluting steel mill that nonetheless is profitable to its investors. They point out that using these financial decision-making rules, the mill operators will freely discharge pollutants into the air and water if there are no fines or fees imposed for pollution. Although there are no costs to the mill owners, these discharges can lead to real costs to society in the form of the familiar health and agricultural impacts of pollution. While Solomon and Pringle still insist that such a course of action must be pursued because it increases the value of the firm,[5] they make it clear with this example that maximizing the value of the firm may not maximize the general welfare of society and that profit maximization does not, on its own, meet broader social needs. To the contrary, it quite often prevents the satisfaction of those needs. The history of capitalism indicates that a single decision criterion leads to a single goal. As business makes its decisions for the maximization of profit, all other values become secondary to that.

One way that profits are maintained is through the avoidance of costs. In the case of the steel mill, the real costs to society from the mill's pollution are not borne by the polluter but by society at large. Costs and financial impacts that fall on society rather than on the responsible business are called "externalities." Much environmental damage, as in this example, is the result of externalities. Generally, opportunities for externalities are readily available to polluters in the form of an atmosphere for gaseous discharges and rivers for liquid wastes. When such opportunities are not naturally available, companies will seek ways to externalize costs. Thus the nuclear industry has worked successfully with the federal government to have radioactive waste accepted as a public (external) cost rather than pay for it as a private cost. Much government "regulation" similarly provides a cost-avoidance service to business. This is a case where the concentration of political power satisfies the demands of the growth economy: as corporations become repositories of increasing economic power, they act to institutionalize their advantages through the comparably concentrated political power embodied in the federal government, which in turn acts to their continued economic benefit.

The imperative for growth is intertwined with the modern faith in the power of technology. The need for profit will lead to the rapid acceptance of new technologies that might increase profit margins. There are, of course, many examples of profitable technologies that proved damaging to health or to the environment and were later withdrawn. Often, problems with technology or products are ignored by the profit-driven corporation. Particularly notorious, for example, are the ongoing efforts of cigarette manufacturers to downplay the many studies showing the dangerous health effects of tobacco use.

In addressing this question of faith in technology, the economist Herman Daly uses a method of decision making known as Pascal's wager. The French philosopher Blaise Pascal sought a rational basis for the belief in God and contrasted the consequences of being wrong as a believer in God to those of being wrong as a nonbeliever. Pascal argued that the mistake of living a potentially unwarranted religious life was insignificant compared to the mistake of failing to believe in an actual God. An error involving a few unnecessary hours a week in church is preferable to an error leading to an eternity of damnation (although, as Bertrand Russell pointed out, there may be a "special place in hell" for those whose faith is based on Pascal's logic). Daly applies the same method to technology. If a technology is good and we delay or fail to develop it, we are probably only inconvenienced. However, embracing the wrong technology can lead to death, environmental damage, or, in the modern era, perhaps even widespread catastrophe. Daly concludes that "it would seem prudent to reject the omnipotent technology hypothesis."[6] But Daly's argument is not widely known and certainly not studied in business school. Profit maximization continues to relentlessly drive technological innovation.[7] High profits require new, highly profitable products and more efficient production techniques, regardless of their impact on society or the Earth.[8]

One of the most instructive descriptions of the profit system comes from Joseph Heller's black comedy novel about World War II, *Catch 22*. The character Milo Minderbinder sets up a syndicate to sell supplies to the U.S. military and its allies in the Mediterranean region. The protagonist, Yossarian, doesn't understand how Milo can buy eggs for seven cents and sell them for five cents and still make a profit. Milo explains:

Because I'm the people I buy them from. I make a profit of three and a quarter cents apiece when I sell them to me and a profit of two and three quarter cents apiece when I buy them back from me. That's a total profit of six cents an egg. I lose only two cents an egg when I sell them to the mess halls at five cents apiece, and that's how I can make a profit buying eggs for seven cents apiece and selling them for five cents apiece. I pay only one cent apiece at the hen when I buy them in Sicily."[9]

This fanciful account reveals that what is termed an invisible hand is really the result of actual hands manipulating the economy. The invisible hand works well for those who know the rules and even better for those who make them.

The Social Foundation of Capitalism

As discussed earlier, the ethics and traditions of the preindustrial community tended to limit the development of technology. The original theory of capitalism presumed that these same traditional community values would provide an infrastructure undergirding the capitalist economy. When Adam Smith first defined the mechanisms of capitalism, he took for granted then-existing restraints not only of law, but also of morality, religion, and custom.[10] Smith presumed the continuity of many of the aspects of traditional society that he saw as limiting the potential harm of self-interested behavior.

This social morality inherited from its preindustrial and precapitalist past was essential for the development of capitalism. Unfortunately, capitalism itself has eroded that morality as it taught the ethic that following one's self-interest would in and of itself ensure the greatest common good.[11] When profit is the means of evaluating an enterprise's activity, other social and ethical values tend to slip by the way. While economic growth has often been examined in terms of the possibility of natural limits to growth, there are social limits as well. Human communities, political systems, cultural institutions, and even ethical norms feel the strain and over time may be lost or perverted by the elevation of self-interest over other values. Additionally, capitalist society de-emphasizes basic human needs by placing a greater value on "positional" goods—that is, goods that reflect the status of the owner—than it does on essential material goods. Newer, less widely available luxury goods such as compact disc players or high-resolution TVs become the locus of economic growth rather than food, clothing, or shelter. To ensure that the market meets social needs, some form of cooperation is needed, whether through the mechanisms of the government or via nonprofit or community organizations. As the social forms that supported the origins of capitalism have been eroded, government has increasingly been seen as the proper agency for this taming of the market. Many of the worst problems of capitalism, such as child labor, sweatshops, and unregulated discharge of pollutants, have been successfully corrected by the government. Unfortunately, government is subject to continual lobbying and other forms of influence by business to diminish any restricting or taming regulation.

One of the most powerful indictments of the free market is found in Murray Bookchin's essay "Market Economy or Moral Economy?" Bookchin argues that the market, rather than being amoral as economists claim, is, in fact, "grossly immoral." The market invades and subverts the most intimate and personal aspects of our lives, insinuating itself into our very thinking.[12] Without oversimplifying, it seems reasonable to suggest that a marriage, for example, viewed as an investment is more likely to be exchanged for one promising "a greater return" than is a marriage seen as "moral and spiritual." As the language of relatedness is replaced by the language of contract, so too is our ability to relate narrowed to mimic the contractual arrangement.

The assault of the market on traditional relations continued even into the twentieth century, as workers experienced a "sense of tension and contrast" traveling from shop to home and from factory to neighborhood. In contrast to the dehumanized world of the factory, the neighborhood still contained a "peripheral vision [of] an older, more congenial, and moral world." This world existed at least into the 1930s, at which time, although the workplace had a dog-eat-dog quality, the neighborhood still maintained a sense of solidarity and support.[13] Bookchin's perspective is not some vague nostalgia for times gone by. Rather, it reflects the importance of searching the history, way of life, and philosophy of diverse cultures to find the principles on which a "moral economy" and an ecological society can be built in the modern era.[14]

Critiques of Growth

At a 1987 conference on "Economics as if the Earth Mattered," Herman Daly declared that some of the most penetrating economic insights are available from television commercials. As a case in point, he offered a familiar ad from the investment firm Merrill Lynch:

> The scene opens with a bull trotting along an empty beach. Now this bull is obviously a very powerful animal. Nothing is likely to stop him. And there's a chorus in the background . . . and it goes "to know no boundaries. . . . " The bull is now trotting across a bridge that spans a deep gorge. There are no cars or bicycles or 18-wheel trucks crossing this bridge. So again the bull is alone, in an empty world, unobstructed by anything."[15]

As Daly interprets this ad, Merrill Lynch is promising a world without limits, "an empty world where strong and solitary individuals have free reign." But of course the real world is not empty. It is full of people, some like us, some different. It is full of other species. It is "a world with countless moral and ecological bonds." The irony is that Merrill Lynch depicts not the world we live in, but rather the world that awaits us as the outcome of the sort of antiecological growth-fixated economics it advocates: a barren, lifeless, lonely landscape.

Conventional economic calculations and the tyranny of the bottom line obscure a number of important real-world considerations. Financial accounting does not recognize the distinction between renewable and nonrenewable resources. Potential future scarcity is of no concern as long as the supply is plentiful today. The costs of environmental degradation are not considered, nor are the needs of future generations or the needs of other species for habitat. For example, those concerned with preserving biological diversity seek to modify conventional economics to come up with ways to confer economic value on the natural world, perhaps assigning other species an "existence value" or some estimate of their use value for future generations. They recognize that, without such measures, the Earth's biological heritage could be lost not only in the financial equation but also in fact.[16]

The growth economy allows profits to be earned from products that are socially or environmentally destructive, such as cigarettes and chemical pesticides.[17] Perhaps the most infamous case of high profits from deleterious products is the guaranteed profit margins offered to military contractors by the Pentagon, culminating in the notoriously expensive screwdrivers and toilet seats that became controversial in the Reagan years. The contribution of such harmful products to the economy forms the basis of criticism that has been leveled at reliance on the familiar gross national product (GNP) as the main measure of economic success. The GNP generally includes any economic activity that has a monetary value attached to it, regardless of whether or not it serves an actual social need. It is the quintessential expression of the way that profit maximization has narrowed values to a single barren standard.

My favorite example of the GNP's shortcomings is the case of asbestos. Asbestos contributed positively to the GNP for many years as it was sold as a building material. Then it was revealed that asbestos dust caused a dangerous lung disease, asbestosis. Asbestosis victims required medical care, the cost of which also contributed positively to the GNP. The victims then sued the asbestos manufacturers for damages. The legal costs again added to the GNP. Today, asbestos continues to positively affect the GNP through the "productive work" of construction crews around the nation that are busy removing asbestos from schools and other public buildings. Thus, the manufacture and sale of asbestos contributed to the economy far beyond the expectation of its manufacturers. Unfortunately, most of the impact was negative. The claim that GNP growth is the measure of a healthy society does not stand. If anything, the opposite may be indicated.[18]

Some economists have offered an alternative to the GNP that deducts environmental and social costs while adding in the value of nonmonetary economic contributions. These economists see a need for measures to guide policy makers and alternatives that provide better guidance than the GNP.[19] Unfortunately, while such measures would provide a more accurate picture of the overall economy, the individual firm would still be following the same rules of profit maximization, seeking to avoid the social and environmental costs of production. These alternative measures would provide little more than a clearer vantage point from which to view the destructive consequences of our economic system. Furthermore, by placing a dollar value on nonmonetary economic activity, they would be removing more of life from the moral sphere and placing it in the market sphere, further eroding what's left of the "congenial, moral world" that is the basis of an ecological society.

Growth economics creates a pressure to bring new products quickly to market that ultimately hurts both society and the environment. In this regard, science becomes subservient to industry as financial pressure devalues even human life. The corporate scientist may well defend the use of inadequately tested pesticides (for example) with the rationalization that industry cannot afford to wait the many years proper testing might require.[20] Product testing must conform to business plans that generally extend no more than five years into the future. Unfortunately, a four-to-five-year testing period is often not enough time to determine ecological effects.[21]

That the safeguarding of human life is not a matter of major concern for industry is evident from Ford Motor Company's notorious comparison of the legal cost of deaths from its poorly designed Pinto with the cost of a design change for safety. The Pinto's gas tank would easily rupture during a low-speed collision, increasing the likelihood of explosion or fire. A preventive measure would have cost $11 per vehicle. Using a U.S. government valuation of $200,000 per traffic fatality, Ford determined that installing the $11 part in each car would cost millions more than would the anticipated 2,100 burning gas tanks each year. Using standard cost-benefit accounting techniques, Ford financial analysts determined that the design change was too expensive. The explosively dangerous gas tank was left in place.

Catch 22 also contributes to this discussion through the character of Milo Minderbinder, who expands beyond the egg business described above and one day contracts simultaneously with the American military to bomb the German-held highway bridge at Orvieto and with the German military to defend the bridge.[22] He later justifies this action to a shocked Yossarian, whose tentmate was killed in the engagement, explaining that "maybe they [the Germans] did start the war, and maybe they are killing millions of people, but they pay their bills a lot more promptly than some allies of ours I could name. Don't you understand that I have to respect the sanctity of my contract with Germany?"[23] Although Minderbinder appreciates the sanctity of a contract, like Ford Motor Company he falls short in his commitment to the sanctity of life.

The question of adequate time for product testing exposes the limitations of the planning horizon of modern business. This five-year "long-range" horizon stands in marked contrast to the understanding of long-range by the indigenous peoples of North America. The Iroquois tribal leaders are said to have considered the impact seven to ten generations into the future when making decisions. That would be two hundred to three hundred years, an astounding time period for a people with a low-impact way of life. This time period makes sense when one considers natural cycles, such as the time it takes a forest to mature. The Iroquois leaders did not need incentives, tax abatements, or fines to induce them to take this perspective. It was an integral part of their culture.

If business decision makers adopted a similar planning horizon, many of the most environmentally destructive practices would likely cease. Certainly the production of wastes that take decades to decompose and of plutonium, which remains deadly for millennia, would be curtailed. Quite likely, the future potential of maintaining the incredible biodiversity of the tropical rain forests would outweigh the short-term profits from raising beef cattle instead. Such longer-range planning conflicts with financial planning tools such as net present value (NPV). The NPV projects returns on investments using anticipated interest rates. At 10 percent interest, an anticipated return has only 90 percent of the value a year from now that it does today. Each year, the return is further discounted, dropping under 50 percent after seven years to 15 percent in the twentieth year. The potential to maximize profit is thus greatest in the shortest possible time period. Because financial decision-making criteria value the present over the future, there is an incentive to deplete resources and invest the earnings in other enterprises.[24] The need for growth demands the speedy exploitation of resources for profit. This profitability increases the value of remaining resources, thus giving impetus to their use and ultimate depletion. While discounting may be a reasonable decision criterion for self-interested individuals with finite life spans, society itself is practically (one hopes) immortal. Thus the greater the impact of an economic decision on society as a whole, the more difficult it becomes to apply a meaningful discount rate.[25]

Short-term profit considerations may even make it desirable for an entrepreneur to make decisions that lead to the ruination of the business enterprise itself. After a quick profit is earned, it may make sense financially to let the business fail, as long as there is another opportunity for investment available.[26] The whaling industry, for example, without the intervention of environmentalists, would quickly eliminate the world's whale population. The oil companies seem quite eager to use up global oil reserves. Another example of this type of destruction involves a business cannibalizing, selling off, or allowing the deterioration of its productive assets for write-off. The cooperation of the authors of government tax laws is important to the profitability of these "losses."

The points I have made amount to a staggering indictment of capitalist economics. Capitalism depends on independent social forms to moderate its impact. Yet capitalism undermines and destroys those forms. Capitalism depends on a healthy planet and ecosphere in which economic activity can occur. Yet capitalism externalizes environmental damage, leaving the repair to disempowered communities. Finally, capitalism depends on the success of businesses but has room for "profitable" decisions that lead to the death of a business or the destruction of its natural or social foundations.

Noncapitalist Nations and the Environment

A predictable response to the suggestion that capitalist economics is, in part, at the root of the environmental crisis is to look around the world for an alternative. Modern economies, whether capitalist, socialist, or mixed, have been destructive to the natural environment. In particular, the environmental destruction in the formerly communist countries of eastern Europe is notoriously vast in scope. Among familiar concerns are devastated forests, cities choked with smog, and polluted rivers, lakes, and soils. Westerners point in smug derision at the terribly polluting automobiles produced by the former East Germany or at the tragic accident at Chernobyl.

Environmentalists could probably argue endlessly as to whether the environmental damage is worse in the East or the West. The point of agreement is that both areas have done their share. While local and regional damage may be worse in the East, the impact of the West has probably been greater on a planetary scale. The few areas where the Western record is clearly better can be attributed to greater opportunities for public intervention in government policy in the Western democracies, rather than to differences in the strictly economic realm. For example, one of the environmental success stories in the United States was citizen pressure to remove lead from gasoline. Such initiatives are not possible in nondemocratic political systems. While it is not difficult to come up with examples of such political measures to protect the Earth, one would be hard pressed to think of a case where the profit-oriented force of the market led to improved environmental policy. While the political systems have clearly differed, at the root of the common environmental legacy of East and West is a generally obscured correspondence between the economic structures and goals of both systems.

First, it must be recognized that all modern economies oriented toward international trade are subject to the rules and constraints of the global economy, which is a capitalist economy.[27] There are no significant global institutions concerned with the socialization of economic activity. The global economy is dominated by the trade of large-scale enterprises, for the most part private corporations but in some cases publicly owned. Whether public or private, these enterprises use the same narrowly economic measures of productivity and profit. In capitalist, socialist, and mixed economies, governments take on a similar responsibility for promoting the competitive trading position of their nation's industry in the global market economy. International finance agencies, most notably the World Bank and the International Monetary Fund, are controlled by the wealthy, industrialized capitalist nations and develop policies geared toward profit, commodity production, and the market. To compete with the West, socialist economies have been forced to seek the same efficiencies, innovations, and economies of scale as the capitalist firms themselves, by and large imitating Western production methods with their environmentally destructive consequences.

These various economies have also shared the modern commitment to materialism as the measure of societal success and to technological improvement as the means to material well-being. As in the West, economic growth has been the measure and the guide for economic planners in the East. Marx and Engels saw socialism as growing out of capitalism, ultimately to replace a system that met the material needs of the few with one that would meet the material needs of the many. Although many countries in western Europe, with strong labor parties and mixed economies, do better than the United States in areas such as workers' rights and quality of life, for the most part economic growth and quantitative measures of improvement guide and have guided those in power. No national economy intrinsically takes the environment "into account," and few provide workers with the power to actualize their concern for the Earth. The lives of working people, East and West, have by and large been subject to division of labor, socially alienating work conditions, and disempowering bureaucratic control.

Communism, as it has been practiced in the twentieth century, does not have the features of worker and community control envisioned by Marx and Engels or by the utopian socialists and anarchists of the nineteenth century. Both industry and government, in those economies, have been dominated by careerist elites and bureaucrats whose point of view, prerogatives, and way of life bear a remarkable resemblance to their counterparts in the corporations and government offices of the United States. These bureaucrats have benefited from their control of the means of production much as the captains of industry profit from their control of capital in the West. Rather than as a form of socialism, these economies may be more accurately described as "state capitalist."[28] The East, as much as the West, has been enthralled to the narrow values and the grow-or-die imperative of the global capitalist economy.

Of course, for the most part, communism is a thing of the past. Most of the world today is made up of noncommunist countries operating under explicitly capitalist economies with varying degrees of state planning, state ownership of key industries and services, and state intervention in the market. Sweden, for example, as the result of a strong labor-socialist movement in the early twentieth century, mixes a significant amount of planning and government support systems with a strong tradition of workers' rights under a growth-oriented market economy. While not avoiding the environmental ills of other nations, Sweden has been able to react more quickly once environmental problems are recognized. For example, Sweden responded to the Chernobyl accident with a plan for phasing out nuclear power and was among the first countries to commit itself to the elimination of chlorofluorocarbons (CFCs). The Swedish experience indicates that the political and economic empowerment of working people, even under a capitalist economy, is good for the earth but that it is not good enough.

Although an ecologically wise economy has not been implemented on a national level, the political climate, particularly in regard to democratic participation, has made a difference. Certainly, the lack of democratic government until recent years in eastern Europe limited citizens' responses to their environmental difficulties. On the other hand, Costa Rica, with a history of almost Jeffersonian land distribution and a strong democratic tradition, has the largest percentage of preserved land in the Western Hemisphere and has become a virtual laboratory for environmental innovation.[29]

The alternative to growth economics has been posed but nowhere realized. Fundamentally, what is needed is to replace the measures of quantity and growth with those of quality and stability. In the natural world there are only two things that grow endlessly: parasites and cancers. Both of these continue to grow until their host is destroyed. The analogy to the impact of growth capitalism on the environment is more than a casual one. By contrast, a mature ecological system is characterized by stability accompanied by a rich, fecund diversity of life-forms. The coral reef and the climax forest are examples of this. Those seeking to apply ecological principles to human society put special emphasis on this quality of stability coupled with diversity.

This approach, termed steady-state economics, looks toward a similar maturation of social systems, "an economy with constant stocks of people and artifacts maintained at some desired sufficient level."[30] The concept of sufficiency is in marked contrast to the more-is-better approach that is the hallmark of Western consumption-oriented economics. It is quite at odds with the growth imperative of capitalism to advocate the view that there might be such a thing as enough. A steady-state economy seeks sufficiency in the context of the requirements of both the social and the ecological systems in which economic activity takes place. It would ensure that the economy supports rather than erodes its social and ecological foundations. As discussed earlier, even were growth ecologically possible, ethical problems remain. Steady-state economics holds to an ethic that would consider the needs of all people, including future generations, and find intrinsic value in the well-being of other species and of the Earth itself.[31]

Another Fork in the Road

Chapter 2 concluded with Morris Berman's image of a fork in the road, one way leading to "salvation through science in technology," the other to "preservation . . . of the environment, . . . organic community structures," and the like. Our ability to choose between these paths is limited by our means of evaluating our choices. If our measure of value is based on profitability and economic growth, how can we differentiate between "the very paradigm that got us into trouble" and the environmentally benign alternatives available to us as we move into the twenty-first century?

This fundamental choice facing society can also be viewed as a choice between an immoral market economy on the one hand and a moral economy characterized by care and responsibility on the other.[32] The choice is not made through the invention of new economic measures and alternatives to the GNP. Rather it is rooted in the social relations, the broader values, and the understanding of nature on which the moral economy is based. Just as the market economy narrows values to the single measure of profit, the moral economy must be guided by and aimed at a broader expression of values. These values will be the basis for applying technology carefully, for restraining economic activity with sensitivity to social and environmental limitations, and for building an ecologically wise society. The communitarian ethic of preindustrial society was eroded over time by the constricting of values under growth-oriented capitalism, resulting in widespread and continuing environmental and social destruction. The application of life-affirming, sustainable values as part of a creative movement toward social and political transformation can begin to reverse that process.

Chapter 6

THE LOSS OF COMMUNITY: LAND AND LABOR AS COMMODITIES

Through the long annals of human history up until the dawn of the modern era, the buying and selling of land was a rare event. Primitive peoples generally understood the land as part of a web of life that included animal and plant species as well as humans of past and future generations. The Ashanti of Ghana have a saying that "land belongs to a vast family of whom many are dead, a few are living, and a countless host are still unborn." A good sense of this understanding of land is found in one of the best-known inspirations to the environmental movement: a speech believed to have been made by Chief Seattle in 1854. Although the chief, for whom the city is named, did give a noteworthy speech in that year, his own words are virtually unknown, while a version written by the screenwriter Ted Perry in 1972 has gained great renown. In this apocryphal speech, Chief Seattle is supposedly responding to an offer by the U.S. government to purchase Indian lands. "How can one buy or sell the air, the warmth of the land? That is difficult for us to imagine. We do not own the sweet air or the sparkle on the water. How then can you buy them from us? We are part of the Earth and the Earth is part of us. . . . When the Great Chief in Washington sends word that he wants to buy our land, he asks a great deal of us." There is a similar sentiment found in the

Judeo-Christian tradition. In Leviticus, God instructs the Hebrews that "the land shall not be sold in perpetuity, for the land is mine." Somehow, much as modern social structures may attempt to incorporate or justify themselves on the basis of biblical injunctions, this limited understanding of property is not widely emphasized.

The sale or purchase of human labor also has been a historic rarity. Although some people's labor was taken from them in the form of slavery or indentured servitude, even then the ability to work was not viewed as separate from the rest of a person's life. Generally, throughout history, a person's labor power was focused on meeting the needs of his or her family and the broader tribal or village community. These communities depended on the common work and interdependency of their people.

Before the capitalist era, land and labor were not even understood as entities separable from the life of the community.[1] Robert Heilbroner, seeking the historic foundations of modern economics, finds that "the whole world until the sixteenth or seventeenth century could not envisage the market system for the thoroughly sound reason that Land, Labor, and Capital—the basic agents of production which the market system allocates— did not yet exist. . . . [They] are as much modern conceptions as the calculus."[2] It is not mere coincidence that Heilbroner compares these "basic agents of production" to Isaac Newton's development of the calculus. Newton's work was part of the foundation of the scientific world-view that helped to dislocate humanity from nature. The commodification of land and labor —that is, the transformation of land and labor into commodities—provided much of the economic basis for that dislocation.

The term *commodity* is a familiar one today, and its definition is simple. Commodities are defined as objects produced for sale on the market.[3] Obviously, neither land nor labor is *produced* in the sense that we normally think of commodity production. Nor can they be said to exist in any fundamental sense merely for market exchange. Labor—that is, work—is a basic human activity regardless of the mode of social organization; nature is the foundation of life, regardless of whether society is itself ecologically sustainable or destructive.[4] Once land and labor have been made into commodities, the institutions and traditions that characterized preindustrial society are devalued and ultimately lost in a society now organized around commodity exchange. The "great transformation" that is entailed in this commodification can best be understood in its historical context.

Enclosing the Land

Land ownership, as we understand it today, is a concept of recent origin. Heilbroner points our that "as late as the fourteenth or fifteenth century there was no such thing as land in the sense of freely salable, rent-producing property."[5] Feudal society had its own stability for many centuries, based on notions of rights and obligations entirely different from those that we recognize today. Land was not subject to purchase or sale, and its use as well as any right of property was determined by a complex of institutional regulations and traditions.[6] Serfs in the Middle Ages generally had several acres of land to farm. Additionally, there were large areas of common land on which they could gather firewood and where their livestock could graze. These commons, as they were called, formed an integral part of the physical and cultural heritage and were a source of sustenance, security, and independence. The peasants had no ownership as such of the common land. Rather, they had a historically recognized right to use the commons to meet the needs of life.[7] The commons were protected by an ethic of stewardship and preservation and were, for the most part, self-renewing without human intervention. The law of the commons was unwritten, not only because writing was itself uncommon, but because the commons were a part of the traditions and communal knowledge of the people.

From the late fifteenth through the early nineteenth centuries, a process known as enclosure changed the face of the Europe, destroying the commons and the traditions that surrounded them. The history of enclosure is best known in England, where, as textile manufacturing became more sophisticated, there was a need for an increased supply of wool. Peasants were driven off the formerly common lands, which were "enclosed" and turned over to pasture land for sheep. The land appropriated by enclosure had often previously been held as common land or under a definite rent that was paid to the community.[8] Once enclosed, land was held under a modern type of deed that allowed it to be subdivided, and bought and sold. Previously, even when the monarch had deeded lands to favor one lord or another, the life of the indigenous peasant community generally continued without interruption. However, the new breed of landlords sought to turn their property over to new forms of profitable enterprise and thought nothing of the violent destruction of homes and communities.

An often-cited case of enclosure occurred in 1820, at the end of the era in question. The Duchess of Sutherland had 15,000 tenants evicted from 794,000 acres of land and replaced them with 131,000 sheep.[9] British soldiers violently forced these people out, destroying their villages and crops.[10] The remaining inhabitants of these communities wound up living on marginal land by the seashore, where they tried to live by catching fish. Heilbroner describes riots against enclosure in which as many as 3,500 people were killed. He concludes that "it is almost impossible to imagine the scope and impact of the process of enclosure" and what he calls "its terrible historic course."[11]

In England, the enclosures were sanctioned by the passing of official acts by Parliament, giving license to actions such as that of the Duchess of Sutherland. In France, the Code Napoléon established new forms of property ownership and made land a good fit for commerce.[12] Writing in the second half of the nineteenth century, Karl Marx concluded that "the very memory of the connection between the agricultural labourer and the communal property had vanished."[13]

The Creation of Labor

As in the case of the families evicted by the Duchess of Sutherland, the impact of the enclosures was catastrophic for the lives of the common people. The dislocation caused by enclosure included the loss of their land, their communities, and their livelihoods. Their lives lost meaning, structure, and coherence as they were driven from their ancestral homelands, no longer able to subsist through farming, often arriving at last, destitute, in the burgeoning cities.[14] With the growing availability of workers and in spite of strong cultural resistance and fear, the emerging forces of industrialism led to the commercialization of labor, ultimately creating the great proletarian work force on which industrial capitalism depends.

The livelihood of the agricultural proletarians and beggars uprooted by enclosure was tenuous indeed. Just as the state had given the landlords license to enclose the land, it channeled displaced workers toward the factories. English statutes, as early as 1547, condemned anyone who refused to work as an "idler" who should be sentenced to slavery. Other laws sentenced vagabonds to flogging or the galleys.[15] Once they were within the embrace of the wage system, Elizabethan law required the poor to take any work regardless of the wage offered. Additional laws mandated maximum wages at a subsistence level, ensuring the impoverishment of the workers. The English state insisted that those driven off the land work whether they wished to or not, and that they do so for low wages. In this manner early capitalism was provided with an abundant supply of cheap labor.

It is the same force of commodification that led to poor laws and maximum wages in the sixteenth century, sweatshops and child labor in the nineteenth, and the relocation of production facilities to the Third World in the twentieth. The low-wage workers of the Third World, infamous as competitors of their more highly paid American counterparts, are, in many cases, the twentieth-century equivalent of the vagabonds described by Marx, forced by the economically and politically powerful to leave their traditional way of life to work for whatever wage they can earn. Both the imperialism of the nineteenth century and the international economic development programs and free-trade agreements of the twentieth have had a similar impact on Third World peoples to the impact the enclosures had on the peasants of western Europe. In the 1830s, the Cherokee, Creek, and Choctaw tribes were among those Native Americans forcibly driven from their ancestral homelands in the southern United States to make room for "King Cotton." Many thousands died as they were forced to the as-yet-unsettled (by Europeans) western lands along what, in the case of the Cherokee, became known as the "Trail of Tears." More recently, in the 1980s and 1990s, Native Americans and environmentalists in Canada have been fighting the expansion of the James Bay hydroelectric project, which threatens to flood thousands of square miles of hunting and fishing territory that is home to a traditionally sustainable Native American way of life. The product is electricity rather than wool or cotton, but the effect of this contemporary enclosure is as devastating as that of its earlier counterparts.

Apologists for the capitalist system hail the creation of labor as a step toward human freedom, allowing people to work where they please and receive the highest wage they can. In fact, self-reliance has been traded for dependency either on the availability of work for a corporation or on government paternalism.[16] The notion of the free laborer is a capricious one. This is highlighted by the North American Free Trade Agreement, which allows corporations to produce and sell goods regardless of international borders but does not grant the same privilege to workers in search of better wages and working conditions. Generally speaking, the laborer is free only to accept or decline available work at the wage offered. More often than not, economic necessity makes this a hollow freedom, particularly for working-class and less-skilled laborers. While highly trained specialists may be the subject of bidding wars between corporations, most workers today compete with each other for a dwindling number of jobs offered at ever-lower wages.

The general availability of labor as a marketable commodity was a major departure from anything that had been known before. Prior to the sixteenth century, wage labor, when found, was a rarity, confined to the margins of the economy. This was especially true outside the larger towns or cities.[17] For the most part, productive activities were integrated with the other necessities of human life and embedded in the life of the community. They were regulated by custom and, in some cases, guild rule. To the extent that, over the years, workers have organized and developed trade unions to influence the price of their labor or how it should be used, they have sought to reverse the commodification of their endeavors, creating a broader social context for their labors and a democratic structure for the workplace.

Thus, the seizing of land and the creation of a land commodity forced the peasant masses from their agrarian heritage, creating the labor commodity in its turn. The centuries-old sustainable, tradition-bound community was obliterated by the closures. Any impulse of the people to recreate it was smas..... by legally enforced labor. Ultimately, the bonds of mutual aid in the form of village and kinship were shattered as the life of the worker was reshaped in response to the requirements of industrial capitalism.

Land as Commodity

Although the creation of the labor commodity is a modern innovation, it is in some sense just the latest version of the historic pattern of "man's inhumanity to man." The invention of the land commodity was a far more revolutionary turn, unprecedented in history.[18] With land seen as a commodity, without the embedded organic relationship of the human community within nature, both the natural environment and human society were gravely threatened. The difference between land as commodity and land as community was well expressed by the environmental pioneer Aldo Leopold, who wrote that "we abuse land because we regard it as a commodity belonging to us. When we see land as a community to which we belong, we may begin to use it with love and respect."[19]

Once land is viewed as a commodity, its use is subject to the short-term profit criteria discussed in the previous chapter. Its fertility and other characteristics can be depreciated just like any other form of capital. The result is that, for example, the amount of topsoil in parts of the United States was reduced from four feet in the eighteenth century to less than one foot today. Soil fertility is not the only aspect of the natural world that is subject to such depreciation. The mature hardwoods of old-growth forests are the result of hundreds of years of natural development. Logging companies "owning" those forests have a clear economic incentive to cut them down for quick profit, replacing them with faster-growing species that can be harvested more often. The impact of the resulting clear-cutting on the ecology of the U.S. Northwest and on wild species has been at the root of the dispute between environmentalists and loggers going on in that area. The loggers, whose livelihoods depend on the continued "harvesting" of those forests, see the environmentalists as valuing spotted owls more than people.

The environmentalists struggle to point out that, once the forests are gone, the loggers as well will be an endangered species. The unfortunate irony here is that while the fate of the forest and the spotted owl is rooted in the commodification of land, the fate of the logger is bound up in his need to market his labor as a commodity. In this manner, these two historically unlikely commodities reinforce each other to provide the basis for both environmental destruction and social dislocation.

The commodification of land also places it within the scope of the modern sanctification of the right of private property. For example, a familiar struggle of environmentalists is for the protection of watersheds, particularly those lands draining into municipal water supplies. To protect a watershed, development of the surrounding land must be limited. Inevitably, land owners cry foul, insisting that their right to dispose of their land for maximum profit is being infringed. In an ecological society, this conflict would not occur, since all parties would feel a fundamental allegiance to the well-being, sustenance, and sustainability of the broader community.[20] Perhaps the best-known philosophic attack on the right to hold land as private property was that of Jean-Jacques Rousseau, who, in a 1754 essay entitled "The Origin of Inequality," reviled the invention of private property.

> The first person who, having enclosed a plot of land, took it into his head to say *This is mine* and found people simple enough to believe him was the true founder of civil society. What crimes, wars, murders, what miseries and horrors would the human race have been spared, had someone pulled up the stakes or filled in the ditch and cried out to his fellow men: "Do not listen to this imposter. You are lost if you forget that the fruits of the earth belong to all and the earth to no one!"[21]

Although Rousseau was not familiar with acid rain or global warming or toxic waste, the environmental crises would readily fall under the rubric of "miseries and horrors" that we might well have been spared.

Twentieth-Century Enclosures

The usurping of the commons did not end with the last of the nineteenth-century enclosures. Much of the contemporary destruction of rain forests in the Third World occurs as lands previously held in common by tribal people are redefined as commodities for private ownership and profit. Ivan Illich has described the contrast he observed thirty years ago between the roads in the older and newer sections of Mexico City, at a time when much of the city was first being modernized. In the old sections, roads were filled with people selling vegetables and charcoal, drinking coffee or tequila, or perhaps holding informal meetings. Donkeys and carts were common. Children were at play in the street. In the newer sections, the scene was one more familiar to the average American. Taxis, cars, and trucks sped by. There was no place for people. The old roads were still commons, the latter merely resources for the circulation of vehicles.[22]

Even today, public or common resources continue to be subject to commodification. The Reagan and Bush administrations promoted a policy of privatization of public programs and publicly owned resources. The opening of national forests to paper companies or of national parks to grazing forms a contemporary version of enclosure.[23] In this case the loss is not human communities but the dwindling preserve of natural areas.

The development of the modern economy and the resulting commodification of labor also underlie much of the current discrimination against women. Prior to the modern era, there were not the differences in economic status between the genders that are found today. While the patriarchal abuse and domination of women is as old as history, preindustrial society generally consisted of autonomous women's and men's domains, each respectful of and dependent on the other. The requirements of the labor market destroyed these gender domains along with the communities that had sustained them.[24] The men then sought to sell their labor as a commodity to enable the women to continue to work at home and look after the small children. Since capitalist society could place a value only on commodities, the unpaid work of women was devalued relative to that of men.

With this transformation came the creation of what Illich calls "shadow work." The products of industrial society are not generally usable without additional inputs of labor by the consumer. Shadow work is thus any labor by which the consumer transforms a purchased commodity into a usable good.[25] For example, in earlier times, food was either grown or collected near the home, ready to be eaten or cooked. Modern convenience allows us to maintain a car to drive to the supermarket, to stand in long lines to purchase groceries, to drive back home, and in the end to pay for the disposal of the packaging. All of these tasks are modern innovations that amount to "the unpaid upgrading of what wage labor produced," without which the commodity could not be used. Shadow work in effect subsidizes the producer of the commodity. For example, when Chapel Hill, North Carolina, started a plastics recycling program, citizens were encouraged to "stomp" on their soda and milk bottles before dropping them off at the recycling center. One local Green activist only half jokingly suggested that the time spent stomping be totaled up and a bill presented to the plastics manufacturer. After all, these citizens' voluntary efforts at recycling help the manufacturer to sell profitable nonreusable containers. Illich points out that the tasks of shadow work have been and continue to be primarily the province of women.

The commodification of the human being did not stop with the sale of labor power. Currently, controversy revolves around the marketing of body parts, fetal tissue, and reproductive capacity. To a great extent, the "supplies" of these "commodities" depend on the economic disadvantage of women, who in fact make up the majority of our poor.[26] For example, the television program "L.A. Law" ran an episode on December 6, 1990, featuring the availability of kidneys for purchase from impoverished women. The ethically fastidious attorneys had little difficulty maneuvering around the inconvenience of the law to obtain this commodity for a wealthy client. The issue of surrogate motherhood has also troubled the courts, most notably in the 1987 Baby M case. A woman's bearing a child for sale is another case of custom and law being overturned for the sake of a commodity.[27] Pregnancy has not yet become an overt service industry, offering babies for sale on the open market, but the forces of commodification and harsh economic necessity press women in that direction.

The march of commodification has been long, nasty, and insidious, from the gross dislocations of late-medieval peasantry to the contemporary loss of public resources and programs to the sale of poor women's body parts and children. Its impact on human society has been thorough. Enclosure has erased the moral economy that characterized most of human history. Commodification is the result of and also further feeds the narrowing of values to the simple, destructive measure of profit. Moreover, commodification fundamentally contradicts the participation of people in a democratic process of determining their fate as a community.

To reverse this process of commodification, a new sense of community must be created. This will not be a merely human community, but an ecological community in which society is rooted in harmony in its natural environment. Such a community will depend on the democratic participation of its people in its definition, its sustenance, and its development. A clear articulation of sustainable, life-affirming values will be basic to such a community. Above all, since the obstacles against such a community are formidable, attaining it will require committed effort and sustained organizing. Since the final form of such a community is today unknown, an active imagination, a willingness to experiment, and the patience to take an occasional step backward along with two steps forward will be needed in order to ultimately achieve an ecological society.

III

ECOLOGY AND POLITICS

Chapter 7

VALUES: THE PILLARS OF EFFECTIVE ACTIVISM

> *Movement toward a lasting society cannot occur without a transformation of individual priorities and values.—Lester Brown,* The State of the World 1990

Historically, a narrowing of values accompanied the rise of a materialistic and profit-oriented economy. Today, broad holistic values do not come easily to us. We are too imbued with the materialistic values and fragmented world-view that characterize the modern era. By contrast, in many cases the societies of the preindustrial era maintained an environmentally sustainable way of life based on life-affirming values that evolved over a long period of time. These values were characterized by a sensitivity to the particular ecological characteristics of a locality and to the sustained livelihood of its people. The values on which an ecological society will be built are not those of some more simple culture that may have thrived in the past. Rather, they are values that must be synthesized from a variety of sources: the experience of many cultures, the complex web of the natural world, an understanding of human history, and lessons from the inquiry and exploration of many disciplines. Formulating the values on which an ecological society can be built is more than an intellectual exercise. The values must be consciously applied and kept close to the heart of our organizing and activity, both public and private.

The philosopher and educator John Dewey described the keynote of democracy as "the necessity for the participation of every mature human being in the formation of values that regulate the living of men together."[1] This participation in the formation of values is also the keynote of an ecological society. To counter the trend toward commodification, competition, and individualism, it is necessary to develop, to teach, and to reinforce values of community, ecology, and citizenship. These must be part of the everyday affairs of life. The power of materialistic values is so great today that the importance of consciously fortifying alternative values must be stressed, and stressed again.

A genuinely transformational movement, whose goal is to change our environmentally destructive society to an ecologically sustainable one, cannot view particular values in isolation from one another. For example, it has often been pointed out that the Nazis were great naturalists. Thus, valuing nature alone is not enough. Similarly, a commitment to global responsibility could be interpreted as requiring the kind of paternalistic neo-colonialist attitude toward the Third World that is prevalent today. Valuing global responsibility alone is not enough. As we have seen, a democratic form of government will not ensure environmentally wise policy when outcomes are evaluated by the narrow measures of profit and growth. Valuing democracy alone is not enough.

The alternative is to place values in a holistic context that can inspire a comprehensive movement toward an ecological society. The Green movement has created such a context. The early European Green parties espoused what they termed their "four pillars:" ecology, social justice, grassroots democracy, and nonviolence. The U.S. Green party, at its founding in 1984, added six more values to make up a list of "ten key values." In addition to the four pillars, the U.S. Greens added the values of decentralization, community-based economics, feminism, respect for diversity, personal and global responsibility, and future focus (or sustainability). The importance of this value orientation to the Greens is well expressed by their introductory brochure:

> This is not a list of ten separate issues but aspects of a coherent unified world view [that] are interconnected in a very basic way. They convey our commitment to a value-based politics, a new politics that seeks to create a shared sense of the common good rather than the old

politics that promotes one sectional interest at the expense of others. . . . [The Greens' organization] exists to promote and embody these values.

This chapter will examine the ten key values as the basis of a movement toward an ecological society. The contention is not that these form the only, or necessarily the best, statement of values. The Greens themselves have modified the list on occasion and will likely do so again from time to time. Nonetheless, these ten values provide the example here because they are inclusive, workable, and relevant in that they are already widely recognized in the United States.

Members of the Green movement often give primacy to one or more of the values over the others, usually corresponding to their own interests. Environmentalists may emphasize ecological wisdom; feminists, feminism; internationalists, global responsibility. This section gives special attention to grassroots democracy, which is viewed as a central enabling mechanism for the success of a transformational movement as well as a fundamental attribute of an ecological society. A major emphasis will also be placed on the concepts of cooperation and community, expanded from the value of community-based economics. Community, in this sense, will be viewed as comprising elements of social responsibility, sustainability, decentralization, respect for diversity, and ecological wisdom. In other words, it will provide a perspective for integrating the various values in a meaningful, pragmatic context.

Certainly, each of the ten values could merit an entire chapter, if not its own volume. The brief treatment here is an effort not to lose sight of the importance of the totality of the ten values and their interconnectedness. The U.S. Greens' statement on the ten key values originally presented each value through a series of questions. Excerpts from these questions, with occasional minor modification, followed by a brief discussion provide the format for what follows. The ten key values are presented as one answer to the question, What are the values of an ecological society?

Ecological Wisdom

How can we operate human societies with the
understanding that we are part of nature? How
can we live within the ecological and resource
limits of the planet? How can we promote respect
for self-regulating natural systems?

A powerful understanding of humanity's connection with the
Earth is generally credited to the Native American peoples. Ironically, the best-known expression of this understanding is the
speech usually attributed to Chief Seattle, whose actual author,
as we saw, is the screenwriter Ted Perry. Perry should be credited with composing a beautiful statement of ecological wisdom: "Humankind has not woven the web of life. We are but
one thread within it. Whatever we do to the web, we do to
ourselves. All things are bound together. All things connect.
Whatever befalls the Earth befalls also the children of the Earth."
These words suggest a sense of relationship and responsibility,
not only of humanity for the Earth, but of people for each
other. They suggest a fundamental ethical sensibility that,
if adopted by contemporary society, would simultaneously
forestall the rampant extinction of nonhuman species and the
spreading impoverishment of human communities. The words
challenge us to understand the connections between the world's
myriad life-forms and the diverse forms of human society and to
make a commitment to their common vitality and preservation.
If its actual authorship had been known, the speech might not
have attained its current prominence. But in a way, it is even
more heartening that such a clear and inspiring vision could be
articulated by a contemporary American.

Ecological wisdom is, in a sense, the goal of this entire book.
The essence of ecological wisdom was expressed with cogent
simplicity by Aldo Leopold: "A thing is right when it tends to
preserve the integrity, stability, and beauty of the biotic community; it is wrong when it does otherwise."[2] By this standard,
much of human activity today must be wrong, wreaking havoc,
as it does, with the natural world, paving over the beauty of
nature, and depleting the rich diversity of life-forms. Yet
Leopold's definition is too simple. One must take care to avoid

a definition of biotic community that might leave humanity out of the picture. Many environmentalists attempt to place a biocentric or life-centered world-view in opposition to what they see as the anthropocentric or human-centered orientation of contemporary society. This viewpoint overlooks the damage that the instrumental world-view has done to humanity as well as to the Earth. It is not the presumed anthropocentrism of the modern world, but rather its materialistic egocentrism and instrumentality that underlie the environmental crisis.

Nonetheless, a discussion of biocentrism leads to an appreciation of the interconnectedness found within the natural world. One popular expression of this is the Gaia hypothesis of James Lovelock. In this view, the life-forms existing on planet Earth, in their entirety, are seen as a "single living entity." This entity maintains the Earth's atmosphere and ability to support life through a vastly complex web of symbiotic relations.[3] That such a web would include human society is well expressed in Ted Perry's rendering of the speech of Chief Seattle: "whatever we do to the web [of life], we do to ourselves. . . . All things connect." Ecological wisdom challenges us to understand the interdependency and inherent value of the Earth's multitude of species. In contrast to the hyperrationalism of the modern world-view, ecological wisdom connotes a respect for the intuitive and participatory experience as well. Ecological wisdom seeks an orientation in which the rational and the intuitive reinforce each other in an appreciation of human society as an integral part of the natural world.

Acceptance of interconnectedness, even without considering the Earth itself as a volitional entity, is quite contrary to the fragmented perspective of the modern world-view.[4] This fragmentation is found etymologically in the derivation of the word "environment" itself. Its French root, *environner,* to surround, implies that nature is something around us, something apart from us. The concept of ecology, by contrast, emphasizes connectedness and firmly places humanity within nature. In this context, the first point in the value statement is critical: human societies are part of nature. The social ecology of Murray Bookchin sees the social attributes of the human species as part of natural evolution. Humanity expresses the qualities of freedom, reason, and ethics in the natural world. Just as human society arises as part of nature, humanity's impact on the natural environment is mediated through its social forms. Behind much of the analysis in this book lies Bookchin's tenet that "all ecological problems will have their roots in social problems."[5]

Respect for Diversity

How can we honor cultural, ethnic, racial, sexual, religious, and spiritual diversity within the context of individual responsibility to all beings?

The importance of diversity in nature is demonstrated in the thriving coevolution of millions of species around the planet. Mature ecosystems such as the coral reef and the climax forest are characterized by a rich diversity of life forms. Respect for diversity thus entails a lesson in environmental and social values drawn from the natural world. The thrust of contemporary society is to have people around the planet eating at McDonald's and watching the same sitcoms on television, forming a uniform global economy of commodity-based consumption. Such a society is fundamentally alienated from the Earth and inevitably misunderstands, devalues, and, finally, destroys the environment. Respect for diversity asserts that differing natural conditions and the different life experiences of diverse locales lead to different cultural experiences, to unique and varying ways of life around the world.

Respecting this diversity goes hand in hand with honoring the unique natural characteristics of a particular ecosystem. Human cultures have historically tended to be well adapted to and supportive of the stability and vitality of their natural environs. Traditional cultures depend utterly upon and therefore respect and value the neighboring biota. They would not be implicated in the wholesale destruction of species that characterizes the contemporary era. It is no wonder that as the modern economy attempts to get everyone living the same way, using the same resources and technology and externalizing environmental and social costs, this sensitivity to the natural world is lost, leading to the destruction of any habitat suited to species other than humans and cockroaches. Respect for diversity will lead to diverse social forms, celebrating and supporting the diversity of life and community in countless ways around the planet.

The value called "respect for diversity" is sometimes also called "inclusiveness." This goes one step farther than merely honoring the differences among people and places. It calls on a transformational movement to actively seek out and include the diverse elements of a community, particularly those who tend to be disempowered and on the receiving end of social and environmental problems. In practice, diversity in itself is often a barrier to inclusiveness. Different ethnic or cultural experiences, for example, will lead to different goals and thus to different political strategies. All groups will not always be included in all projects. Respect for diversity is a fundamental principle. Inclusiveness is an important, but sometimes elusive, goal. The commitment to inclusiveness of the U.S. Greens is embodied in their bylaws' guarantee of representation to various minorities on all decision-making bodies of the movement.

Decentralization

How can we restore power and responsibility to individuals, institutions, communities, and regions? How can we encourage the flourishing of regionally based culture, rather than a dominant monoculture? How can we have a decentralized, democratic society with our political, economic, and social institutions locating power on the smallest scale (closest to home) that is efficient and practical?

Arising naturally from ecological wisdom and respect for diversity is an appreciation of decentralization. It is obvious from the most casual observations of the natural world that different things grow, and grow differently, in different locales. Thus, an ecologically oriented society will be decentralized so as to be sensitive to both environmental and social diversity. Historically, the traditions and folklore of indigenous people often provide for the preservation of the natural environment through their responsiveness to local conditions. Even the U.S. National Research Council has recognized that the important environmental goal of preserving biodiversity depends on understandings that may only be found in the local knowledge systems of traditional communities around the world.[6]

Decentralization asserts that those living closest to environmental conditions have the best knowledge of them and should have the power of policy-making and stewardship. To be effective, the principle of decentralization must be applied to political and economic power as part of a movement of reinvigorated grassroots democracy. National and international organizations in an ecologically responsible world order must be reoriented to support the development of organizational forms that allow direct grassroots democracy to function at the regional or even the global level.

Environmentalists organizing around the principle of decentralization have formed a movement known as "bioregionalism," which seeks a way of life that is responsive to the unique ecological requirements of diverse places. Bioregionalists would structure society around geopolitical entities known as bioregions, defined not by arbitrary political factors but with a sensitivity to natural conditions, such as watersheds, changing flora and fauna, and differing soil types or geological formations. Bioregionalists maintain not only that the unique characteristics of a locality lead to a particular way of meeting the needs of human life but also that culture will take correspondingly unique forms in a society that is harmonized with the natural world.[7] The principles of bioregionalism can be applied to urban as well as rural life.

Decentralization also has a tactical aspect for a movement seeking a transformation to an ecological society. Put simply, the closer one gets to the arena of centralized, concentrated power, the less chance there is to contend successfully with that power. A major obstacle to success is the fact that transformational movements, like efforts at independent politics, tend to be ignored at the national level. For example, in the 1992 U.S. elections, there were twenty-one independent or third-party candidates on the ballot for the presidency in at least one state. Only H. Ross Perot, who spent some sixty million dollars of his multibillion-dollar fortune, received any serious attention from the news media and the pundits. Similarly, thousands of environmental groups are engaged in daily struggles around the United States, but only a few large national organizations receive even negligible attention. Operating in a decentralized manner at the local or regional level, both environmental organizations and political campaigns can get the attention they deserve. Even if a transformational movement succeeds in gaining attention in the national arena, it must face the likelihood of co-optation, marginalization, distortion, and even violent suppression by the state, as has been the fate of such movements in the past.[8] A decentralized movement can better control communications to its membership and to the public. It can also better differentiate itself from its mainstream opponents. Decentralization makes it more difficult for opponents to find leaders to discredit or eliminate or to sow dissension through infiltration.

These, of course, are the more negative and defensive reasons for decentralization. In a positive sense, decentralization is important in providing the scale necessary for participatory democracy. It provides a home for community-based economics and an awareness of the characteristics and needs of the diversity of life and culture as they vary from place to place.

Future Focus and Sustainability

How can we induce people and institutions to think in terms of the long-range future, and not just in terms of their short-range selfish interest? How can we encourage people to develop their own visions of the future and move more effectively toward them? How can we judge whether new technologies are socially useful and use those judgments to shape our society? How can we make the quality of life, rather than open-ended economic growth, the focus of future thinking?

Sustainability relates to a number of concepts presented earlier: sufficiency, steady-state economics, and the Iroquois notion of seven generations as the basis for decision making. Recall that for the Iroquois, considerations of the distant future were not part of some abstract analysis like our own cost-benefit ratios but were an intrinsic part of their culture. For us, in a culture characterized by planned obsolescence and the annual model change, sustainability must be consciously and intentionally made a part of our thinking.

Sustainability entails meeting the needs of the present without compromising the ability of future generations to do so. The simplest expression of sustainability involves asking in regard to each policy or decision, Will my grandchildren also be able to enjoy living in this way? This clarifies many issues. Of course, chemical-based agriculture, which depends on the limited resource of petroleum and which is rapidly eroding our topsoil, is not sustainable. Of course, fossil-fuel-based transportation and energy systems are not sustainable. Of course, an economy that annually pours billions of tons of pollutants into the air, land, and sea is not sustainable.

Advocates of the "grow or die" imperative like to equate sustainability with stagnation. In their view, only a robust and growing consumer demand will lead to innovation and improvement. But when development is motivated by profit, innovation is driven by the need for capital accumulation, regardless of the nature of the overall social and environmental consequences. In reality, the commitment to an unsustainable way of life has, in some cases, slowed innovation. For example, oil and nuclear interests have steered federal research and development funds toward their products and away from renewable energy sources. In addition, profit-driven organizations, with their emphasis on hierarchy and control, tend to stifle creativity. A sustainable society will be one that, rather than relentlessly turning human and natural resources into captital, frees people from the alienation of the rat race, providing the time and opportunity for continuing education and exploration that can unlock a wellspring of human imagination and inventiveness. The foundation of such a society is an understanding of sustainability that implies not only respect for the natural environment but also a fair distribution of economic and social rewards and opportunities so that all people have a stake as well as a share in a common future.

Sustainability is also an important criterion for grassroots organizing for those seeking an ecologically wise, socially just society. Organizing must be done in a way that increases participation, prevents burnout, is financially tenable, and consciously faces obstacles to its continuity. The transformation to an ecological society requires building sustainable organizations that can serve as models for a sustainable society. The quality of sustainability in this sense is not the same as indefinite persistence and is quite different from the notorious ability of bureaucracies to sustain themselves by ensuring their own continued existence, regardless of whether any useful purpose is served. What is required is activist organizations that see their role as not just bringing about change but also embodying the change that they seek, organizations that understand the need not only to organize for but to model and promote a just and ecological society.

Feminism

How can we replace the cultural ethics of dominance and control with more cooperative ways of interacting? How can we encourage people to care about persons outside their own group? How can we promote the building of respectful, positive, and responsible relationships across the lines of gender and other divisions? How can we encourage a rich, diverse political culture that respects feelings as well as rationalist approaches and respects the contemplative inner part of life as much as outer activities? How can we proceed with as much respect for the means as the end?

Feminism entails a commitment to the liberation and empowerment of women, understanding the fundamental disparities in respect, opportunity, and power inherent in the gender roles of our patriarchal society. Those embracing feminism ally themselves with the many struggles of the women's movement: for reproductive freedom, for pay equity, for health care, for child care, for humane family-leave policies, and for an end to rape and violence against women. Feminism recognizes that whether it is through abuse in the home, harassment and wage discrimination in the workplace, or inequity of funding and support in government programs, women continue to experience oppression in all contemporary social, economic, and political settings.

As well as these somewhat traditional meanings of feminism, Greens generally subscribe to a feminist perspective known as "ecofeminism," which recognizes the relationship between the exploitation of women and that of the Earth. Ecofeminism is an understanding of feminism that developed along with increasing environmental awareness in the 1970s and 1980s. Ynestra King, one of its leading proponents, has characterized ecofeminism as "an urgent, angry critical feminist movement propelled by a powerful sense of historical urgency to end the domination of human over human in order to end the domination of people over nonhuman nature and make possible the continuation of life on earth."[9] Thus, ecofeminism places the common association of women with nature in the context of an extensive history of hierarchy and domination. Human beings, men as well as women, arise out of and remain part of nature. It is not that patriarchal society forges an identification of women with nature so much as that it represses the sense of men's and society's connection to nature. Such a dissociation is required by a mechanistic world-view. Ecofeminism resituates humanity in its natural context, while asserting that there are no hierarchies in nature. It places a prominent focus on the status of women in society, while affirming that the battle against the oppression of women and the battle against the defiling of the Earth are two aspects of a common struggle.

Although rooted in the modern rationalist tradition, ecofeminism rejects the preeminence of rationalism as a way of knowledge. In the words of Ynestra King, ecofeminism is "informed by all ways of knowing—intuitive *and* scientific, mystical *and* rational. . . . [It holds] the potentiality of a *rational reenchantment.*"[10] It is significant that ecofeminism's embrace of the intuitive and mystical couples those sensibilities with the rational and scientific. The nature-based spirituality of some environmentalists has been justifiably criticized as having the potential for supporting an authoritarian naturalism similar to that of the National Socialists of the 1930s. Ecofeminism, by linking an ecologically oriented spirituality with a social ethic based in feminism (especially significant for its critique of hierarchy), ensures that its potential for "rational reenchantment" is consistent with human freedom and empowerment.

An important feminist contribution to the discussion of values, though not of the ecofeminist school, is found in the work of the psychologist Carol Gilligan. Reviewing a number of studies that indicate differing concepts of self and morality among men and women, Gilligan concludes that the morality of men is one of justice, individuality, and rights, while that of women emphasizes care, relatedness, and responsibility. Women view relations as weblike; men view them as hierarchical. Although some interpret Gilligan's work as indicating a fundamental moral difference between the genders, for our purposes it is important in that it reinforces the ecofeminist's equation of hierarchy and patriarchy and leads environmentalists to think of the nonhuman world in terms of what kinds of care and relatedness are meaningful between humans and the rest of nature. This relatedness is based, not on a patriarchal concept of rights, but on an expanded emphasis on humanity's connection to nature.[11]

Thus, the lessons for ecological politics from feminism are based on care, knowledge, and relatedness. In a hierarchical society, an ethic of power is promoted. Power over people implies power over the Earth. It is not necessary to argue whether the domination of women precedes the domination of nature or vice versa in order to assert the obvious fact that, in the modern world, the two go hand in hand. A caring society will not be one that depends on coercing people into a competitive struggle for socially scarce rewards. Rather, it will be based on mutual respect and understanding and will be made up of people who work cooperatively for the common good. A society made up of caring and cooperative people will be a society that cares for the Earth.

Social Justice

How can we respond to human suffering in ways that promote dignity? How can we encourage people to commit themselves to lifestyles that promote their own health? How can we have a community-controlled education system that effectively teaches our children academic skills, ecological wisdom, social responsibility, and personal growth? How can society be organized to meet the needs of all its people, allowing each the opportunity for self-expression and personal well-being?

As the ecological society learns to value the Earth, so it values all of the people of the Earth. Valuing the people of the Earth in turn leads to a commitment to social justice. Social justice asserts the right of each individual, of each community, and of every people to the rewards and opportunities of life. More than a fair distribution of goods, social justice implies equitable access to health care, education, food and shelter, cultural enrichment, personal and community expression, and political power. At its most idealistic, in a socially just society no person would seek status or material accumulation at the expense of another, understanding fully that the well-being of all enriches the well-being of each individual, and vice versa.

Social justice has an environmental aspect as well, embracing the endeavors and concerns of what is known as the environmental justice movement. Around the world, the poor and disenfranchised are the primary victims of both environmental destruction and social inequity. Environmental justice insists that it is not acceptable for one society or community to achieve environmental health at the expense of its less affluent neighbors. In the United States, the environmental justice movement has focused primarily on fighting the placement of waste facilities in poor and minority communities. It is well established that such communities have for decades been and continue to be targeted for landfills, incinerators, and toxic-waste dumps. Polluters and their allies in government seek to exploit the economic and political weakness of minority communities by subjecting them to facilities that more affluent and powerful communities would never tolerate. For example, in the early 1980s, the state of North Carolina dumped many tons of PCB (polychlorinated biphenyl)-contaminated dirt in Warren County, a majority-black rural county. Unsuccessful legal challenges followed by mass demonstrations and hundreds of arrests were not able to prevent the dumping. Ten years later, a firm charged with finding the best site in North Carolina for a radioactive-waste dump scoured the state using as its criteria, not just geological and environmental conditions, but also the political and economic power, sophistication, and organization of areas under consideration. In reaction to experiences like these, many communities around the nation, with the help of organizations such as the Citizen's Clearinghouse on Hazardous Waste, the Jobs and Environment Campaign, and Greenpeace, have organized successful grassroots campaigns overcoming the legal and scientific expertise and the political and economic power of polluters and preventing the siting of waste facilities. The environmental justice movement has cast off the pejorative label "NIMBY" (not in my backyard) by asserting that hazardous waste should not be dumped in *anyone's* backyard. The movement sees itself as fighting for homes and family and views its work as "democracy in action."[12]

In 1991, the United Church of Christ's Commission for Racial Justice hosted the first National People of Color Environmental Leadership Summit. As well as opposing the deliberate targeting of minority communities for waste facilities, the conference blasted the major environmental organizations for their long-time failure to include people of color in leadership positions. The six hundred participants asserted that the environmental exploitation of African American and Native American communities goes hand in hand with the economic, social, and political exploitation that are part and parcel of a racist society. The summit was an indication of the strong moral and organizational leadership that people of color must play in resolving the environmental crisis. At the same time, it carried a clear challenge to the primarily white mainstream environmental organizations to broaden their vision, their commitment, and their inclusiveness.

When originally formulated, the key value of social justice was called "personal and social responsibility." This original conception provides a bridge from the popular notion of individual environmental responsibility as exemplified in the "fifty simple things" approach to a broad political orientation. Personal responsibility entails a withdrawal of support from destructive aspects of the "pentagon of power" and the lending of support to alternatives.[13] But while personal lifestyle change is important to developing an ecological society, it will most effectively contribute to that goal only as part of a broad-based movement for social and political change. Personal responsibility, the value statement implies, must be enacted in a framework of social responsibility, the understanding that our actions are most effective when developed in the context of our social relations with others. Excessive focus on individualistic action is, to an extent, the disease, not the cure. Ultimately, it is society, social structures, and social decisions that wreak havoc with the Earth.

Personal and social responsibility also conveys the sense of developing the ability to respond. It emphasizes learning from early childhood through old age and fosters community self-reliance rather than dependence on professional bureaucracies or paternalistic corporations. It promotes the sense of personal and social empowerment as an active goal of the ecology movement.

The coupling of social responsibility with social justice demands human rights and far-reaching democratic rights for all people. It recognizes that environmental well-being is not possible without political self-determination and economic self-reliance, and thus it requires an end to the exploitation of poor people and insists on providing all with the means to health and well-being. The value of social justice challenges the environmental movement to understand that the environment is, in one sense, truly that which surrounds us. The ravaged landscapes and neighborhoods of the inner city represent the same basic disease that afflicts the mountaintops denuded by acid rain. The U.S. Greens, in recognition of this, focused their 1992 National Action Plan on "Detroit Summer" in support of the efforts of grassroots community groups in inner-city Detroit. Detroit Summer activities included rehabilitating homes, marching against crack and crime, planting urban gardens, and celebrating the rich cultural and ethnic heritage of Detroit. The ecological society will be a just society, empowering all people with the means for a healthy, fulfilling, and sustainable way of life, wherever they live.

Nonviolence

How can we, as a society, develop effective alternatives to our current patterns of violence, at all levels, from the family and the street to nations and the world? How can we most constructively use nonviolent methods to oppose practices and policies with which we disagree and in the process reduce the atmosphere of polarization and selfishness that is itself a source of violence?

To countenance violence against people, in any form, is to condone violence against the Earth. To do violence to the Earth is inevitably to do violence to its human inhabitants. The nonviolence expressed in this value statement derives from a holistic approach that does not view violence narrowly as the province of the military, on the one hand, or of police and criminals on the other. It is a nonviolence that opposes violence in all social relations, from the family to the workplace to the international arena. It understands the inherent contradiction in the stance of the politician who rails against crime on the streets while at the same time extolling the use of military force. It entails an understanding of structural forms of violence that bring disease, injury, and death to the economically disadvantaged. In particular, in keeping with the lessons of feminism, violence against women and children is seen as integral to the ethos of domination and oppression that characterizes the modern era. To end such a culture, violence must be eradicated both at the fundamental level where it enters the lives of individuals and at the institutional level where it upholds unjust structures of power and is legitimated through the voice of the corporate media.

Nonviolence, as the Greens understand it, does not imply passive behavior or acceptance of injustice, nor does it exclude active social resistance. It expressly includes the tactic of nonviolent civil disobedience in the tradition of Thoreau, Gandhi, and King. The Green movement in both Europe and the United States was in part developed by the organizers of the intensive struggles of nonviolent civil disobedience in the 1970s and 1980s that opposed nuclear power and the escalating arms race. Greens would replace militaristic defense policies, which lead inevitably to armed conflict, with nonviolent strategies involving mass civil disobedience, noncooperation with aggressors, work stoppages, and perhaps even sabotage. Such policies, if developed with the organizational rigor of our current military defense program, could prove quite effective in both deterring and, if need be, overcoming aggression.

As to the far-reaching transformation of our political and economic systems required to achieve an ecological society, it has been a controversial point whether a nonviolent approach can succeed against the often-brutal response of an armed and repressive state government in service to the status quo. Some Greens have advocated an approach they call "strategic nonviolence," which would condone tactical violence in certain circumstances. In their view, those in the citadels of power will not hesitate to use violent means to maintain their position, necessitating a violent response. For example, after pointing out that "ecological consciousness [cannot] be created through the barrel of a gun," Gary Sisco goes on to assert that while "the struggle for a free, ecological society will be primarily a nonviolent political struggle, . . . [this] does not rule out the use of armed self-defense against official violence and armed reaction."[14] Unfortunately, such a tactical acceptance of violent means may serve to provoke a reaction, including discrediting by its opponents and disruption by agents provocateurs, as was the experience of the Black Panther movement in the late 1960s. More importantly, the goal expressed in the feminism value statement of proceeding "with as much respect for the means as the ends" reminds us that a nonviolent society will not be attained by violent means. A movement whose goal is to end the violence done to the Earth must embrace a value system that is committed to nonviolence toward people as well. Such a movement must incorporate a nonviolent approach in its organizing, both strategically and tactically.

Personal and Global Responsibility

How can we be of genuine assistance to
grassroots groups in the Third World? What can
we learn from such groups? How can we help

*other countries make the transition to self-suffi-
ciency in food and other basic necessities? How
can we promote these ten Green values in the
reshaping of our global order? How can we
reshape world order without creating just another enormous nation-state?*

Think globally and act locally. The first principle of global responsibility is that "we all live downstream." There is no one's
backyard besides our own in which to dump pollution. Acid
rain from U.S. emissions kills lakes in Canada. Fallout from
Chernobyl contaminates milk in distant Lapland. The uranium
used to produce electricity in New England or Florida leaves
deadly tailings in the Native American lands of the Southwest
from which it is mined. Without global thinking, environmental
integrity will never be sustained. Global responsibility means
more than thinking about planetary ramifications. It also implies a holistic thinking that transforms both public policy and
citizen activism from their typically fragmented, single-issue approach.

Global responsibility encompasses the social as well as the
environmental impacts of our actions. A sound environment
depends on the economic viability and political enfranchise-
ment of all people. Foreign policy and international economic
activity must support the economic and democratic potential of
other people, particularly those in the Third World, whose labors and resources have undergirded a global economy that
returns little to them. Neither First World affluence nor a clean
First World environment can be maintained on the backs of
others. Global responsibility fundamentally opposes the economic or political exploitation of any people anywhere, understanding not only the unacceptability of such conditions from a
humanistic standpoint but also the pragmatic reality that under
such conditions environmental integrity cannot be sustained.
Global responsibility recognizes the injustice done to Third World
and native peoples through colonialism and through contemporary international economic policy (neocolonialism) and seeks
actively to rectify it. Global responsibility asserts the right of all
people to live according to life-affirming values and supports
their realization of community-based economics, grassroots

democracy, sustainability, and the other factors that contribute to an ecologically and socially healthy and meaningful way of life.

Grassroots Democracy

How can we develop systems that allow and encourage us to control the decisions that affect our lives? How can we ensure that representatives will be fully accountable to the people who elected them? How can we encourage and assist the "mediating institutions"—family, neighborhood organizations, church group, voluntary associations, ethnic club—to recover some of the functions now performed by the government? How can we relearn the best insights from American traditions of civic vitality, voluntary action, and community responsibility?

For a movement to succeed in building an ecological society or even to achieve environmentally beneficial reforms, it must find the power to affect both public policy and the organization and development of political and economic life. Thus, grassroots democracy is more than a strategy for influencing government. A movement and a society that value the Earth will value each human person who inhabits the Earth, empowering all people to participate actively in the realization of their own well-being and fulfillment. Grassroots democracy is antithetical to the identification of people merely as passive consumers. It entails an active citizenship that transforms the character of the citizen through the process of participation in the public life of the community.[15]

Grassroots democracy turns our usual top-down approach to public policy on its head, giving people and communities the power to determine their ecological and social destinies. It empowers people to find an environmentally and socially responsible way of life. Grassroots democracy is the keystone of the key values, the enabling factor through which the broader vision of the ecological society can be realized. Such interrelated issues as citizenship, leadership, conflict, and consensus will be discussed at length in chapter 9 in the context of developing an understanding of participatory, grassroots democracy.

Community-based Economics

How can we redesign our work structures to encourage employee ownership and workplace democracy? How can we develop new economic activities and institutions that will allow us to use our new technologies in ways that are humane, freeing, ecological, and accountable and responsive to communities? How can we establish some form of basic economic security, open to all? How can we move beyond the narrow "job ethic" to new definitions of "work," "jobs," and "income" that reflect the changing economy? How can we restructure our patterns of income distribution to reflect the wealth created by those outside the formal monetary economy: those who take responsibility for parenting, housekeeping, home gardens, community volunteer work, and so forth?

Just as an international, competitive economy has gone hand in hand with environmental destruction, a community-based, cooperative economy will be the hallmark of an ecological society. Community-based economics implies cooperative enterprise, workers' self-management, and human-scale organization fitted to the ecological characteristics of the particular locale. An ecologically oriented, community-based economy will emphasize self-reliance to promote environmental stewardship and social responsibility. Community forms the basis for self-reliant economic activity, the basis for political life, and the foundation of an ecological society. Just as grassroots democracy enables ecological living, community provides it with a context and a home.

An expanded understanding of community will place human society harmoniously within its natural setting. Some fear that to view humanity as part of nature is to abandon our sense of the dignity and value of the human being. On the contrary, to embrace a commitment to a view of human beings and human society as able to love, nurture, and sustain one another and our natural environs is to take on a very lofty idea of human nature. The ecological community is based on an understanding of home, not as the edifice we inhabit, but as the place in which we live, a place of interpenetrating social and natural characteristics, a place that we know and cherish as our own.

The Big Picture

It is important to view the key values holistically. Viewed in isolation, some of the values may seem to contradict one another. However, careful analysis usually reveals an approach or understanding that can surmount the contradiction. For example, respect for diversity is often misconstrued as supporting notions that are contrary to other values. Respecting diversity, on its own, might seem to imply that we should respect those who might choose authoritarian political forms. Of course, that contradicts the commitment to grassroots democracy. Respecting diversity might seem to allow for a diversity of production methods according to a business manager's choice, including methods that are polluting. But that would violate the value of ecological wisdom.

Similarly, the commitment to grassroots democracy may seem to empower citizens to choose public policies that violate the other values. After all, the Nazis were voted into power in the 1930s. Could not a democratic majority, even in a local political arena, vote against the ecological position? Of course it could. By the same token, a community in and of itself is not necessarily either ecological or humane. This is why the entire range of values must be consciously developed and continually reinforced as interconnected "aspects of a coherent . . . world view." People who value ecological wisdom and sustainability, as well as community and grassroots democracy, would not vote, for example, to allow development to threaten their water supply. Add the value of global responsibility, and they would assume careful stewardship of waters flowing to their neighbors downstream. Although at first it will be necessary to bring consciously to bear the perspective gained from the full complement of values when deliberating any important decision, ultimately the values must become an almost reflexive part of our awareness, much as the values of materialism and competition are today. Chapter 11 will give an example of how the ten key values can be used to develop an approach to a particular issue.

These seeming contradictions also bring home the fact that the use of values is for guidance and not for rigid definitions. The final determination of how the values must be applied in any situation will be made by the people concerned with it. Just as the ten amendments in the U.S. Bill of Rights are variously interpreted by the changing Supreme Court, the ten values of the Green movement will be applied differently at different times by different people. Working out such differences in a manner that promotes human and natural well-being is what ecological politics is ultimately all about. While it would be easy to conclude glibly that the ten key values are, after all, not the Ten Commandments, it should be remembered in this context that the Talmud records centuries of debate and guidance from learned rabbis on just how to interpret and apply the commandments and other biblical injunctions in day-to-day affairs. Placing holistic, life-affirming values at the core of our social and political life offers a similar challenge.

Chapter 8

COOPERATION AND COMMUNITY

The word "community" is heard a lot today. It is applied loosely to such entities as the "black community," the "gay and lesbian community," the "community of nations," the "business community," and others. Almost any collection of people may be labeled a community. By contrast, understood in the more traditional sense as they have flourished in the past and around the world, communities have had very specific characteristics. They are united, not primarily by shared interests or by physical or ethnic type, but by a sense of mutual support, by a shared culture and way of life, by shared values, and by a historic rootedness in a place called home. The colonial America beloved by Jefferson was characterized not so much by rugged individuals and self-made "men" as it was by an independence that rested securely in the cooperation of family, friends, and neighbors in an interdependent community.

Today, community organizing is part of the social and political landscape across the United States. Such efforts have linked volunteer groups, neighborhood organizations, and churches in such diverse places as the barrios of San Antonio, the old neighborhoods of Brooklyn, and the schools and churches of San Francisco. Within a given city or locale, community organizations nourish, support, and empower one another through a shared process involving communication, problem solving, and the discovery of common values.[1] They seek to discover new ways of working together for the common good, to recover lost traditions and skills, and to repair their homes, their schools, and their local economies. Their efforts often convey a sense of community as something lost, as something that can be regained with specific steps, and at the same time as something built anew on a contemporary foundation.

For many, community tends to be a hazy ideal, simply conveying an image of people joining together for a better way of life.[2] An ideal of community is important to the extent that it stirs our imagination and motivates our endeavors, but the problems of our times require more than a vague romanticism or fanciful imagery. They require a practical understanding of the dynamics of community, the obstacles and opportunities for community building, and specific ways in which the principles of community can be applied to healing the relationship of humanity with the Earth.

Defining Community

A landmark in popular awareness of community as a topical issue came with the 1987 publication of *The Different Drum: Community Making and Peace,* by the psychiatrist M. Scott Peck, the author of the perennial best-seller *The Road Less Traveled.* Peck also established the Foundation for Community Encouragement, which holds community-building workshops. For Peck, a community must be inclusive, embracing all genders, races, and creeds. It requires a commitment that will carry members through bad times as well as good, much like the commitment of a marriage. It is built around a consensus of members, honoring each individual's unique needs and ideas as well as those of the group as a whole, transcending individual differences to find common ground. A community, in Peck's view, also requires a kind of collective contemplation that is similar to personal introspection. The community reflects on itself, asking such questions as How are we doing? and Are we a healthy group? Finally, a community is a place of safety for its members in which "no one is attempting to heal or convert you, to fix you, to change you. Instead, the members accept you as you are."[3]

These elements capture the qualities of the community experience in a way that resonates with the hope for community life held by many people. Certainly, feelings of inclusiveness, commitment, and safety are social experiences most of us would like to have. Nonetheless, the incompleteness of Peck's definition becomes apparent as he takes off in some unexpected directions, seeking the practical applications of his theory of community. Peck advocates a national "community presidency" in which a presidential candidate campaigns with a vice president and cabinet selected because they can work as a community rather than solely because of their expertise in the responsibilities of government.[4] He believes that the president sets the tone for the rest of government and that a community presidency would change the climate of society in general. A president with a commitment to community would in effect spread the gospel of community building to the people. This position is reminiscent of the trickle-down mystification of Ronald Reagan's supply-side economics: build community at the top and it will eventually reach the masses. Unfortunately, Peck does not clarify the mechanism by which a sense of community might be established in a top-down manner. He does not consider that concentrated power in the form of a national presidency could be part of the historical process that destroyed community in the first place. (Indeed, a historical perspective is not to be found in Peck's book.) Even were a community presidency to be desired, Peck overlooks the grassroots work necessary to elect such a president. To properly educate enough of the electorate to find value in and to vote for such a presidency would be tantamount to developing an understanding of the experience of community through much of the nation. In other words, rather than electing a community president to change the climate, the climate would have to be changed first in order to be able to elect a community president.

Tellingly, Peck also advocates a "supranational government," which will be the sole military force on the planet and provide a "police force in the event that a nation-state commits an illegal or immoral act."[5] He never raises the question of likely abuses of power by a centralized world government or problems of administration and democratic control. For Peck, a faith in the power of community becomes a panacea, allowing him to overlook both the lessons of history and the modern structures of economic and political power.

The experience of the community-building workshops at Peck's Foundation for Community Encouragement in Knoxville, Tennessee, reveals similar shortcomings. In 1988, Marion O'Malley and Tiff Davis of the North Carolina Center for Peace Education (CPE) took up the challenge of attending a three-day workshop in Knoxville to experience community. Ostensibly, over the long weekend some fifty strangers would become a community with the help of a trained leader. Writing in the CPE newsletter *Peacetalks*, O'Malley and Davis described a weekend of frustration, discouragement, and disappointment as the workshop participants interacted from a position of pain and "brokenness," omitting the healthy, happy, and productive aspects of their day-to-day lives.[6] Davis characterized the weekend as one of feeling "alienated from where and who we are." Finally, the workshop seemed to take on an almost cultlike demeanor as the discussion of developing action plans for participants to take home with them "focused on encouraging others to come to a community-building workshop rather than creating community with folks back home." O'Malley suggested that an addiction to community building with strangers might be a way of avoiding life's problems. Both Davis's and O'Malley's accounts depict the workshop as disconnected from the reality of their everyday lives.

Marion O'Malley left the community-building workshop thankful "particularly for the community I already have here at home." In spite of all their disappointment, however, both O'Malley and Davis indicated an interest in conducting community-building workshops as part of the program at the CPE, feeling that they had learned principles that could be applied to their work for peace. The lesson they learned seems to be that the exercises and facilitation of community building can be worthwhile but need a context in the lives, work, and aspirations of the participants. Although modern life often connects people across long distances thanks to telecommunications and rapid transportation, the most likely place for this context to be found is in the local setting where most people work, play, and raise their children. The missing element in Peck's analysis, and thus in the community-building workshop as well, is rootedness, the sense of place, the understanding of community as home. This understanding of rootedness brings to our definition of community a sense of shared values and traditions, of a shared political capability, and of responsibility toward one another.

Such an understanding is suggested in the work of another psychologist, Erich Fromm. In his classic book *The Art of Loving*, Fromm describes love as having four characteristics: care, responsibility, respect, and knowledge. These four attributes might also characterize a healthy relationship of people with one another and with the Earth in an ecologically oriented community. Care entails "active concern for the life and growth of that which we love." Responsibility is "my response to the needs, expressed or unexpressed, of another." Respect is the ability to see and value a person on the basis of unique individuality. Finally, knowledge, "to know a human being objectively . . . in his ultimate essence", provides the basis on which care, responsibility, and respect can be built.[7] Fromm is not describing a superficial or merely objective form of knowing. Only continued contact over time can provide the knowledge of another from which genuine love can blossom. So it is with community. Only in a sustained, lived relatedness, in which one comes to know others intimately, can meaningful community be found. Understanding the importance of this intimate form of knowledge guides us away from supranational governments, away from a community presidency, and away from distant weekend workshops. All of these are too remote from people's actual roots and relationships, too far from the possibility of intimate knowing, to provide a genuine sense of community. One must look closer to home for that sense of community, particularly for a community that joins people in a caring relationship to the Earth. It is a matter of course that the knowing that Fromm finds necessary to care for another person is also required to truly care for the Earth.[8]

Bioregionalism: The Politics of Place

The trend in the environmental movement that best captures this sense of place, of commitment, and of home is bioregionalism. Although it sounds like a term from an advanced program in environmental studies, bioregionalism describes both a movement and a fundamental orientation toward attaining an ecological society. Quite simply, bioregionalism advocates that human society be consciously oriented to natural life (bio-) and that this consciousness be based on an understanding of a particular locale or region.

The phrase "the politics of place" is often used descriptively in lieu of bioregionalism and provides a sense of concern for home in the broader sense. The ecological issues that seem remote and impersonal or merely philosophical when addressed at the national or global level become immediate and personal when viewed at the regional or local level.[9] For bioregionalists, the very concept of home must be changed from a salable commodity to a place where one puts down roots, a place one calls one's own. No longer acceptable is the view of home as an exchangeable piece of real estate that goes along with exchangeable jobs in exchangeable "communities." Bioregionalism demands the commitment to a place required for the intimate knowing on which care, respect, and responsibility can be based.

Bioregionalism originated in the 1970s. Its popularity grew among environmentalists, leading to the first North American Bioregional Congress (NABC) in 1984. The NABC continued to convene biennially, changing its name to the Turtle Island Bioregional Congress at the 1990 meeting. (Turtle Island is a Native American term for the North American continent.) The importance of the bioregional movement as a catalyst for environmental activity can be gleaned from the fact that the U. S. Green movement was spawned at the first NABC.

A bioregion is itself a sort of geopolitical entity, one in which boundaries are set not by arbitrary political factors but with a sensitivity to natural conditions. These boundaries might follow the definition of a watershed, changing flora and fauna, differing soil types, or geological formations. Most likely it will be a combination of these and similar factors. The identification of a bioregional entity will always be somewhat arbitrary, particularly as some bioregional criteria contradict others. North Carolina, for example, is commonly understood to have three geographic sections: the sandy coastal plains, the rolling hills of the piedmont, and the wooded western mountains. The rivers typically flow through all three. The solution, of course, is that a bioregionally oriented community would apply different criteria to different needs. Those in the coastal plains might work together on coastal protection and issues to do with marine life. Then, coastal communities surrounding the rivers might also work with those upstream on water-quality issues or questions of permissible effluent.

In an engaging passage in *The Once and Future King*, T. H. White has his characters discuss this question of boundaries. Wart, the young King Arthur, has been transformed by the wizard Merlin into a goose. A companion goose explains to him that geese do not have warfare because "there are no boundaries among the geese." "What are boundaries, please?" asks Wart. "Imaginary lines on the earth," the goose replies.[10] Flying high above the Earth, Wart cannot find the, to him, familiar boundary lines. Wart's experience as a goose, created by White in the 1940s, anticipates the awe reported by astronauts twenty years later on seeing the Earth from space for the first time, without the outlines of nations they'd grown to expect from the familiar pages of an atlas. But while they would certainly not recognize a boundary as such, migratory birds such as the geese described by White successfully travel thousands of miles, year in year out, to reach a specific location across the globe. They apparently possess a very keen sense of place.

Commitment, one of the principles of community building, in this case a commitment to place, is the first step toward attaining the understanding of place advocated by bioregionalists. This understanding of and commitment to place leads to an emphasis on a self-reliant and sustainable way of life within the natural context of a particular region. Since each region has unique geological and biological features, its inhabitants will develop a unique way of life to ensure an ecologically sustainable community.[11] These natural features will determine the way basic human needs—food, clothing, shelter, and energy—are met, which will in turn lead to a unique culture and economy. Certainly, the thousands of distinct cultures that have existed around the planet can at least partially be explained as having arisen in response to the natural qualities of distinct bioregions. The sustainability sought by bioregionalists requires a rootedness that persists over generations, during which time the politics of place can become well established. Bioregionalists believe that well-rooted people will work to ensure the viability of their communities.[12]

Although the bioregional movement per se is of recent origin, born in the wake of mounting environmental concern, the concepts it represents are not new. Alexis de Tocqueville, in *Democracy in America*, discussed the importance of the politics of place, which he contrasted with the politics of the nation-state. For de Tocqueville, the state is remote and poorly understood, an infertile ground for active political concern. People will have little incentive to take an interest in the general welfare of the state. However, "If it is a question of taking a road past his property, he sees at once that this small public matter has a bearing on his greatest private interests."[13] While de Tocqueville's analysis is founded on a belief in humanity's self-interest, bioregionalism, based on a more optimistic view of human nature, seeks a caring, cooperative relationship with one's neighbors and with the Earth.

Lewis Mumford was an early proponent of something akin to bioregionalism, although he would not have called it by that name. In the 1920s, Mumford was active in an organization called the Regional Planning Association of America (RPAA). The RPAA saw the solution to modern problems as requiring a return from congested urban centers to a system of population and economic activity dispersed across regions. Mumford, writing for the RPAA in 1925, defined a region as "being any geographic area that possesses a certain unity of climate, soil, vegetation, industry and culture,"[14] in other words, a bioregion. Although the RPAA lasted only from 1923 to 1933, regionalism continued to be a factor in Mumford's thinking. In his 1938 book *The Culture of Cities*, he again discussed the region in terms similar to those I am using, calling for a society that unites people in their regions by a common landscape, literature, and language. This sensitivity to their own region, he felt, would give them a sympathetic orientation toward the peculiarities of other regions.[15]

From Region to Neighborhood

Most of us do not view ourselves as living in a bioregion. We see ourselves as living in a city or town, and, closer to home, a neighborhood. Most of us do not have the intimate knowledge of environmental conditions necessary to rigorously determine the outlines of our bioregion. For most, bioregionalism will begin as we work with our neighbors to develop cooperative, environmentally sensitive modes of living with one another and within the particular ecological niche in which we reside.

In recent years, a number of cities have been experimenting with what is called the "green city" approach. In San Francisco, the Planet Drum Foundation held a series of green city meetings in 1986, bringing together over 150 individuals and representatives of groups active in various fields related to sustainable living. These meetings were open and inclusive, involving a diverse cross section of San Francisco and taking advantage of the fact that "these days most individuals, citizen organizations, businesses and labor groups are aware of urban decline and care strongly about some aspects of sustainability," as expressed in the resulting publication, *A Green City Program for San Francisco Bay Area Cities and Towns*, a collection of ideas and visions for urban bioregionalism.[16] The *Program* is a short (seventy-page) handbook that provides a description of problems, a vision of change, and a program of action in nine different "areas of sustainability," such as urban planting, recycling, neighborhood character, and celebrating life-place vitality. Although bioregionalism is almost intuitively associated with rural settings, the green cities approach insists that cities too "need to become 'green.' They must be transformed into places that are life-enhancing and regenerative."[17]

A *Green City Program* is chock-full of innovative ideas for revitalizing neighborhoods and cities. For example, the *Program* suggests replacing neighborhood through streets with cul-de-sacs that can be crossed only by bike or foot traffic. This has the benefit of slowing the pace of the neighborhood, increasing safety, enhancing the sense of the neighborhood as a shared space, and promoting environmentally benign transportation choices. The *Program* calls for the establishment of neighborhood common areas as centers for urban gardens, recreation, public meetings, celebrations, and fairs. It suggests building community identity through the celebration of local history, geology, flora and fauna, and people. Finally, the *Program* concludes with a discussion of socially responsible cooperative businesses as key to the development of a green city. A *Green City Program* demonstrates clearly that there are a multitude of opportunities for making our way of life more ecologically sound and that these opportunities will vary from neighborhood to neighborhood, city to city, and bioregion to bioregion. The green cities approach contradicts the notion that ecological living is not possible in the city.

Cooperation and Self-reliance

The development of community depends on some organizational model in which people can work together to ensure their common well-being, to create a sense of relatedness, and to establish a process for collective activity and decision making. The competitive form of economics currently practiced is based on the commodification of land and labor and the view of people and the Earth instrumentally, as objects to be manipulated to the advancement of the corporate enterprise. This objectification of people and the Earth underlies our contemporary social and environmental problems. Competition is part and parcel of the hierarchical orientation that places the Earth at the bottom of a pyramid of exploitation and abuse. Continued emphasis on competition will not likely be the way out. Certainly, it is difficult for those at odds with one another through a competitive relationship to put their care for each other at the forefront. It is unlikely that those competing for the means of survival will give highest priority to sustaining the Earth.

Of course, the alternative to competition is cooperation.[18] San Francisco's *Green City Program*, for example, was created through a cooperative, citywide effort. What persists today of community does so in the form of cooperative activity, whether through neighborhood cleanup efforts, food drives for the hungry, or the actions of citizens to protect the local environment. But in a society that gives preeminent value to the commodity sold for a profit, these projects are the exception rather than the rule. Quite simply, anything we do for ourselves or band together to accomplish with our neighbors, rather than purchase from industry, detracts from the national economy as measured by the GNP. Sharing becomes unlikely when the goal of the economy is to sell each person at least one of each commodity, to be replaced periodically due to style changes, obsolescence, or deterioration.

A test of the unlikeliness of cooperation in contemporary times can be made in any suburban neighborhood. Merely walk down the block and count the number of lawn mowers per household. The ratio is generally close to one to one, with each mower in use perhaps a few hours a week. It is doubtful that it has occurred to these suburbanites that several families might come together to share a lawn mower, an extension ladder, a chain saw, or whatever. In twentieth-century America, each of us is supposed to own the things needed for life.[19] Everyone knows this.

Most of the limited cooperative behavior found in the modern era is reactive. It develops in response to the assaults of modern society on people's safety, health, or well-being. Neighborhood-watch programs, in which people look out for the safety of their neighbors' property, are a stunted relic of the community's role of self-protection that flourished in a less complex era. They amount to a recognition that the individualistic isolation of modern society has definite pitfalls.

Similarly, home schooling cooperatives grow in response to a perceived deficiency in bureaucratic educational systems. Then again, the political formation with the greatest vitality in most American communities is the school board or the PTA. People work together to ensure that the needs of their children are well met. Day-care cooperatives are a common response to the lack of affordable child care and the uncertainties tied to placing small children in unfamiliar institutions.

On another front, those concerned with the food choices available at the megasupermarket of the late twentieth century may form buying clubs or natural-food cooperatives. Buying clubs often have the strictly economic goal of low prices, providing their members with little more than a cheaper can of Spam, although some do look at quality as well as quantity. Natural-food cooperatives, which rose in the wake of the 1960s counterculture, tend to provide otherwise unavailable or overexpensive items to their members. Although food co-ops originally depended entirely on the cooperative efforts of their members, recently some have adopted flexible structures, allowing paid membership without a work requirement and mixing their volunteer base with paid staff.

Just as a community must be grounded in cooperative activity, cooperation must be informed by the understanding of community and ecology that is the essence of bioregionalism. Cooperatives that give people only better access, for example, to mass-produced food laden with pesticides and grown and sold by huge, distant agribusinesses will not contribute significantly to the development of community or ecological wisdom. On the other hand, a co-op that emphasizes locally produced, organic food grown on small family farms or by local farming cooperatives is strengthening the local community and supporting those who care for the environment.

It is important not to mistake cooperative organizing for a group effort to "shop for a better world." Cooperatives, at their best, take us far beyond the image of individual consumers checking the ecological merit of products as they stroll through a mall. Cooperatives create the social forms from which a genuinely sustainable society can be built. They challenge their members to seek ways to achieve common goals while avoiding the seductive offer of the faceless global economy to do it all for them (the price: merely their health, their communities, their planet). Although cooperatives formed as part of a program for social change must guard against becoming insulated enclaves that do not affect the larger global picture, by their very nature they give people the opportunity to explore, express, and actualize their values in the economic arena. The potential scope of cooperative activity is as broad as our imaginations.[20]

An important aspect of cooperative organizing and of a bioregional orientation is self-reliance. Cooperatives tend to rely more on their own labor, collective abilities, and the sharing of resources than on distant corporations or government agencies. To the extent that the members of a cooperative have an environmental commitment, they are more likely to implement it locally than is a distant corporation. When self-reliance is in a cooperative framework, self-interest is placed in a context of interrelatedness and care for other members of the community. Murray Bookchin is perhaps neither too poetic nor too bold in his comparison of the cooperative community to a lover who "experiences the joy of the beloved in the very fact that a desire is satisfied."[21]

Self-reliant organizing has economic benefits beyond the immediate savings of the participants. Much of the benefit of economic activity currently leaves the community. For example, much of the price paid for a typical commodity goes to distant producers, transportation companies, and the dividends paid to unknown stockholders. A retail chain buys from centralized producers, uses professional services in the home office, and often transfers in managers from other locations. With self-reliance, transportation costs are limited and profits stay in the community, recirculating and increasing the local wealth. Local businesses are more likely to use local services and products. When profit leaves the community, it is gone for good. If it stays in the community, it can be spent again and again, each time contributing to the local economy. Self-reliance can, of course, be implemented through traditional institutions or governments. San Jose, California, for example, found that it could save $25 million by setting up a community-based fire insurance program, using the program's revenues for local investment.[22]

Cooperative organizing also decreases shadow work, that work which Ivan Illich defines as necessary to turn a commodity into something useful. If, instead of standing in line at the supermarket (shadow work), one works in a community garden or at a food cooperative, work in service of the global economy is replaced with work more directly connected to one's own needs and to the community.

A major concern of cooperative economics is access to the three pillars of the capitalist economy—land, labor, and capital—the lack of which can be a major obstacle to cooperative organization and to the use of economic activity for social transformation. Primary among these obstacles is the lack of capital for starting and developing cooperative businesses. A small but growing number of alternative credit unions, such as the Self-Help Credit Union in Durham, North Carolina, seek to overcome this problem. These institutions offer customers a range of conventional banking services, such as savings accounts and retirement accounts. With the funds on deposit, they provide loans to cooperative businesses, worker-owned businesses, minority-owned businesses, and others with limited access to conventional sources of capital. The Self-Help Credit Union also provides business and technical assistance through its companion organization, the Center for Community Self-Help, thus addressing the fact that new enterprises often lack the training or experience to effectively manage and develop a business. By supporting such financial institutions, concerned citizens ensure that cooperatives will have funding available for their needs.

The community land trust (CLT) is a model for the kind of relationship to the land that can sustain a cooperative economy. A CLT purchases land and places it in a trust, taking the land off the speculative market, removing it from private ownership, and returning it to individual or common use subject to the provisions of the trust. The CLT then leases out land on a long-term or lifetime basis. Leaseholders do not own the land but may own the structures they build on it. Land trusts ensure affordability of land and housing by requiring that buildings be resold only for their original cost, factoring in inflation and the value of any improvements. Low-income housing that is placed in a land trust is sure to remain affordable for future owners. Land trusts are usually established with strict legal covenants imposing a stewardship ethic in regard to the land itself. They have been successful in both urban and rural areas.

The reclaiming of labor from commodity status is at the heart of cooperative economics. An important step in this direction is taken when workers organize cooperatively to own their business. Worker ownership has a number of advantages. Worker owners generally live in the local community and are less likely than absentee owners to take actions that are destructive to the local environment. Worker owners will not close their plant and relocate it to the Third World for cheaper labor. Worker ownership provides a more environmentally and socially stable form than private or corporate ownership. There is a difference between worker ownership, in which workers manage as well as reap the benefits of the business, and various schemes of employee ownership, such as employee stock ownership plans (ESOPs), in which corporate employees merely become vested in industry profits. Worker ownership changes the nature of the workplace as well as the relationships among the workers. It engenders in workers a sense of responsibility for the enterprise, for one another, and for the broader community.

Many bioregionalists advocate the trading of labor through something called a Local Exchange Trading System (LETS). An LETS maintains a labor account for each participant. One does work for another member, receiving a credit to one's own account. This credit provides access to the skills of any other LETS member, usually without any cash payment. A more open system is one that replaces credit and membership with the use of a local currency to pay for services. For example, a growing number of businesses and independent businesspeople in Ithaca, New York, accept the local "Ithaca dollar" in lieu of cash. These various systems allow people to work even when traditional paying jobs are not available. They enable people low on funds to obtain services by trading their own work. Barter, of course, takes place informally throughout the economy. Prior to the modern era, it was the predominant mode of economic activity.[23] While the individualistic exchange of labor embodied in an LETS or local currency falls short of the genuinely cooperative effort to meet needs that is the basis for a fully realized sense of community, there is still an important element of cooperation and trust found in the commitment to these alternative economic processes. Those individuals and businesses belonging to an LETS or accepting Ithaca dollars can be recognized as making an active commitment to the community. By placing buyer and seller in a community context, these alternatives represent a significant step away from the faceless commodification of labor that characterizes most work in the modern economy.

Hybrids have been formed between worker ownership and self-help cooperatives. Weaver Street Market in Carrboro, North Carolina, for example, encourages all its employees to become worker owners. The worker owners have two representatives on the board of directors and participate actively in the management and operations of the store. Meanwhile, shoppers at the market are encouraged to become consumer owners by purchasing membership shares (and thus providing the store with needed capital) or working as volunteers. Consumer owners receive discounts and also have two representatives on the board. Weaver Street Market struggles to balance democracy and efficiency in the workplace and to turn shoppers into active members of a cooperative. Incidentally, It received start-up loans from the Self-Help Credit Union mentioned above.

Expanding the Cooperative Endeavor

The examples of cooperative organizing we have looked at thus far tend to be isolated endeavors without a broad reworking of cooperation into the many facets of life and of the economy. A well-known example of a regional cooperative movement is the Mondragon cooperatives, started in the Basque region of northeastern Spain in the 1940s.[24] Mondragon has since grown to include some 21,000 workers involved in 166 cooperatives with $1.6 billion in sales (1988). These cooperatives are engaged in heavy industry, services, housing, retail, education, and agriculture. The scope of the Mondragon system allows one to work, learn, and find the necessities of life within the cooperative framework. Mondragon was born in the vision and efforts of Father José María Arizmendi, who saw cooperation as "the authentic integration of people in the economic and social process that shapes a new world order."[25]

Mondragon started in 1943 with a training school to provide education for workers. Education has remained an important emphasis of the movement. Workers contribute to the capitalization of the Mondragon system and have an entrepreneurial mind-set, seeking opportunities for new cooperative businesses and services. An average of four new cooperatives are developed annually, and only a handful have failed, producing a failure rate far below that of the traditional business sector. Although 20 percent of Mondragon's sales are made internationally, community-oriented economics has been a historically important aspect of the cooperatives. The cooperatives themselves provide for democratic control and ownership by the workers, although they do not necessarily challenge the traditional work roles or industrial activities of contemporary society.

Father Arizmendi's vision is based on a principle he termed "equilibrium." Equilibrium is a sense of balance, of the individual cooperative enterprise with the system, of the needs of the workers with those of the cooperative, of the Mondragon system itself with the natural environment and with the global economy. While contemporary thinking tends to view freedom and community as opposed to each other, equilibrium intertwines them. In a sense, equilibrium is an attempt to base a radical approach on not ten key values, but a single key value.

The record of Mondragon is that while equilibrium has led to an improved quality of work life as well as to increased environmental sensitivity, it has fallen short in some areas. In particular, Mondragon's acceptance of a niche in the global capitalist economy has led to a growing international trade, with ecologically damaging overutilization of resources and high transportation costs. Unresolved is the need for the cooperatives to compete for workers with traditional businesses. This competition has driven Mondragon's wage differentials from 3:1 up to a controversial 6:1. If this trend continues, it could undermine the cooperative spirit.

Nonetheless, the existence, growth, and success of Mondragon are enormously important. Mondragon's experience takes cooperation from the margins of the economy and places it firmly in the center. Mondragon contradicts the widely held notion that democratic workplaces are inefficient. It shows that a cooperative culture can be entrepreneurial, depending on the development of diverse technical, administrative, creative, and social skills among workers. Mondragon frees the individual to succeed within the cooperative context. It demonstrates the importance of a cooperative culture interpenetrating the various spheres of social life and of education to ensure the success of the cooperative endeavor.

Cohousing: A Case in Point

One of the most innovative developments in cooperative organizing in recent years is an approach to community housing called *cohousing*. First developed in Denmark in the 1970s, the cohousing idea has spread across northern Europe. Today, a cohousing movement is growing in the United States.

Cohousing brings together a group of people who want their homes to be part of a community. They work together to collectively design a living space that will include both their individual homes and shared facilities. There are four major characteristics of cohousing.[26] It is a participatory process in which residents plan and design the project and are responsible as a group for all final decisions. It involves intentional neighborhood design, a design based on the residents' understanding of their shared goals as a community. Cohousing includes extensive common facilities designed for daily use to supplement private living areas. Finally, cohousing involves complete resident management, in which residents control the project and provide for common needs, making decisions about common concerns at community meetings or in working groups.

Cohousing offers a number of benefits to community members. The mix of shared and private space allows for better meeting of social needs without sacrificing privacy. Cars are generally left at the periphery of the site, providing a better environment for children to play and adults to work or socialize. The design of the neighborhood usually encourages spontaneous social interaction. For example, the common building is generally placed between the parking area and the living areas so that those returning from work or errands can easily see if anything is going on there.

Cohousing allows residents to actualize their concern for the environment. Land use in cohousing projects usually concentrates buildings in one section, conserving natural areas. Participants can design for renewable energy use and conservation. Shared facilities lower environmental impacts of commodity and energy consumption. It is easier to develop group efforts to support projects such as recycling or composting.

Finally, cohousing has economic benefits. Participants are able to design the features they want as a community while minimizing costs. Common facilities reduce both construction costs and the operating costs of individual households. Cohousing developments usually allow as much or as little sweat equity as a participant would like to put into a home. Design features of cohousing generally lead to reduced land development and site infrastructure costs.

The key to the success of a cohousing project is the planning phase, when a core group of potential participants come together to define their project. These people, often inexperienced in both collective decision making and construction, have their hands full.[27] Generally a two-year process is required from the initial meeting to ground-breaking. Cohousing groups tend to operate by consensus, seeking to reach decisions that best meet the needs of all members. Decisions to be made include identifying the general goals and strategy of the group, developing an organization, selecting a site, and choosing consultants, architects, and builders. Although attending weekly meetings over a two-year period seeking consensus on fundamental issues of lifestyle sounds harrowing, the result is that, according to a participant in a Seattle cohousing project, "we've succeeded in creating a wonderful, flexible, supportive community of all ages and status."[28]

The experience of the Danish cohousing movement provides an indication of how powerful a force cooperation, self-reliance, and community can be. For example, although most cohousing projects have room for a washer and dryer in each home, very few homes actually have the appliances. Members prefer to save the expense and use the common facilities. The trend over the two decades of cohousing has been reducing the size of the private homes and increasing the size and facilities of the common buildings. Members take extensive advantage of common meals. A thirty-unit project may require each member to cook the common dinner only once per month. Thus, in exchange for cooking one night a month, a resident can come home all the other nights to a fresh, healthful dinner with friends. While this saves time as well as food and energy costs, many cohousing members would attend for the congeniality alone.

Born out of cooperation, cohousing lends itself to continual opportunities for new cooperative endeavors. Community gardens are common. Day-care facilities can be provided cooperatively and located on site. Children have available a level of care and safety in an auto-free neighborhood of friendly, sharing families that harks back to the "Leave It to Beaver" era that most Americans consider lost forever. The common building may contain computer facilities, libraries, and reading rooms. Guest rooms in the common building remove the need for each individual home to have a separate room for guests, allowing members to entertain guests while still having a measure of privacy in their homes. Many cohousing groups also maintain a supply store of essential items. Thus, running out of toilet paper no longer requires a drive to the shopping center but only a short walk to the common building.

Cohousing might sound like a middle-class phenomenon limited to those with funds for conventional home ownership. In fact, it is amenable to various forms of development and financing, whether public, private, or nonprofit. For example, public-housing agencies in Denmark have developed cohousing projects to provide rental homes to those with lower incomes. Some projects have mixed owner-occupied and rental units. The experience has been that turnover and participation levels have been about the same for owners and renters. Banks in Denmark have found cohousing to be a preferred risk because of the stability of the community.

An important lesson from cohousing is that when people develop their community cooperatively from the ground up, they have a basis for all sorts of cooperative activity in the future. Those participating in cohousing apply cooperative solutions widely within the cohousing community. The cohousing experience appears to impart an understanding of and sensitivity to the fact that cooperation, community, and environmental responsibility go hand in hand. The cohousing community can also be a force for grassroots democracy and sustainable values in the broader political arena, since members have proven skills in participation, organization, and cooperative decision making.

The example of cohousing clarifies another aspect of my argument. Much of the discussion thus far may seem to idealize or convey a sense of nostalgia for a past era, when a more organic society united human communities with the Earth. Some might read into this discussion a suggestion that we somehow return to that society, giving up our modern way of life, lock, stock, and barrel. On the contrary, community is not some fixed form lost in the past, to be recreated in the future. Rather, it is a way of relating, of organizing human affairs, and of living that is defined anew by the evolving sensibilities of the people who experience it. Community, while rooted in the history and traditions of a place, is nonetheless a uniquely evolving creation of its participants. Indeed, one of the exciting things about studying cohousing is the discovery of such a wide variety of cohousing communities, each vitally unique. The cohousing experience contradicts any nostalgic romanticism about community, demonstrating that it is possible to organize a modern living environment in a way that creates community and that is socially and ecologically sustainable.

The point in presenting cohousing as an example is not to suggest that everyone should go live in a cohousing community to "save the planet." The experience of cohousing has only been touched on here. Nonetheless, it is clear that there are opportunities for cooperation and for ecological living that most Americans are not aware of. The fundamental lesson of the cohousing movement is that life in a cooperative community is richly rewarding and both environmentally and economically viable in a way that is rare in contemporary society—and that there are ways that we can begin today to develop similar communities.

A cohousing project in Denmark or Seattle seems remote from environmental catastrophes taking place in Valdez, Alaska, over the Antarctic ice cap, or in the Amazon rain forest. But the more we cooperatively take care of our needs, the less power and opportunity faceless multinational corporations and nameless bureaucrats caught in the web of alienation and power will have to continue their destructive practices. The more we create a sense of ecological community, among our neighbors and with the Earth, the more likely it is that human affairs will be conducted with environmental sensitivity. Still, the corporate powers are active in the world's capitals, writing the regulations that continue to omit the impact on the Earth from the profit-loss equation, that continue to subsidize the importation of mass-produced commodities so that they seem less expensive than the products of local economic activity, and that limit the power of communities to do things for themselves and to preserve their social and natural integrity. Ultimately, if an ecological society is to be achieved, community organizing must enter the political arena, returning power to the grassroots through the process of direct democracy found at the heart of any truly cooperative organization.

Chapter 9

PARTICIPATORY, GRASSROOTS DEMOCRACY

*Democracy . . . is the idea of community life
itself . . . a name for a life of free and enriching
communion.* —John Dewey

Public-opinion polls indicate that an overwhelming majority of Americans care for and would sacrifice to preserve the natural environment. Yet our efforts to do so are often waged defensively and carried out against great odds. Thus, the democratic empowerment of citizens to effect change is at the heart of our ability to actualize our concern for the Earth. An ecological society will rest on the ability of its citizens to create a caring, sustainable community through active participation in self-government. This process, in which citizens take part in their own governance, is called direct or participatory democracy. Since it involves the mass of people in their day-to-day lives, it is also called grassroots democracy. Just as the development of community can lead to a direct understanding of and care for the Earth, participatory democracy gives people the power to translate that care into public policy. Any movement or organization whose goal is an ecologically wise and socially just society must seek to establish forms of direct democracy both in its internal affairs and in society at large.

We are educated in modern society to function and to think of ourselves as individuals rather than as members of a community or broader sociopolitical body. It is therefore critical to create forms of participation that we embrace as individuals but that bring us into an awareness of community and to a lived experience of democracy. Participatory democracy requires a renewed sense of citizenship and an emphasis on the common interests of the community along with an ability to resolve conflict through democratic processes that respect differences and the rights of minorities.

Like community, democracy is an idea that everyone subscribes to, even though most would find it difficult to define. People usually identify democracy with the political process, common in Western nations, in which citizens periodically go to the polls to elect representatives. There is an alternative viewpoint, held by Thomas Jefferson and others, that democracy is the active participation of all citizens in self-government. One's notion of democracy is very much tied to one's understanding of politics and of the structures of governmental authority and decision making.

A simple yet insightful analysis of American politics has been provided by the sociologist Robert Bellah and his associates. Based on interviews, they have identified three distinct conceptions of politics in the United States.[1] The first of these is the "politics of community," which seeks to understand the moral consensus of the community and to bring that consensus into practical application in the day-to-day affairs of the community. This consensus is reached through free face-to-face discussion, much as in the New England town meeting, the wards of Thomas Jefferson, and the self-governing towns discussed by de Tocqueville. The politics of community is inherently small-scale and local, depending on the ongoing relations among participants and on their shared understanding of common concerns.

Contrasted to this image is that of the "politics of interest," in which "politics means the pursuit of differing interests according to agreed-upon, neutral rules." This is the familiar politics of interest groups, often competing, sometimes forming fragile coalitions. It emphasizes conflict rather than consensus. The activities of interest politics, such as adversarial struggles, alliance building, and interest bargaining, are more complicated and more highly professionalized than are the activities of consensual democracy.

Finally, in the "politics of the nation" is found "the realm of statesmanship in which the high affairs of national life transcend particular interests." This is the world of "Nightline," National Public Radio, the *Washington Post,* and the *New York Times.* The politics of the nation is a politics of leadership rather than a politics of citizenship. The politics of the nation, like the politics of interest, generally accepts the status quo in terms of the relations of power. Both leave the ordinary citizen out of the picture. For most people, the politics of the nation contains a powerful symbolism. It often unites citizens in the spirit of patriotism or allegiance embodied, perhaps, in the person of the president or a victorious general. Most people today have minimal experience of the politics of genuine moral consensus in the community. To compensate for this, the politics of the nation is enhanced with an aura of national unity that creates a feeling of consensus and community otherwise lacking in people's lives.

An interesting picture of the relationship and conventional valuation of these three types of politics can be obtained from any of the major news media, whether print or broadcast. The headline stories almost invariably highlight the politics of the nation, focusing on "inside the Beltline" news from Washington and international affairs. Immediately following, but clearly of secondary importance, is the politics of interest, as competing interest groups are observed in their efforts to influence public policy. Finally, often consigned to human-interest features or the back pages, is the politics of community, in which the grassroots efforts of citizens organizing for their own political empowerment or social and economic betterment are reported. The self-fulfilling prophesy of the major media is that the politics of the nation is important and that grassroots politics is not.

What is needed is to turn this perspective on its head. Of course, the national news media, owned for the most part by a handful of giant corporations, cannot be expected to report on local grassroots politics. But a reinvigorated polity will assert the importance of its own work. Recall that the nineteenth-century Populists communicated their message via thousands of lecturers and independent newspapers. Grassroots politics in the community finds its own value through the word-of-mouth communications and day-to-day interactions of the participants and through the forms citizens create to educate and inform themselves and their neighbors: newsletters, independent journals, public-access television and radio, study groups, public programs, festivals, and cultural events.

The message in the slogan "Think globally, act locally" is not that national and international events are unimportant. Rather, it is that effective citizen action is rooted in the politics of the local community, as well as that local action has global ramifications. Both the politics of the nation and the politics of interest assert a myth of politics as a realm of experts, as if the 535 members of Congress, for example, were somehow better qualified to make policy than are the citizens who elect them. As seen in the history of the drafting and ratification of the U.S. Constitution in the 1780s, mistrust of the democratic participation of the people is deeply embedded in the American form of government. An ecological society will assert with Jefferson that well-informed citizens should be entrusted with their own government.

The importance of participation in self-government is well expressed in Marge Piercy's novel *Woman on the Edge of Time*. The protagonist, Connie, who has time-traveled to a utopian future, asks how scientific decisions are made. Her friend Luciente tells her that it is "the town meetings. That's how general questions of direction of science get decided." Incredulous, Connie replies, "You mean by people like me? How could I decide if they should build an atom bomb or something?" The simple answer is, "Of course you could decide. It affects you— how not?"[2] Even today in the real world, an exciting moment for people working in grassroots movements is the discovery that, sorting through the jargon of expert opinion, ordinary citizens can understand technical material and, more importantly, the impact of technical decisions on their lives and communities. At the foundation of grassroots politics is the development of a sense of the political power, personal worth, and competency embodied in the mere exercise of the prerogatives of citizenship.

Citizenship

The practice of democracy is a learned one. It is learned in making the decisions that affect one's life in a face-to-face context. Participatory democracy is a bioregional phenomenon: it is best practiced close to home, in the place where community and politics meet. It is not a question of whether citizens have the political understanding or competency to participate. Rather, participation itself creates a citizenry proficient in the ways of democracy. Direct democracy depends not so much on common interests as it does on a common understanding of and commitment to the political process itself.[3] The democracy of ancient Athens, for example, placed civic education in reasoning, argumentation, ethics, and martial arts at the heart of its political system, developing a knowledgeable and dedicated citizenry.[4]

In America today, we spend most of our lives in hierarchical, authority-based organizations, where, far from learning participation in self-government, we learn obedience and conformity. Most schools provide lessons in hierarchy as they separate classes for "gifted" students from those for average or "disadvantaged" students. Schools are organized around the authority of teacher and principal. Even those alternative schools consciously oriented toward student participation must overcome deeply rooted tendencies toward authority. For example, I sent my son to a Quaker school in the hope that he would have an experience of participatory decision making, but by the time he was a teenager, he had grown frustrated with school meetings in which student participation involved little more than discussing, after the fact, policies developed previously and privately by faculty and administration.

After graduation, we Americans find ourselves well educated for workplaces organized around the authority of a boss. While much has been said in recent decades about participatory workplaces and innovative management styles, the fact remains that the vast majority of Americans work in an environment where "the buck stops" on someone else's desk. It is no wonder that this experience, coupled with our centralized, representative form of government, turns us into passive, apathetic citizens who think we live in the ultimate democratic political system merely because we've been told so. It is in part because the lessons of authority and obedience are a fundamental aspect of our social conditioning that the discussion of democracy here has been preceded by a discussion of cooperation and community. Participatory democracy, to be recovered politically, has to be part and parcel of the social organization of each aspect of our lives.

These two qualities, citizenship and participation, reinforce and depend on one another. Although citizenship is learned from participation, it is clear that participation, to be meaningful, requires a minimal level of citizenship as the foundation of a self-governing community.[5] In most instances, people become active politically through organizing to defend their rights or homes, revealing the rudimentary awareness of the rights of citizenship that exists today. However, these efforts often lead to an awareness of the possibilities for collective problem solving, and a new understanding of the promise of self-government and citizenship can be found.[6] The power of democratic participation is readily discovered in the work of grassroots activists. It can also be observed through the history of community groups and even, in some cases, that of nations.

Democracy in Switzerland

The most significant example of participatory democracy in modern Western history is the Swiss commune. Switzerland has practiced some form of participatory democracy since at least the thirteenth century; and it provides an excellent case study in direct democracy, although it is one that should be regarded as suggestive rather than exemplary.[7]

In Switzerland, the locus of political power for most of the modern era has been jurisdictional communes and the autonomous neighborhoods of which they are composed. The average commune contains three thousand citizens and the average neighborhood six hundred. For the Swiss, politics is a neighborhood phenomenon. In contrast to the powerful parliaments of the modern nation-state, the Swiss system has kept power at the lowest possible level and is committed to a process of face-to-face consensual decision making.

The history of Swiss politics reveals a tendency toward self-reliance that is an understandable response to the country's geology. Swiss communities, isolated from one another by high mountains with steep passes, could not practically depend on even their closest neighbors. The self-reliant communes that developed maintained a democratic standard in which communal decision making incorporated both the development and the implementation of policy. Thus, if the community needed a new bridge, the decision to proceed represented a commitment by the citizens to construct it themselves.

The federal government in Switzerland has limited authority, which is determined by referenda in the communes. The Swiss referendum serves as the sovereign voice of the people. In the United States, we think of the referendum as a ballot initiative to be voted up or down by a majority of citizens. The Swiss referendum is different in several important ways, which exemplify the vitality of Swiss democracy.

First, the vote on a referendum is not counted in the (to us) familiar one-person, one-vote manner. Instead, the referendum's success depends on a count of the votes of the communes themselves. In each commune and in its constituent neighborhoods, the referendum is debated in public assembly in which citizens discuss the resolution, seeking the consensus of the democratic body. Even in federal matters, Swiss democracy is founded in, and in turn reinforces, face-to-face democracy.

Unlike U.S.-style referenda, the Swiss referendum does not permit a simple yes-no vote. Each commune submits a long, well-developed statement that provides background on the issues, elaborate arguments, and a discussion of relevant precedents and principles.[8] This is similar to a decision of the U.S. Supreme Court, in which each justice may deliver a detailed opinion. Each Swiss citizen, through the local commune, is able to propose modifications of or alternatives to the referendum. Unlike an American, who might emerge from a polling booth to say, "I didn't vote for *any* of them; it only encourages them," a Swiss citizen might more likely say, "I didn't vote for any of *them*; I voted to introduce a different set of options that will give us a meaningful choice."[9] While the American citizen has become notoriously apathetic and passive, by contrast the Swiss citizen is well informed, having grown up surrounded by political discussion and debate. The Swiss feels the confidence to grapple with complex referenda and civic questions.[10]

In the twentieth century, Swiss democracy has to some extent fallen victim to the forces of modernization that press toward centralization. While the eighteenth-century villager might have been called on to decide the price of timber, his twentieth-century counterpart instead might have to debate the purchase of fighter-bombers for the national air force. In the past, "a vote for a new common meant building it, just as a vote for war meant waging it." By contrast, "gangs of well-meaning citizens cannot build reinforced concrete buildings or cantilevered bridges."[11] In the commune itself, a citizen has trouble maintaining the integrated political-economic perspective of earlier centuries. Modern economics and technologically sophisticated industry fragment the knowledge of workers and limit their ability to make informed decisions as well as to carry out many projects.

The Swiss certainly foresaw the threat that modernization was to their democracy. In 1911, for example, one commune outlawed the automobile, a ban that stayed in effect until the 1930s. The Swiss were not reactive Luddites. Rather, they refused to evaluate progress solely on the basis of efficiency. They preferred to ask whether new technology would interfere with their self-sufficiency and autonomy.[12] For the Swiss, a broad community perspective remained important to the adopting of technology.[13]

It would be easy to look at the diminishing of democracy in the Swiss commune and take a pessimistic view of the prospects for democracy in the modern era.[14] Swiss democracy has been weakened by the forces of a global economy that thrust a technology and way of life on it running counter to self-reliance and to the interdependencies that are the foundation of participatory democracy. The technological and economic forces that have assaulted the decentralized Swiss democracy are geared toward centralization, fragmentation, and profit.

Fortunately, as we have seen in the cases of cohousing and Mondragon, it is possible for communities to plan intentionally for the promotion of cooperation and self-reliance, to design themselves in ways that minimize reliance on the more alienating forms of technology, and to encourage self-help, mutual aid, and interdependence. Additionally, as such communities, and the broader constituency for an ecological society, interact with the forces of central government, they can work for reversing the trend of subsidizing the large-scale technologies that are destructive to democratic communities as well as to the Earth.[15] If research and development were guided by values of decentralization, self-reliance, and ecological wisdom, technological development could support the social and environmental integrity of bioregionally based communities.

Thus, the destruction of communities and direct democracy by the forces of modern technology and the global economy is not inevitable. Communities can promote environmentally sensitive technology that supports decentralized democratic politics and cooperative economics in several ways: through community design, through selection of technology for use by the community, and through influence on government policies. Over the long haul, the transition to sustainable communities committed to an ecological, democratic society based on cooperative economics will reduce the relative power of multinational corporations and provide the political foundation for systemic change.

Adversary Democracy

The participatory democracy of the Swiss, even as it struggles against the forces of modernization, is unusual in the history of nations. More common is the system of adversary democracy familiar in the United States. This is the system where representatives are elected and make decisions on the basis of majority rule.[16] Adversary democracy assumes that politics is about resolving an inevitable conflict of interest among citizens. It goes along with the politics of interest discussed above. Adversary democracy rose to prominence during the period surrounding the rise of capitalism and the industrial era. A process based on resolving conflicting interests could only appear with the legitimation of self-interest that is found in modern society.[17] The self-reliant communities of preindustrial society had no need for the adversarial system.[18]

Since an adversary system assumes a conflict of interests, the question of power becomes critical to the protection of competing groups. If people are seeking only their own self-interest, then to the extent that power is distributed equally, people have equal power to achieve their interests.[19] This is the rationale behind "one person, one vote." Of course, in reality under a self-interested system, some will gain more power than others and will use that power to further increase the discrepancy.

It is ironic that, while those advocating cooperation and common interest are often pejoratively labeled utopian, it is the equal distribution of power that has proved to be a truly utopian, in the sense of unattainable, ideal. The strategy for creating an ecological society must depend on a cooperative, bioregional approach that replaces the drive for competitive advantage with a restored sense of common interest within the local community. This must be combined with a political art of participatory democracy that attempts to equalize power and resolve conflicts, while sustaining the diversity of the citizenry.

Strong Democracy

Just as the natural world contains both symbiosis and parasitism, an ecological society requires a participatory democracy that can contain and resolve conflict. The theory of strong democracy, which was developed by the political scientist Benjamin Barber, is an effort in this direction. In strong democracy, all citizens participate directly, rather than through representatives, in their own governance. Strong democracy is based on a belief in the common-sense wisdom and competency of citizenship.[20]

Strong democracy places an acceptance and experience of conflict at the heart of political participation. The fundamental social consensus of a strong democracy values difference, seeking solutions that address the needs of the many while protecting the rights of the few. Strong democracy would place the right of dissent, guaranteed by the U.S. Constitution's First Amendment, in a framework that sought to glean the best from competing viewpoints through a participatory process.

In strong democracy, public ends are determined through public participation and public deliberation. This process can include activities such as neighborhood assemblies, electronic balloting, selection of local officials by lottery, and workplace democracy.[21] In strong democracy the most basic and unifying common interest is found in the commitment of the community to the success of the participatory process of self-government itself.[22] Meeting the criteria for a strong democracy, the future society described by Marge Piercy in *Woman on the Edge of Time* is one of fully participating, self-governing citizens, for whom there is no final authority. In Piercy's future utopia, those who disagree argue for as long as it takes to reach a resolution. After what could have been a debilitating town meeting finally comes to a close, the adversaries are described as sharing food and exchanging gifts, celebrating the resolution of a difficult problem. In strong democracy, the political process is celebrated as the lifeblood of the community.[23]

Developing a system of strong democracy will depend on four types of leadership: transitional, natural, facilitative, and moral. Transitional leaders are similar to those who today function effectively as representatives and who have the skill to guide people toward greater self-government. They understand the workings of the adversary system yet must be committed to a transition to more participatory forms. Natural leaders are those who inevitably will have better-developed articulateness, will power, or experience, even in the most egalitarian communities. Facilitating leadership addresses the need for participatory institutions to work actively to overcome the skewing effects of natural and traditional leadership skills, seeking to engage the less proficient in the democratic process on an equal footing. Finally, moral leadership identifies and promotes the values of the community and the freedom and dignity of its citizens, ensuring that these broader goals are not lost in the details of day-to-day affairs.[24]

Strong democracy has three key elements, each of which is crucial to a fully participatory process. Strong democratic talk includes participation in deliberation, agenda setting, and information exchange, emphasizing listening and speaking skills and empathy. Strong democratic decision making involves participation in the actual determination of policy and the exercise of public judgment. Finally, strong democratic action entails common work, community action, and citizen service to implement policy decisions.[25]

The theory of strong democracy answers our need for forms of participation that attract us as individuals but at the same time bring us into an awareness of community and to a lived experience of direct democracy. Placed in a face-to-face context, strong democracy can create the empathy and maximized sense of common interest that is vital to a sustainable community and to environmental responsibility. Yet it is not enough to focus on government as the ultimate ground of democracy, omitting the broader dimensions of social, cultural, and economic life. A genuinely strong democracy cannot fragment the political arena from the rest of experience. It must be developed holistically through the many opportunities for meeting human needs by the efforts of cooperative, participatory organizations.

Unlike most of the needs of contemporary society, democracy cannot be picked up off the shelf and applied as needed. Society itself must build a foundation of democratic culture that includes information, skills, and attitudes instilling a sense of democracy into all social activities and institutions. Of course, the hierarchical structures of capitalist enterprise are antithetical to a democratic culture, teaching neither the toleration nor the respect, cooperation and solidarity needed for democratic participation. The market itself emphasizes choosing among given alternatives rather than establishing what choices are available. This undermines participation and is contrary to a dynamic democratic culture.[26] Democratic culture is at the heart of the comparison of American and Swiss voters drawn above: the Americans choosing not to choose because they lack the participatory options of the Swiss.

The fundamental importance of democratic culture can be gleaned from the assertion of the women's movement that the personal is political. Our political relations are modeled and reproduced in the various patterns of daily life, whether in the home, the school room, or the workplace. Thus, as feminists would confront male domination, whether it is expressed in government, business, or the family, those seeking a participatory democracy must forge democratic culture as a pattern of life. This perspective transforms politics from an affair of the state to the concern of citizens in all areas of life. A democratic culture must penetrate each aspect of social life. The greatest obstacle to a democratic culture remains the forces of commodification and materialism that tend to colonize all areas of human experience, turning them into objects for exchange on the market and advancing consumerism at the expense of citizenship. Thus, the economy must be a key arena for establishing the culture of democracy.

Economic Democracy

Although our constitution ensures each person the equal power of a single vote, vast economic inequity gives some citizens substantially greater influence. An adversary democracy requires an equality of power to protect the competing interests of its citizens. Even in an ecological society, recognizing adversarial situations within a community context, equalization of power will go hand in hand with the search for common interest. As we seek participatory forms of self-government, we must work to level the economic playing field to provide the basis for genuine democracy.

The capitalist economy can be viewed as conferring three significant types of power on the controllers of capital. Command over production involves organizing the workplace and controlling the activity of workers. Command over investment determines which enterprises receive financial support. Influence over state economic policy allows the financially privileged to limit the impact of democratic forces on economic regulation and government investments.[27] Each of these areas of socially consequential power (production, investment, and state policy) would, under economic democracy, be returned to the workplace and to the community. The earlier discussion of worker and community ownership and community-based financial institutions touched on aspects of changing economic-power relationships. Certainly a community must have the power to influence production and investment decisions in order to develop an environmentally sustainable way of life. A bioregional orientation, however, more than merely giving communities influence over state policy, would also reduce state power as much as possible to allow genuinely democratic bodies to discuss, determine, and directly implement policy, tying democratic talk directly to democratic action.

A program for economic democracy will naturally be resisted by those benefiting from concentrated economic power. Their near monopoly on command over production, investment, and state policy can block challenges from less-powerful political formations. Additionally, the possibility of capital flight—the removal of production and investment from an offending community—can bring devastating consequences to a local economy. Capital flight is already a common response to labor organizing and environmental regulation and has led to the resiting of much U.S. production in the Third World.

The most direct defense against the threat of capital flight is the building of a self-reliant economy. Local production for local needs will strengthen the local economy and make it less dependent on large corporations. Simultaneously, legal reforms can place community members on the boards of distant corporations or can tie the siting of production facilities to a commitment to the community. Communities offering incentives to corporations should negotiate for increased democratization of production and investment as part of the corporate commitment to the economic sustainability of the community.[28]

The benefits and obstacles to economic democracy are highlighted by the case of municipally owned electric utilities. Although most Americans receive power from private utilities, there are over two thousand public, nonprofit electric systems serving fifteen million customers, representing approximately 10 percent of households.[29] These public power corporations make the interests of the owners and the consumers, who are in this case the same people, identical. Private utilities have a profit incentive to sell electricity and thus, for example, aim an energy-efficiency program at replacing gas and oil heaters with electric heat pumps (thus increasing total sales of electricity). Municipally based utilities are more likely to invest in energy-efficiency programs that actually lower the total consumption of energy, such as free energy audits for homeowners, assistance for insulating, and incentives for efficiency improvements. They also look carefully for the least expensive source of energy, as opposed to private utilities, which seek the most profitable source (unless constrained from doing so by state law).

Thus, the case of municipal utilities demonstrates the benefits of economic democracy in the form of direct community ownership at the local level. The environmental benefits of locally owned utilities are obvious, in that an emphasis on efficiency causes much less damage to the environment than does an emphasis on increased sales, and thereby use, of electriciy. Unfortunately, since the dawn of the electric age over a century ago, the public-power movement has waged a mostly losing battle against the giant private utilities.[30] The power industry took off in 1892, when the financier J. P. Morgan formed General Electric. Today, there are over one thousand directorial interlocks between banks and private utilities. The high profitability and capital intensiveness of power production have made the private utilities a favorite on Wall Street. When private utilities battle citizen referenda that would close inefficient power plants or limit utility profits, they are actively and extensively supported by the big investment firms. This combined power of the major institutions of energy and finance is well able to influence state economic policy to protect their interests from the threat of economic democracy.

For example, in 1987 Commonwealth Edison of Chicago lobbied Congress's Joint Taxation Committee, chaired by Illinois representative Dan Rostenkowski, to promote legislation restricting towns' ability to purchase electric utilities with traditional tax-exempt bonds. This would put a damper on the move toward municipalization, since capitalization of the purchase becomes more difficult and more expensive. The restrictive legislation was opposed by the American Public Power Association (APPA) and a coalition of fifteen civic, consumer, and environmental groups, including the National League of Cities and the U.S. Conference of Mayors.[31] Although their efforts softened the impact of the bill, they were not able to prevent its passage. The success of Commonwealth Edison in this case is typical of the ability of corporations to use their power with the federal government to stop a threat to their profits and control coming from the local or state level.

Still untapped in the municipal-power movement is the possibility that the thousands of communities involved could bring an influence to bear on Congress that might rival that of Commonwealth Edison. A single municipality is not able to compete with the corporate power of the giant utility. At the same time, the organizations comprising the APPA tend to be bureaucratic, and their lobbying efforts are not based in the grassroots. Their power is no match for the big utilities. However, the affected cities contain many millions of citizens who, if working together from a basis of grassroots participation, could voice a loud and powerful demand for federal policies more in their favor. The active involvement of the millions of customers of the public power companies could provide an effective counterweight to the moneyed interests. If public power were based in a participatory municipal democracy, citizen activism could be engaged on questions of policy at many levels. These democratic municipalities could then cooperate with one another to forge the power of the grassroots citizenry into an effective political force to hold national representatives more accountable to the needs of citizens and communities.

Confederal Municipalism

The municipality, or local community, is the breeding ground for democracy and citizenship. It is at the right scale for participatory democracy. An ecological society will avoid a narrow or parochial localism, asserting that self-reliance is not the same as self-sufficiency and that decentralized communities must still be dependent upon one another.[32] To combine these characteristics of self-reliance and interdependence, municipalities based on participatory democracy must join with one another in democratic confederations.

At the heart of the idea of confederalism is a democratic process whereby delegates to confederal councils are elected by democratic assemblies in the constituent municipalities. Larger municipalities might be composed of confederations of neighborhoods similar to the Swiss communes. The confederal councils administer the policy of the confederation, with each delegate acting on the mandate of the community assembly. A system similar to this is described in *Woman on the Edge of Time*:

> We arrive with the needs of each village and try to divide scarce resources justly. Often we must visit the spot. Next level is regional planning. Reps chosen by lot

from township level go to the regional to discuss gross decisions. The needs go up and the possibilities come down. If people are chilled by a decision, they go and argue. Or they barter directly with places needing the same resources and compromise.[33]

Fundamental to structures of participatory democracy is the ability of those "chilled by a decision" to have the opportunity not only to argue their position, but to have some ability to influence the outcome as well.

Confederal municipalism builds up from the participatory foundation of the municipality to create in confederation the ability to address regional and even global issues through the form of direct democracy. It places decisions as close to the local level as possible. Thus, much of the day-to-day policy-making of society can be conducted in a face-to-face democratic manner close to home. Regional decisions, for example those concerning the use of a major river, would be made by delegates mandated to act on behalf of their constituent municipalities. Issues with an even broader impact, perhaps, for example, concerning a continental power grid, could be made in a similar manner through interregional confederations, with delegates chosen by the regions. In each case, the authority of the higher confederation is strictly limited and the decision-making power is exercised bottom-up from the grassroots. Municipalism, readily adapted to the bioregional perspective, is based on maintaining the scale and organization that allow for popular control of policy in a context of community ownership and worker self-management.

While direct democracy is at the heart of the municipalist approach, an equally great challenge is withdrawing authority from state and national governments and returning it to local communities and regional confederations. In Bookchin's view, confederal municipalism is initially developed as a counterpower to the state, challenging its centralized and hierarchical power with the moral power of grassroots democracy.[34] Existing municipal leagues in some ways anticipate the potential of the confederal approach, but they have been stymied by a lack of authority to implement a wide range of innovative programs.

The structures of state government are often opposed to the democratic, ecological, or social priorities of confederal municipalism.

For example, in February 1990, Peter Berg of the Planet Drum Foundation spoke to a group of local officials in Chapel Hill, North Carolina, about San Francisco's green city project. Hearing about the innovative programs, the North Carolinians shook their heads, saying they'd need special enabling legislation from the state to be able to undertake such things. The difference comes from the fact that California has home rule, in which powers not specifically granted to the state are retained by localities. In North Carolina, all powers belong to the state unless expressly granted to counties or towns; special legislation to enable localities to exercise new powers is viewed as something difficult to obtain from a busy state legislature and thus is rarely proposed. Clearly, initiatives geared toward cooperation and community, toward increased grassroots democracy, and toward environmental and social sustainability require home rule. Home rule brings politics within the scale necessary for participation.

As well as confronting state power, grassroots groups must press for changes in the process of local government. Currently, citizen involvement is too often limited to public hearings at which elected officials condescend to listen to the opinions of citizens prior to making what is often a preordained decision. At their best, public hearings are an adversarial process, setting citizens against one another. They provide no means for the discovery of common ground and shared solutions. Cooperative meetings are needed that are based on dialogue, brainstorming, and an appreciation of the interdependence of the members of the community. A citizens' movement creating new institutions of cooperation and community will seek the legal space and power to implement and support its initiatives. The insistence of an activated citizenry can lead to a resurgence in town-meeting-style government. The inability of the existing structures of government to accommodate the direct democracy and broad local jurisdiction needed for the confederal municipalist approach may ultimately require structural and even constitutional change.

Putting the Pieces Together

An ecological society will be based on a participatory democracy rooted in a bioregional understanding of place and the interdependency of confederal municipalism. From strong democracy it will draw an understanding of citizenship as the basis for a democratic community. Strong democratic theory offers valuable perspectives on the dynamics of leadership, the relationship of policy-making to implementation, and the reality of conflict. From adversary democracy is gleaned the importance of equality of power to maintain the democratic nature of the community, particularly as power is exercised in the economic realm. The bioregional emphasis on place and scale leads to an appreciation of the municipality as the proper home for a confederally oriented democratic movement. With this understanding of participatory democracy as a foundation, citizens can begin to introduce a democratic culture into their public lives, lending strength and meaning to their efforts at cooperation and community and providing both the context and the power for developing an ecological society.

At this juncture, it is important to emphasize that participatory democracy, by itself, will not necessarily lead to an environmentally wise society. Certainly, a democratic decision could be made to remove an ancient forest for quick profit or to send wastes downstream into someone else's water supply. The culture of the ecological society will be one that embraces participatory democracy as one piece in a set of broad, life-affirming values. These values, such as ecological wisdom, nonviolence, future focus, and respect for diversity, will lead to socially and ecologically just and sustainable policies. Just as the democratic process provides an avenue for citizens to actualize their concern for the Earth, the key values of the ecological society will inform and guide the workings of its democracy.

The possibility of building a democratic movement from the grassroots up runs counter to all our received notions of centralized power and to the officially sanctioned view of politics as an unassailable fortress ruled by experts. Murray Bookchin offers a challenge to those who would build such a movement: "In an era of growing power in nation-states and corporations, when administration, property ownership, production, bureaucracies, and the flow of capital as well as power are notoriously centralized, how can we invoke a localist, municipally oriented society without seeming to be starry-eyed visionaries?"[35] While the vision must be maintained, it is nonetheless crucial to address the strategic issues faced by locally based citizens' movements confronting the enormous power of the nation-state and global capitalism. It is necessary to place the vision of an ecological society in a practical context that gives both meaning and functionality to the slogan "Think globally, act locally." To this context we now turn.

Chapter 10

FROM PARTICIPATION TO POWER: GREEN POLITICS

The largest, most widespread, and perhaps longest-lived occurrence in the United States of a cooperatively oriented, democratic political movement was that of the Populists in the nineteenth century. Born of economic necessity, this agrarian movement was politicized by the difficulty of meeting the financial needs of its agricultural cooperatives. Ultimately turning their attention to national banking policy, the Populists were thrust into the political arena. There, on the stage of national politics, the Populist movement gained prominence and perished, its issues coopted by its opponents, defeated by the vast resources of the major parties and their corporate backers. In this light, a challenge to those seeking social, environmental, and political transformation today is to recognize that the United States' republican form of government is fitted to the centralizing force of the capitalist economy. It is an inhospitable arena for a movement seeking to develop a cooperative society.

A sober awareness of the history of the Populists as well as that of the twentieth century's more radical movements for social change will caution a transformational movement to ground itself firmly and continually in a local and bioregional context in order to build an alternative and present a challenge to the forces of concentrated power. In this manner, a movement can develop human and organizational resources to match the financial resources of the vested interests. It can engage the citizenry in issues that have a day-to-day relevance. It can counter mass media with door-to-door canvasing, grassroots media, and word of mouth. Organized in such a manner, transformational movements will keep the principles of participatory grassroots democracy, cooperation, and community as part and parcel of all aspects of organizing. At the same time, to succeed politically, care must be taken when citizens' movements have their inevitable dealings with state and national government. To achieve an ecological society, it is not sufficient merely to approach the government with the stance of yet another interest group lobbying for a particular policy. There is too much history of government pacifying a movement through adopting a policy that turns out not to have teeth or that is quickly reversed. While important battles are fought at the state and national levels, such struggles must be combined with efforts to increase the role of direct democracy and return power to local communities and regions, where participation is meaningful and where social and environmental needs can best be understood.

Bioregionally oriented efforts must guard against the threat of marginalization and the label of irrelevance, which can undermine the extended commitments they require for success. Slowly evolving cooperative and democratic alternatives can lose support as citizens are bombarded by news glorifying power struggles in the global arena. Transformational movements may not always seem relevant to these global events or may be portrayed as being at the fringe of serious political concerns. Grassroots efforts must also guard against a kind of localism that creates pockets of alternatives but that never really challenges the status quo.

The contemporary political movement that has best addressed this discrepancy, coupling a radical commitment to an ecological society with a sense of national and global power relations, is the Green movement. While the Greens have not fully resolved the dilemma of combining decentralized grassroots organizing with an effective global focus, they are attempting both theoretically and programmatically to do so. For those seeking an ecological society, whether or not they are personally identified as Greens, the Green movement offers an important model for organizing and strategy. Its successes and failures, its level of coherence, and its areas of controversy have much to teach the ecological activist. The discussion that follows is very much from an insider's perspective, based on the author's experience with Green politics, both in theory and in practice. At the same time, it is not intended to be a thorough description of the Green movement, but rather to outline a model for a practical, real-world strategic and organizational approach to developing an ecological politics. Readers seeking a more complete treatment of the Green movement per se should consult Brian Tokar's seminal introductory work *The Green Alternative*.

Green Politics

The Green movement arose in western Europe, most prominently in what was then West Germany, in the late 1970s and early 1980s. It developed from a coalescing of movements for peace, ecology, citizens' initiatives, and feminism.[1] The importance of these various constituent movements can be gleaned from the early endeavors of the German Greens. The Greens' rootedness in the peace movement was highlighted by their prominent role in the opposition to the deployment of Pershing missiles in the early 1980s. The young Green party was galvanized by the millions who took to the streets of Frankfurt and Bonn to protest the deployment. Their ecological roots can be seen in their opposition to nuclear power and concern with acid rain, and even in the simple act of Green delegates bringing plants to their seats in the otherwise staid German parliament. In 1984, feminists on the Green women's council were able to establish briefly an all-female leadership structure for the Greens, unprecedented for a major party. Further expressing their feminist commitments and roots, Greens later stood out in the German parliament with their insistence on strict punishment for the crime of marital rape. The Greens' constituent movements shared a number of concerns, including the recovery of community, a strategy of nonviolence, and a disenchantment with politics as usual.[2] The groups forming the Greens were brought together around a critique of the structures of modern society, a distaste for both conventional politics and conventional political ideologies, and a commitment to developing alternative forms.

The Greens are well aware that government is only one aspect of the structure of national and global power. They see their path as one of transforming institutions and social relations throughout society. The German Greens describe themselves as having two legs: a "playing leg" in parliament, which raises issues, helps forge movement consensus, and legitimatizes the movement; and a "standing leg" in grassroots movements, which builds the alternative structures of power. The Greens raise issues and influence policy in the legislative sphere while simultaneously developing democratic initiatives in the community. Electoral success provides the Greens with a legitimacy that both empowers and politicizes local struggles. Green activity in state and national politics is geared toward supporting the development of ecological alternatives at the local level.

The Green movement represents a radical approach to politics in the etymological sense of seeking the roots of political and social problems. It does not accept any aspect of the status quo as a given but seeks to understand how economic, political, and cultural institutions are intertwined in causing environmental and social problems. Green politics is rooted in a number of historical traditions, including social democracy, Marxism, anarchism, and populism. At the same time, the Greens do not rely on the failed, outdated, or incomplete analyses of the past, but seek to integrate them with the understandings of modern movements, particularly feminism and ecology.

Green politics is a holistic approach. As the ten key values of the U.S. Greens indicate, Green politics seeks to develop "a coherent world-view." Greens believe that social and environmental problems cannot be solved in isolation and are rooted in our public institutions, our private enterprises, and our personal lives. Green politics, as its origins indicate, is heterogeneous. The Green value of respect for diversity (or inclusiveness) demonstrates a commitment in principle to including all people in its organizing. It is a challenge to Green organizing to unite diverse points of view and constituencies around a common political program in a common movement. While programmatic interpretations may differ, the key values provide an important level of unity to the Greens.

Important to the Greens' diversity is their independence. The Green movement is organized to be independent both of conventional political parties and of single-issue movements. This allows the Greens to develop their programs and processes without the need to compromise with other organizations, which may be wedded to the status quo. Greens may work in coalition with other groups and in so doing may make tactical compromises to obtain particular goals, but they will avoid making compromises in principle that might undermine their more radical positions. For example, Greens have no problem joining mainstream conservation groups in a call for improved environmental protection. However, alliances with other political parties lacking a radical approach have proved controversial and in some cases have caused Greens to sacrifice their own principles in order to maintain the coalition.

Green politics is still in a formative stage. Green parties in Europe struggle to resist the pressures toward bureaucracy that accompany parliamentary participation. The German Green party, in particular, has found the necessities of administering the nation-state to be antithetical to fostering an emphasis on grassroots democracy. It is still struggling to find the balance that allows a grassroots movement to hold elected legislators accountable. In the United States, Greens are groping in many states and localities to find a way to engage politically in a nation whose electoral laws make third-party success virtually impossible. Meanwhile, those who want to run candidates for president have found themselves at odds with those who prefer competing for offices at the municipal level, while both struggle to integrate their efforts with nonelectoral, movement-building activities.

The Green movement as it exists today may ultimately be little more than a stage in the development of a diverse grassroots movement that can work effectively for a fundamental transformation to an ecological society. The practice of Green politics is still being shaped by a number of contending forces. Some seek only an alternative political party, a party of reform. Others work toward building a broad-ranging transformational movement for an ecological society. As an activist, I lend my efforts toward the latter tendency, in full awareness that a decentralized, grassroots approach leads to uncertainty as to the organizational outcome. Still, the principles of Green politics represent the most far-ranging and radical formulation on the current political scene. They are important to any movement, organization, or individual seeking to work toward an ecological society.

Transformation and Transition

A grassroots-based transformation to an ecological society is a vast organizational task, extensive in scope and promising decades before fruition. Green politics couples its transformational goal with a transitional program, geared toward gains that can be achieved in the short term and that have the characteristic of increasing the power and viability of the grassroots movement. The transitional program speaks to the short attention span and casual acceptance of the status quo that are characteristic of modern society. It focuses on goals that can be readily achieved, primarily through conventional means. For the Greens, however, it is crucial to view these short-term goals as part of a transitional stage en route to the more fundamental transformation to an ecological society. For example, the Green economic program takes both a long-term and a transitional approach. In the long term, Greens seek to transform the job economy so that human well-being is not dependent on alienating paid employment, as it generally is today. In the short term, Greens have called for a shortened work week with no loss of pay, to decrease unemployment and to attain a more equitable distribution of wealth.

This idea of a transitional program is critical to the success of a transformational movement. It addresses head-on our cultural preoccupation with national and global affairs, capturing public attention at that level and seeking to adapt public policy to ecologically and socially responsible ends. The transitional program seeks to use state and national policy to empower the transformational strategy. For example, state-funded job-training programs can be developed that, rather than producing workers for large corporations, train workers in skills needed for the local economy, furthering efforts at local self-reliance. State banking regulations can encourage and support the development of community-based, cooperative credit unions.

In the transitional program, national policy is developed to promote solutions that tend to be small-scale and bioregionally oriented, such as solar power, energy efficiency, and organic agriculture. Greens would institute a number of public-sector programs to meet the need for health care, housing, energy, and public transportation. However, unlike traditional federal programs, they would be administered in a decentralized manner, tailored to the unique requirements of each community and subject to grassroots democratic control and the broad values of the transformational movement, such as ecology, social justice, and sustainability. In developing these public programs, the Greens would challenge accepted notions of private property, asserting an ethic of stewardship and placing natural resources under common ownership for the common good.

A transitional program would not be confined to the economic arena. For example, it would seek to remove state limitations on grassroots organizing, calling for home rule, for proportional representation, for citizens' initiatives and referenda, and for easier ballot access for political parties and independent candidates at every level. Green groups around the United States have been working in various manners and contexts for these goals. The California Green party, for example, after obtaining ballot status, successfully challenged state law to allow it to provide a "none of the above" option in its primary elections. In a sense, the playing (or parliamentary) leg of the German Greens is part of the transitional program, seeking reform through traditional institutions, while the standing (or movement) leg is the transformational strategy, working directly to build the foundation for an ecological society.

A good example of a transitional strategy is found in the evolving global cooperation in the labor movement. A coalition of Mexican and U.S. labor organizations has been seeking to combat the exploitation of cheap Mexican labor by U.S. firms. Hundreds of factories just south of the U.S.-Mexican border, called *maquiladoras,* have been described by the *Wall Street Journal* as causing "abysmal living conditions and environmental degradation."[3] The Maquiladora Coalition unites labor organizations on both sides of the border in the recognition that these factories are damaging to both American and Mexican workers. It calls for labor to stand in international solidarity to raise the standards for workers in all countries, not just in regard to work conditions but in a broad sense of quality of life.

The Maquiladora Coalition recognizes the importance of an international approach, similar to that of the Greens, geared toward cooperative organizing, democratic participation, and environmental sustainability.[4] Its program places the goals of improved working and living conditions in the context of a far-reaching transformation of the maquiladora system. The coalition believes that it is important for labor success in one country to include the promotion of policies favorable to labor organizing in another. Thus, the coalition uses its local struggles against particular plants or corporations to build international solidarity and to push for policies that will increase the power and improve the quality of life in the broadest sense of workers everywhere. The Maquiladora Coalition, like the Greens, is committed to the philosophy of the slogan "Think globally, act locally." Its efforts exemplify the fundamental characteristic of transitional organizing: seeking to utilize all victories to increase the power of the grass-roots movement to achieve its transformational goal.

A combined transitional and transformational orientation like that of the Greens can guide single-issue movements toward more effective strategies for change. While traditional lobbying efforts and direct action may ease certain problems or highlight structural difficulties, new relations of power depend on the development of alternatives.[5] On a day-to-day basis, those working toward an ecological society can reach out to those involved in conventional politics of protest and reform through a transitional program, engaging with them in common struggles while offering a model of social and political transformation.

This wedding of transition and transformation holds the promise of breaking the impasse met by all social-change movements. Reform movements, if they do not integrate a long-range radical perspective, rarely achieve more than short-lived, superficial, or cosmetic changes in a destructive status quo. Radical movements, if they do not have a strategy for addressing the day-to-day concerns of citizens in a familiar context, become marginalized outsiders, strident voices railing against politics as usual, or they become isolated enclaves of utopian dreamers cut off from the rest of society. Combining these two approaches holds the promise of meaningful reform designed to advance the work of those committed to the ecological transformation of society.

Green Internationalism

The combined critique of the nation-state and the transnational corporation as agents of ecological and social destruction is fundamental to Green politics. This is in part a response to modern problems that transcend national boundaries: acid rain, species loss, global warming, world hunger, and so forth. Green parties, while active in national governments, tend to cooperate internationally. Greens in Europe and the United States have called for strengthening the United Nations and the World Court, making them more democratic and less easily controlled by superpowers. The German Greens have called for abolishing the right of veto (held only by the five permanent members) in the U.N. Security Council. Greens from nations around the world actively participate in international environmental initiatives such as the U.N. Conference on the Environment and Development, the "Earth Summit" held in 1992 in Rio de Janeiro.

Still, the description of the Green movement as international is somewhat misleading. In both its economic and political programs, the Green movement combines principles of regionalism and global responsibility that transcend the nation-state. Greens in Europe have consistently opposed the establishment of a unified European economy, seeing it as playing into the hands of antiecological transnational corporations. The German Greens stood out among political parties in their opposition to the reunification of Germany, viewing the creation of a large nation-state and potential superpower as contrary to both social and environmental well-being. Greens have called for a regionalized Europe, in which most political and economic activity would be coordinated in areas significantly smaller than the typical nation-state.

The Green emphasis on global responsibility leads to a particular concern with Third World relations. Greens argue that international economic forces place developing nations in a position of economic dependency on the industrial West, which forces them to exploit their natural resources and labor force for the needs of a global market. Cash-hungry Third World countries turn traditionally maintained fields and forests over to cash-cropping. This leads to many of the familiar environmental problems in those countries, including soil depletion, desertification, deforestation, and species loss. The German Greens call for economic decentralization and national self-reliance as a way to reduce imports from the Third World and to reduce the power of multinational corporations.

While freeing Western economies from the necessity of exploiting the Third World is important, decentralization by itself does not address the need to make amends for the centuries of stealing human and material wealth from those peoples. The program of the U.S. Greens addresses this, calling for cancellation of Third World debt, export policies that promote renewable energy and ecologically sustainable technologies, and aid policy geared toward self-reliance for developing nations. While Third World self-reliance will not eradicate environmental problems, such a program will mitigate the antiecological pressures currently arising from the global economy.

Green Strategy

Green politics, of course, is more than a theory of social change. As an activist-based political movement, the Greens subscribe to strategic and organizational principles and practices that are important to those working to achieve an ecological, just, and sustainable society. The statement of purpose of the Orange County Greens (North Carolina), of which I am a member, lists five aspects of Green strategy: education, nonviolent direct action, alternative-institution building, citizen activism, and independent electoral campaigns. Each of these five aspects is considered an integral part of a comprehensive orientation toward political activism. Taken together, they provide the basis for a combined transitional and transformational approach in the context of building a broad-based movement for change.

Green educational programs are geared toward informing the public not only about issues, but also about political approaches and alternatives. Most political and current-events information today is received passively from the broadcast and print news media and from the school systems. Green educational programs tend to be participatory, since for Greens the process is as important as the product. For example, the Orange County Greens in their monthly public forums have offered presentations and discussions about cooperative ownership, social ecology, hazardous waste, the German Green movement, energy policy, and archeological records of the local indigenous way of life. These forums emphasize dialogue and the creative, thoughtful participation of all. Greens consider their message different and radical to an extent that requires an educational component in all their activities. Green educational programs emphasize the idea that reform is not enough and continually assert the importance of social and political transformation. Thus, when the Greens organized in support of a boycott of General Electric, they developed educational materials emphasizing the connection of the boycott issue to each of the ten key values and to political change. While even single-issue movements will seek to educate the public, the transformational orientation of the Greens reqires a continual emphasis on the interrelatedness of issues and on the structural changes required to fully resolve them.

Study groups are also important to the development of citizen activism, group cohesion, and a well-articulated political perspective. They transform knowledge from something that is passively received to something that is developed by interaction. Green study groups tend to focus on Green politics itself, especially the key values. Many Green locals offer an introductory study group, usually based on *The Green Alternative*. Study groups may be used to educate Green activists on issues of local importance. Groups also study important works of political, economic, or environmental theory to hone their theoretical understanding. A valuable accompaniment to this sort of reading is works of fiction, particularly utopian novels depicting an ecological society, such as Marge Piercy's *Woman on the Edge of Time* or Ernest Callenbach's *Ecotopia*. These works tend to engage the imagination and open up one's perspective on the possibilities for change. It is important to distinguish study groups from individualized self-teaching. The study group becomes a laboratory of participatory democracy as participants challenge or elaborate each other's ideas, leading to a deeper understanding of the subject at hand and to an important experience of democratic culture.

Nonviolent direct action includes rallies, vigils, sit-ins, boycotts, civil disobedience, and other forms of public protest and demonstration. The Greens' commitment to direct action grows from their roots in the civil rights and antiwar movements of the 1960s and, more recently, in the antinuclear movements of the late 1970s and early 1980s.[6] In particular, many Greens have backgrounds in such organizations as the Clamshell Alliance, which opposed the Seabrook nuclear plant in New Hampshire, and the Abalone Alliance, which tried to stop California's Diablo Canyon nuclear plant from opening. As part of diverse strategies to prevent or delay the plants' licensing, both of these organizations used tactics of nonviolent blockades and sit-ins leading to mass arrests. In 1992, the U.S. Greens began to incorporate into their annual national gatherings direct action supporting a concern of the host community, that year participating in a demonstration against Northern States Power's plan to store radioactive waste on the banks of the Mississippi in a Sioux community in Minnesota.[7] Direct action is important to put pressure on decision makers, mobilize forces of support, dramatize issues, and help raise the consciousness of the citizenry. Along with lobbying, it is the bread and butter of traditional single-issue and protest movements. But on its own, direct action will not yield fundamental change. It must be part of a broad strategy that is developing alternative institutions as well as agitating around the existing structures of power. For example, direct action has interfered with the logging of old-growth forests. However, only a much broader political struggle can change industry's policy of clear-cutting these forests.

Alternative-institution building covers the entire range of cooperative, community-based activity. The Orange County Greens, for example, have worked to support the cooperative grocery mentioned above, Weaver Street Market, which attempts to combine worker and community ownership. The Greens were instrumental in the development of a community newspaper, the *Prism*, organized around Green values and principles. Other Green groups have worked to establish barter systems, land trusts, and alternative financial institutions. Alternative-institution building sows the seeds of the ecological society in the form of democratic, cooperative organizations. The final goal of Green politics, the ecological society itself, can be viewed as the ultimate alternative institution. Of course, not every institution must be built anew. Greens also work to reform existing institutions to make them more democratic, to establish cooperative structures, and to make them more responsible to the community and to the Earth.

Citizen activism conveys the sense of citizenship in a participatory framework. It is the expression of the value of personal and social responsibility. Green organizing depends on the active participation of members rather than on fund-raising for activity by paid professionals. This is not to say that there is no place for paid staff, but the emphasis of the Green movement is on the political engagement of citizen activists. Green members are encouraged to initiate projects and to bring a Green perspective to other organizations and activities. As part of the transitional program, Green citizen activists may engage in traditional forms of lobbying to move government and legislative bodies toward the Greens' goals. The Green organization encourages imagination, initiative, and risk taking on the part of its members. Additionally, as Greens place programs and initiatives before the public, these are designed to broaden the understanding and attainment of genuine democratic participation and citizenship.

Finally, requiring a more lengthy discussion is the relevance of electoral work to the Green movement. Any movement engaged with political issues will eventually come face to face with elected government, possibly as an opponent or an obstacle, potentially as an ally. From that point, electing those friendly to the cause tends to become an important goal. For the Greens, electoral involvement is important both because elections offer a major educational opportunity and because government is an institution of power and influence that can be used to advance the transitional program of the movement. While Green electoral work is usually viewed in the context of running candidates, there are other ways to use the attention focused on elections to educate the public and promote the Green agenda. The Orange County Greens, for example, have conducted forums and presented questionnaires to non-Green candidates in races in which Greens were not running. This allows the Greens to differentiate the Green position and to place the Green perspective in the public eye. It also provides a basis for placing pressure on these candidates once they are in office. During one campaign, the Orange County Greens organized a candidates' forum in coalition with the local Sierra Club and the Rainbow Coalition. The forum, held in a public building in the black community, was the first cooperative venture between those two groups and, in form as well as content, conveyed the message that social and environmental concerns are intertwined.

Most people, informed by the news media only of the electoral activity of U.S. and European Green parties, are not aware that elections represent only one aspect of the Green strategy. Because of this misperception, Greens are under continual pressure to field candidates in political races, regardless of whether the necessary grassroots development has been achieved or whether it fits with the strategic requirements of the Green group in question. Nonetheless, the misperception necessitates a special focus on the place of electoral work in Green politics.

Green Electoralism

Today, thousands of Greens hold local office throughout western Europe and the United States. Many more sit in state and national legislatures. Green electoral success, built throughout the 1980s, has grown steadily with increasing environmental awareness. Thus, it was a shock to many when, in the 1990 German national elections, the Green party won only 4.8 percent of the vote, falling below the 5 percent threshold needed to win seats in the Bundestag (national parliament) for the first time since 1983.[8]

The West German Greens had entered the Bundestag in 1983 and increased their representation in 1987. Their involvement within the structure of national government proved an immediate challenge to the Greens. Commitments to grassroots democracy through rotation of delegates and accountability to the base movement were difficult to maintain in a system that makes celebrities of elected leaders and offers them a power independent of the party that elected them. Jutta Ditfurth, a former Green spokesperson and candidate, described a change in emphasis between the two legs of the Green movement. No longer did the Greens have two equal legs: the playing leg in parliament became all, while the standing leg in the grassroots movement atrophied.[9] The demands of electoral success and participation in government exerted strong pressures on the Greens. The possibility of coalition with the more mainstream Social Democratic Party (SPD) was immediately controversial. Some Green officials were willing to compromise such fundamental Green positions as opposition to nuclear power and to NATO for the sake of building a coalition with the SPD. The German and international news media began to judge the Greens primarily on their ability to elect candidates to office and to wield power in government.[10]

In a sense, the cards were stacked against the German Greens from the beginning. Although they operated with an explicit and extensive commitment to grassroots control, national government is structured in a clear hierarchy of concentrated power. Additionally, those most likely to get votes, even on a Green ticket, were individuals who were already well known and primed for the role of elected celebrity. Once it was established that the Greens were raising popular issues, it was easy for the Social Democrats to add those issues to their platform (at least in word) and co-opt the Green position. In 1990, the Greens were running against the euphoria of reunification and the emerging status of economic superpower. These various problems were exacerbated by organizational problems and infighting within the Green party.[11] Still, the persistence of Germany's environmental woes and the economic problems in the former East Germany are likely to lead to an electoral rebound for the Greens and to the strengthening of radical ecology movements.

An understanding of the history and predicament of the German Green party bears on our notion of the nature of political parties and of electoral politics. Political parties are defined according to rules made by the government. Their activities conform to and afford legitimacy to those rules, while providing elected leadership that is willing to administer the status quo. Parties have the effect of guiding citizens' movements into predictable channels and away from the more radical aspects of their programs. On the other hand, although national parties conform to the structure of the nation-state, the Green emphasis on decentralization and grassroots democracy holds out the potential for parties that can be sustained as vehicles for transformation because of their rootedness in locally based activist organizations.

In the United States, fewer than one hundred Greens have so far been elected to office. But with these numbers, the Greens have been more successful than any other national movement in over half a century. Greens struggle with their identity in relation to party politics and with the difficulties of building a third-party movement. While many push for a third party within the existing system, others call for some form of proportional representation that would allow minority parties representation in government. At the same time, Greens of a more anarchist bent point critically to the German experience and argue that the United States' more restrictive electoral laws may prevent U.S. Greens from following their European counterparts down what they view as a primrose path of overemphasizing elections.

The Green dilemma regarding electoralism may be resolved by revitalizing and elaborating the concept of the parliamentary playing leg. There is no question that electoral work is valuable for educating the public and for mobilizing support. Certainly, elected officials adhering to Green values will influence policy formation in a positive direction, possibly implementing some of the transitional programs of the Greens. Nonetheless, a transformational movement must recognize the pitfalls and limitations of entering government, particularly at the national level. It must not be forgotten that holding national office is a part of the transitional program leading to the creation of more direct and participatory forms of government. Greens must assert that electoral work is only one aspect of a broad strategy for social and political change. In response to the mainstream's emphasis on the overarching legitimacy of participation in government, Greens must continually reaffirm the primacy of grassroots organizing. The German Greens, while wishing to playfully enter parliament, held their delegates to very serious and, in the end, unrealistic standards of rotation, limited terms, and grassroots accountability. Greens should expect to lose some elected leaders to the seduction of celebrity status. For Americans, it is instructive to remember that the nineteenth-century Populists had problems with their national leadership similar to those of the German Greens a century later. In response to the unaccountability of elected leaders, the Populists worked for the right to recall officials by petition. Thanks to their efforts, recall is possible in a number of states, and, while a recall petition is hard work, it can be an important part of the electoral repertoire of the Greens.[12] In most cases, rather than getting bogged down in debates about how to control legislators, Greens should be prepared to occasionally disavow certain elected leaders and move on, seeking out and celebrating those who view their elected position in the context of the broader strategy of a radical movement, who use their personal victories to further empower the grassroots.

In 1986 the Orange County, North Carolina, Greens elected John Hartwell, a new member of their group, to the county commission. Once on the commission, Hartwell virtually stopped attending Green meetings. By 1988 the Greens, finding themselves opposing Hartwell on public-policy issues, were forced to write him off. Hartwell for his part, while doing some good work on the commission grew frustrated by his ineffectiveness and chose not to seek a second term. By contrast, in 1989 and again in 1993 the Greens, in coalition with community and environmental groups, elected an active member, Joyce Brown, to the Chapel Hill Town Council. There has been no need for formal rules of accountability, since Brown and the other Greens are friends, are accustomed to working together, and are comfortable with an informal give and take. Brown's position allows Greens to raise issues simultaneously within and outside local government. Brown's presence has lent increased legitimacy and effectiveness to the grassroots groups that elected her, brought their issues into the mainstream, and led to more environmentally sensitive policy.

Thus, by taking the playing leg a bit less seriously, by being willing to take occasional losses on the chin, and by placing electoral work within the context of a broad organizing strategy, Greens can orient electoral efforts to the strengthening of the grassroots. Of course, state and national government is serious work. The playfulness required of the Greens is not a denial of the importance of policy issues decided in those arenas. Rather, it is a defense against the co-optation, bureaucratization, and erosion of grassroots strength that "come with the territory" of electoral activity. Naturally, it is much easier to maintain relations and a sense of accountability with elected officials at a local level than at the state or national level. Also, at that level it is much easier to integrate public-policy goals with an alternative strategy. As Greens succeed locally, they will form the basis for the confederal organizations that can better achieve their objectives in the regional, state, national, and global arenas.[13]

The efforts of a transformational movement will be aided by the election of people to office at every level who are committed to its goals. These efforts will be frustrated unless the limitations of electoral politics and of administering the status quo are recognized. By properly placing electoral work in the context of a broad organizing strategy, these pitfalls can be acknowledged and their potential damage to the movement can be avoided. It is all too easy to lose a grassroots movement through an overemphasis on elections. Aware of this, wise activists orient their electoral work toward furthering their grassroots efforts.

Prefigurative Organizing

At the root of the five elements of Green strategy is the commitment to value-based, community-oriented, democratic and cooperative organization. Believing firmly that ends will always reflect means, Greens try to embody in their organizing the characteristics of the society they seek to create. They reject the idea of discrete stages of development for social and political transformation (such as the Marxian concept of a dictatorship of the proletariat leading to a withering of the state). Alternative forms must be built in decentralized units, where citizens can meet face-to-face. These units will then provide the building blocks of the broader ecological society, each part having the characteristics of the developing whole. In this sense, the Green movement seeks to prefigure the ecological society, believing firmly that a decentralized society will be attained only by decentralized organizing; a nonviolent society by nonviolent means; and a democratic society by an organizational process that develops the democratic culture of its participants.[14]

Political and social change often arises unexpectedly. This was seen in the transformation of eastern Europe in 1989 and 1990, when millions of citizens rose up to topple seemingly secure communist regimes, as well as in the breakup of the

Soviet Union in 1991.[15] Such upheavals create a vacuum or a window of opportunity in the social and political organization of society. Unorganized citizens at such times can be overwhelmed by aggressive demagogues and totalitarians. After the fall of communism in eastern Europe, nations rushed to emulate the market economies of the West, without any other model available. Prefigurative organizations can be critical at such tumultuous times, providing a model for change and preventing the crisis from being resolved in a regressive manner. It is difficult to create a prefigurative movement in response to a crisis. Such times are generally too chaotic to permit a transformational movement to be established and assume a leadership position. When hard times hit, the prefigurative organization must already be in place.

A transformational movement can use moments of crisis to provide leadership to those reacting to the immediate predicament, to those working toward reform, or to those seeking merely to cope. For example, when the Persian Gulf war was first threatened, a diverse set of peace groups and other progressive organizations came together to develop a broad-based antiwar position. The first mass demonstration did not take place until the sixth month of the crisis. A strong national movement with a holistic orientation would have been in a position to offer a ready strategy and unifying program tied to a sustained effort toward social change. Such a movement would offer to those becoming politically activated by the crisis a model of democratic process, leadership accountability, and grassroots organizing, as well as a comprehensive political program and analysis. In Germany, the Greens in fact provided such leadership to the antiwar movement. In the United States, local Green organizations in some cases provided leadership. The Missoula, Montana, Greens, for example, organized the first local antiwar demonstration, held nonviolence workshops and conscientious-objector training, and worked to connect the antiwar sentiment to energy and transportation issues. The Missoula Greens viewed their work as encompassing movement building and networking for the long haul, not merely for the duration of the war.[16]

The Greens' prefigurative strategy is part and parcel of its commitment to the ten key values. Green organizing seeks to be sustainable, sharing responsibility, rotating leaders, and minimizing the impact of the Greens' activities on the Earth. The prefigurative orientation recognizes that, while government policy has frustrated Green efforts to rotate elected leaders, movement leaders can be rotated successfully, in practice usually alternating by gender. Green organizing respects the inclusion and participation of all members, seeking involvement of women equal to that of men and using a style of meeting facilitation that gives voice to the shy, the quiet, or the less articulate. The Greens seek diverse participation, actively addressing imbalances in the participation of minorities and women. For example, the U.S. Greens have organized a Green Justice Caucus, which includes people of color, lesbians and gays, youth, women, the handicapped, and others who are usually not well represented. The national Green organizational structure guarantees seats for members of the Green Justice Caucus on all national bodies.

Green organizing emphasizes self-reliance, avoiding professional services and seeking to develop the skills and participation of members. For example, the 1989 town council campaign of Joyce Brown spent only five hundred dollars in a race that averaged three thousand dollars per candidate. Instead of relying on expensive advertising, activists canvased door to door. Instead of printing campaign posters, Greens held a poster party at which campaign workers painted posters with their own unique messages. These tactics would sound almost too simple or unsophisticated, except that they worked: Brown, a political newcomer, came in third in a field of eight, ahead of one of the three incumbents seeking reelection and capturing one of the four seats to be filled.

The Green struggle has been, and continues to be, to wed electoral politics to grassroots activism, to build alternative institutions while challenging state-corporate power, and to create structures of direct democracy that can effectively address national and global issues. This is not a process that will be completed in a single decade, or perhaps even in several. Still, the Green movement currently represents the most comprehensive and well articulated effort at building an ecological society. Its success will depend ultimately on the commitment, the consciousness, and the imagination of citizens in many nations and diverse cultures. Today, Greens in local organizations around the world are attempting to create the building blocks of the ecological society. The Green movement offers a vehicle for community-oriented activists committed to ecological wisdom and social justice to obtain information, resources, and organizational models and to identify and make common cause with their allies regionally, nationally, and globally. More fundamentally, Green politics offers those seeking an ecological society the ideas and experience to begin thinking and working effectively for change.

Certainly any organization working for ecology and justice can apply the principles outlined above: embracing a holistic, radical, and independent approach; combining a transformational strategy with a transitional program; developing a comprehensive, multifaceted organizing strategy; placing electoral work in the context of strengthening the grassroots movement; and applying the principles of prefigurative organizing. Thousands of such organizations are needed to develop the political strength and organizational ability to effect change in communities around the world. From that basis, working together, they can build the regional and global institutions and policies, rooted in a participatory, bioregional politics, that can at last put humanity on an ecological, just, and sustainable course.

Chapter 11

FROM PRINCIPLES TO PRACTICE: ENERGY STRATEGY

Up to this point, I have given no particular issue special attention or in-depth treatment. Conventional thinking on the environment emphasizes individual issues rather than the big picture. Here, by contrast, the emphasis has been on developing the general principles of a politics geared toward the transformation to an ecological society. Examples have been given only to illustrate various points in the discussion, avoiding a mere laundry list of issues or a slanted approach that gives some environmental concerns priority over others.

Nonetheless, it is important to discuss how the principles of ecological politics can be applied to organizing around particular issues. Even a comprehensive political program must in actuality take the form of a specific plan of action to address particular areas of concern. Such a focus can be placed on any of a wide range of contemporary issues, such as sustainable agriculture, biodiversity, public control of media, availability of housing, or nonpolluting transportation, to name a few. But more universally accessible than these, affecting the lives of each individual in a variety of ways every day, is energy.

It is well known that our existing energy system is expensive, polluting, highly centralized, and not sustainable. Reserves of oil and natural gas are measured in decades. Coal, while more plentiful, is dangerous to mine and terribly polluting when burned. Emissions from coal-powered plants are a major contributor to global warming and acid rain. Nuclear power creates deadly radioactive wastes that take millennia to decompose. The impacts of oil spills, acid rain from coal-powered plants, and radiation exposure from nuclear wastes are well known. The supply of these fuels depends on massive exploration, distribution, and refinement capabilities. These forms of energy are in the hands of huge corporations whose influence with the government is legendary. Their control is beyond the scope of individuals, communities, states, and at times even nations. In the undeveloped areas of the Third World, peasant peoples, uprooted from traditionally sustainable communities, often depend on firewood, which their burgeoning populations gather from ever-smaller forests.

Amid the growing concern about energy following the 1973 oil embargo and the 1979 accident at Three Mile Island, it has been clear that there is another way. Opportunities exist for energy systems that are clean, sustainable, nonpolluting, and decentralized. Since the 1970s, a number of organizations have been promoting a sustainable energy policy. Prominent among them are Public Citizen, the Rocky Mountain Institute, Worldwatch, the Institute for Local Self-reliance, and the Union of Concerned Scientists. These organizations and others provide a wide range of publications and services to help citizens keep up with new developments in energy technology and to promote wise energy policy.

Based on this considerable body of work, it is possible to envision an approach to organizing around the energy issue that provides a model for ecological politics. The criteria for such a model were discussed in the previous chapters. It must include an explicit articulation of comprehensive alternative values; a long-term or transformational strategy, one that is participatory and community oriented, aimed at achieving an ecological society; and a transitional strategy that gears short-term or intermediate victories toward the transformational goal. The development of a sustainable energy strategy will embody each of these elements.

While the following discussion will identify its goal as sustainable energy, sustainability by itself is not a sufficient criterion for a transformational strategy. Nuclear power might be developed in a way that is economically sustainable but environmentally devastating. Even solar power could be developed in a manner that is sustainable for the affluent but excludes the poor. The sustainable energy strategy that is sought will embody each of the values at the foundation of an ecological society.

Energy and the Ten Key Values

To develop a strategy for dealing with an issue, we must first ask how the resolution of the issue relates to our vision of an ecological society. The ten key values provide a good format for exploring this question. An application of these values will lead to a broad definition of the transformational strategy. We begin by asking how each of the values can be expressed in the area of energy.

That we would seek an ecologically wise energy policy goes without saying. In particular, the development of the energy resource should have minimal environmental impact at the source, minimal pollution or waste when used, and minimal impact from its transportation and distribution. This philosophy clearly eliminates oil tankers, radioactive-waste dumps, and coal burning—that is, most of the conventional energy repertoire.

The implication is that energy sources should be clean, renewable, and available close to where the energy will be used, that is to say, decentralized. The key value of decentralization will lead to a variety of energy-production strategies, depending on the characteristics of different locales. Some areas are better suited for solar power, some for wind power, others for geothermal or small-scale hydropower. The use of energy also differs from place to place: New England uses most for space heating, the South for air-conditioning, northern California for hot water. A decentralized energy strategy will be built on the differing needs for and sources of energy.

At first glance, the value of nonviolence may seem remote from energy policy, but that is in fact far from the case. The United States has built fleets, maintained military bases, and finally gone to war in the Persian Gulf to protect its oil supplies. The costs of these efforts are a hidden subsidy for the oil industry, paid not at the gas tank but through tax dollars. In a militaristic society, an economy that depends on foreign energy supplies presents a clear threat of violence. Nuclear power was initially developed as part of the Atoms for Peace program, which both rationalized the use and increased the supply of nuclear material. The threat of the continued building of nuclear weapons would be diminished by the elimination of nuclear power. The worst consequences of conventional energy sources take the shape of a violent impact on the least powerful in our society: black-lung disease inflicting coal miners, radioactive debris from uranium mining making Native American lands in the Southwest uninhabitable, and the worst air pollution blanketing the ghettos of the inner city.

The energy policy we are seeking will be grassroots democratic, giving the people direct control over their energy supply. In this context, the smaller the scale of the energy source, the more amenable it is to direct democratic control. For example, a neighborhood or cohousing community could be fitted with photovoltaic cells to provide the energy needed by each home. Surplus energy could be stored in a common solar pond or subterranean tank. The community then controls its own energy, allocates the costs as it sees fit, and develops the supply according to its needs. In the transitional program, grassroots democracy will insist on turning utilities over to public control, municipalizing power systems, and breaking up the giant multinational energy empires. Grassroots democracy is both a means and an end for the transformational movement.

At its best, grassroots democracy resides in the community, on a foundation of community-based economics. The community-oriented economy will use a strategy of import substitution to replace products originating in distant locales with those that can be produced in the more immediate vicinity, thus lowering transportation-associated energy costs. Improved energy efficiency and conservation often have strong local impacts. For example, weatherization and insulation programs can be developed as cooperative neighborhood endeavors, a twenty-first-century equivalent of the nineteenth-century barn raising. Contractors providing such services tend to be small-scale and locally based. The sustainable energy strategy, by encouraging small-scale development and a bioregional sensitivity to place, will depend upon and in turn support the cultivation of community awareness.

The critique of hierarchy and domination embodied in feminism leads to the understanding that large-scale, hierarchically organized energy corporations serve the system of domination and exploitation that is destructive to our society and to the planet. An emphasis on renewable energy reveals that energy is not a scarce commodity for which we must compete. Rather, it is an abundant resource that can be made available to all through cooperative effort.

The transformational energy strategy will be inclusive, providing energy for all, and will respect the diversity of individual energy users and communities. An emphasis on a variety of energy strategies and systems will meet the varying needs of diverse communities and people. By developing the best local and regional energy supplies and emphasizing efficiency in use, energy costs will come down and energy will therefore be more accessible to all citizens.

Social justice will insist that the energy needs of all people be given equal priority. It will lead to the availability of warmth and light in the inner cities as well as the suburbs. Environmental justice demands that the dangerous by-products of energy production, much as they must be eliminated entirely, not in the meantime be dumped on the communities of the poor and disempowered. Social justice will reach out to the developing nations of the world, helping them to meet their energy needs through sustainable, nonpolluting technologies.

A sustainable energy policy cannot be built on fossil fuels that will run out in decades. A future focus toward the seventh generation cannot condone the use of nuclear power, which leaves behind lethal wastes that persist for centuries. The energy policy we seek must be based on sources that are abundantly available and that, as much as we use them, will remain abundant, sources that can be used without leaving behind pollution for others to deal with. A sustainable energy policy will value the needs of future generations along with those of the present.

Personal and global responsibility will lead to wise use of the energy we have and careful stewardship of its potential. Personal responsibility will guide those concerned with energy to commit themselves to the goals of the broader energy strategy while limiting their own energy use and choosing environmentally benign energy sources. From this foundation, working cooperatively together, they can build the structures of social responsibility that will change public policy, create new institutions of participation, and provide the resources needed for a comprehensive transformation to an ecologically wise energy system.

As we learn to take local action while considering global consequences, the commitment to global responsibility will withdraw the onerous burden of our energy needs from the rest of the world, and with it the spurious profits that come from accepting our wastes. It will engender the understanding that the pollution we send downstream is as much our concern as that found in our local air or water. Simultaneously, it will provide Third World peoples with technical assistance and aid to develop their own indigenous, clean, sustainable energy sources. Ending peasant populations' dependency on wood gathering for cooking and heating fuel will decrease deforestation, thus helping to slow both the rate of species extinction and the trend toward global warming.

In sum, the perspective derived from the key values provides a basis for the transformational goal. The sustainable energy strategy will emphasize small-scale, clean, renewable energy sources under democratic control. It will be bioregionally oriented, utilizing the best local energy sources to meet local needs. It will stress cooperative endeavors and a participatory process to both determine and develop the needed energy supplies.

A number of transitional activities are implicit as well. Certainly, the federal government, which provides huge subsidies to nuclear power and oil but only minimal support to renewable energy sources, must be challenged to change its priorities. Tax dollars must go to renewables and increased energy efficiency, which, as well as improving the energy horizon, will add new jobs and give a boost to the economy.

Regulatory procedures must increase rather than lessen citizen involvement. For example, the nuclear industry favors a one-step licensing process for nuclear power plants, allowing citizen intervention at only the earliest stage of the process. This posture is in response to local communities putting up obstacles to plant licensing, such as refusal to approve evacuation plans. Note how the concentrated power of the nuclear industry wishes to centralize the regulatory apparatus in

Washington, where it is more easily manipulated. Note also that grassroots citizens' groups will use whatever procedural avenues are available to prevent the siting of antiecological nuclear plants in their communities. Obviously, such a change in the rules must be opposed and, if anything, the licensing process opened even more to citizen participation and local authority.

Boycotts such as the consumer boycott which challenged General Electric's nuclear-weapons program should be joined, with the goal of improved availability of efficient and renewable products as well as the elimination of the antiecological energy conglomerates and their nuclear operations. It should be noted that the missing component in the "shopping for a better world" guides is the simple rule of thumb of supporting those institutions that directly contribute toward the transformational goal and withdrawing support from those that do not. While it is helpful to evaluate conglomerates on their environmental and social policies, it is better still to support small-scale, regional, and preferably cooperative enterprises that serve the same needs.

Another part of the transitional program will take advantage of the ability of utilities to provide financial support for the purchase of more efficient products. Southern California Edison gave away hundreds of thousands of highly efficient compact fluorescent light bulbs to low-income households because the energy savings offset the need for new power plants.[1] Often, state regulations must be changed to allow utilities to profitably undertake alternatives. Pacific Power and Light of Portland, Oregon, received permission from the Oregon Public Service Commission to make loans to customers to finance energy-conservation measures.[2] A representative of the utility works with a customer to identify cost-effective conservation improvements. The customer selects a private contractor to do the work, who is subsequently paid directly by Pacific Power. The amount of the loan is then added to the utility's rate base, from which its profits are computed. This allows the utility to earn profits on investments in energy efficiency in the customer's home. The customer is not required to repay the loan. If the house is sold, the loan amount is included in the sale price and removed from the rate base at that time. This innovative program expands the role of the utility beyond the traditional one of selling power to that of a more comprehensive energy service.

Local governments can also work with citizens' groups to support improved energy strategies. In Springfield, Illinois, under the cosponsorship of the city and Sangamon State University, over two hundred people attended an initial meeting to develop a citywide energy-planning effort. Ten task forces were established in such areas as residential use, business use, transportation, and waste. The outcome of a two-year process was a plan calling for a 40 percent cut in energy consumption and local production of 50 percent of energy by the year 2000.[3]

A number of Springfield's specific goals have already been reached. The Springfield City Water, Light, and Power Company has offered a one-hundred-dollar credit for the purchase of high-efficiency air-conditioning. The local natural-gas distributor offers low-interest loans for energy-conservation improvements. The zoning ordinance has been changed to allow maximum solar access.

Springfield also instituted a 1 percent gasoline tax to fund improvements in the transportation system. In states without home rule, permission would be needed from the legislature to implement such a tax. At the state level, the city could expect to be challenged by lobbyists of the auto and oil companies, who would correctly view such a tax as hurting their sales. Just as these industries, with their economic stake in polluting technologies, have held back federal efforts to improve automobile fuel efficiency, they would likely succeed in blocking initiatives at the state level. Home rule to empower local communities to implement ecologically wise policies thus becomes an important part of the transitional program.

A municipal power program that has acquired almost legendary status is that of Osage, Iowa.[4] Osage produced an economic-development program at the heart of which was energy conservation. Typical of its success is a local grocery that competes successfully with chain stores by using energy efficiency to keep prices down. The municipally owned utility gives away water-heater jackets and shade trees. It provides infrared scans of buildings for improved efficiency. Jaycee volunteers go to low-income homes and install weatherstripping and water-heater jackets, supplied free by the utility. Osage's persistent pursuit of improved conservation and load management has led to five reductions in electricity rates over a ten-year period.

Springfield and Osage are two of a small but significant number of cities around the country that have implemented cutting-edge energy programs. For example, Austin, Texas, saved participating residential users several thousand kilowatt hours yearly through an aggressive conservation program.[5] Municipal programs such as these are neither new nor particularly radical. As early as 1980, the Department of Energy published a handbook on "forging energy programs for communities" that emphasized citizen organization and initiative.[6] Yet progress remains slow, and programs like those of Springfield, Osage, and Austin are still a rarity.

Three factors have combined to slow the progress of the sustainable-energy movement: resistance to change, particularly on the part of the bureaucracies that govern most communities; the persistence of the "more is better" approach that is fundamental to our culture; and the opposition of the corporations that have a huge vested interest in the sale of energy and of energy-using products.

All of these are directly challenged by movements geared toward citizen participation and empowerment. Citizens' groups voluntarily working for the good of the community do not have the level of resistance to change that municipal bureaucrats, who generally view their job as one of administering the status quo, tend to have. Citizens are able to give a broad sense of quality of life priority over a strictly economic orientation. They are more likely to substitute self-help efforts and activities that increase the fulfilling aspects of community life for reliance on the services of distant corporations. Finally, citizens' groups, once aware of the actual financial impacts, are eager to disengage from the utilities and keep their energy dollars in the local economy.

A Multilevel Strategy

Citizen organizing for a sustainable-energy policy will focus on four fronts: the community, the municipality, the state government, and the national government. Each of these areas will, to varying degrees, embody aspects of the transitional and the transformational strategies. To a great extent, the particular approach, other than on the national level, will vary from place to place, depending on a number of local conditions. These factors include the political climate, the regulatory climate, the nature of the existing utilities, the particular energy needs and sources of the area, and the resources of the community in question.

On the national level, the goal of citizen organizing will be exclusively a part of the transitional strategy. Whenever possible, the national government should be made to use its authority to tax, regulate, and subsidize to promote environmentally and socially beneficial activities. Specifically, national subsidies for fossil fuels and nuclear power must be curtailed. Strong regulations must require nonpolluting power generation, support for the health claims of workers, and use by utilities of sustainable, environmentally sound methods. Federal policy can support the use of less-polluting natural gas as a transitional fuel while developing a renewable-based economy.[7] To the extent that polluting power plants remain in use, tax policy should exact from them the cost of their pollution to society. Mainstream economists will argue that these taxes are merely passed on to consumers in the form of higher rates. In fact, such a policy will make the hidden costs of pollution directly apparent and thereby improve the economic argument for clean, renewable energy sources.

Federal law should also recognize the right of states and localities to restrict polluting activities and bar access of polluters to their area. Federal interstate-commerce regulations should be redefined so that "fair trade" includes a sense of healthy trade, both for communities and for the Earth. Federal law should support the establishment of municipal power cooperatives and permit the use of tax-exempt bonds to finance their development. It should again be noted that there are a number of national organizations developing strategies and programs and lobbying on these and other energy issues. Grassroots community-based organizations can work in coalition with these groups to identify and achieve their common goals.

State policy initiatives, while varying among the fifty states, will to a great extent address concerns parallel to those on the federal level—that is, using tax, regulatory, and subsidy policy to promote the transitional strategy. An important distinction on the state level is the states' closer regulation of utilities. Utilities must be required to obtain energy from the least expensive source and to provide financial and technical support both for the increased use of renewable sources and for improved energy efficiency. Of course, an important concern for environmental activists will be to secure home rule for municipalities, so that each can develop the best energy policy in response to local conditions.

The municipal level is the proving ground for the ecologically wise energy policy. At its heart is the cooperatively organized, democratically controlled public utility.[8] The mandate of this utility will be to develop an optimum energy strategy in terms of both the best renewable energy sources and the most efficient energy use. Currently, public-power customers pay an average price 21 percent less than that charged by private utilities. This differential will become even more profound as municipal power cooperatives emphasize efficiency in use as well as cost of supply. The specific sources and uses of energy will vary with local conditions. The municipal utility will seek to use local resources and skills to substitute for energy imports. The value to the community of creating local jobs in the energy-efficiency business must be weighed against any short-term cost savings offered by the large utilities.

Existing public power companies often narrowly define their mission as consisting only of the provision of energy. This has led some of these companies to hurt both their customers and the Earth by supporting vastly overexpensive nuclear power plants and other energy-industry boondoggles. By contrast, the ecologically oriented municipal power cooperative includes environmental and social policy goals in its mission statement and will develop criteria for their ongoing evaluation. Democratic control by the community it serves will ensure that its activities are continually scrutinized and held to a high standard. In effect, the cooperative, democratic structure seeks to remove distinctions among energy producers, energy consumers, and municipal government. All are working toward a common goal of a healthy community, with ample energy used wisely for local needs.

The municipality can also use its authority to zone and establish design guidelines as a way of supporting a sustainable energy strategy. Cities can establish a right to solar orientation and provide development perks for the use of renewables. Environmentally conscientious developers will respond by designing new neighborhoods or subdivisions for optimum energy qualities, emphasizing not only active energy systems but passive qualities in the design that reduce energy needs. For example, the use of well-placed deciduous trees can be part of a strategy for decreasing energy for heating and cooling. A municipality can establish staff positions to support its energy strategy. Municipal staff or community volunteers can identify residential energy loss by taking infrared scans of homes and businesses or by using blowers that attach to a doorway and send a harmless colored gas through a house, thereby revealing air leaks.

Municipalities are also often involved in supporting low-income or affordable housing. With a commitment to social responsibility, municipally sponsored housing developments can empower their future residents by allowing them democratic participation in the planning, design, and management of the community. Such projects can be offered technical support and financial incentives to become models of wise energy use. Municipally supported financing agencies can take into consideration long-term energy costs in their evaluation of the overall costs of ownership and mortgage qualifications, thus allowing the less affluent to take advantage of the best approaches to energy use.

Finally, the community level of organizing will vary most according to local conditions, the size of the community in question, and the characteristics of the municipality. In towns with well-organized neighborhoods, a strong tradition of citizen activism, or visionary elected leadership, the community and municipal strategies will dovetail neatly together. Communities will participate in the development of the municipal strategy, and the municipality will actively support and encourage community-based efforts. As in Springfield, Illinois, citizen task forces can lead the way to innovative energy programs.

If, on the other hand, a municipality is not generally well disposed toward developing an energy policy, neighborhood and community groups may begin self-help efforts aimed at improving energy efficiency or the use of renewables. Unorganized neighborhoods might conduct workshops on weatherization and conservation. Such workshops could provide a forum for beginning to address some of the broader issues of energy policy, building a constituency for change. Within neighborhoods and communities, there is certainly a lot of room for initiative along the lines of the "fifty simple things" approach. Self-help efforts can lead to improved use of daylighting, energy-wise landscaping, and a variety of generally low-tech and inexpensive energy-saving measures.

Cohousing provides an excellent opportunity for developing a sustainable energy strategy on the community level. The Sun and Wind cohousing project in Denmark was organized with an explicit goal of exemplary use of renewable energy.[9] Among the seven planning committees was one charged solely with energy issues. The result was a community of energy-efficient homes with strong solar orientation. Forty percent of Sun and Wind's energy comes from solar panels and a windmill. Solar energy accumulated in rooftop collectors is piped to heat-accumulation tanks located under the common house. This stored energy is returned to the homes, providing hot tap water and radiant space heat.

Sun and Wind applied for grants and received $59,000 from the European Economic Council and the Danish government to support the prototype energy systems. With the grants came a requirement that Sun and Wind monitor energy savings and be open to visitors interested in renewable energy. This stipulation ensured that Sun and Wind's success would provide a model for other communities.

Sun and Wind's grant support is a good example of how transitional strategies at the national level can promote community-level transformation. The Danish government had a program of support for renewable energy that bypassed large-scale energy providers, reaching out directly to a small cohousing project with a strong cooperative and democratic orientation.

As neighborhoods and communities organize for improved energy use, they will naturally turn to their local government and utilities for assistance. Organizing can start around the transitional strategy of turning resources and power over to grassroots groups. Working with the municipal government and utilities will reveal where state and federal policy limit the development of a sustainable energy program, causing a grassroots organization to press for change in those arenas. Ultimately, such an approach will lead grassroots groups to work to elect to office at all levels people who support their goals.

Actively engaged across each of these four strategic levels will be a citizens' organization concerned with sustainable energy. Such an organization can be either a single-issue group, a task force of a multiissue organization such as the Sierra Club, or an action arm of a wide-ranging transformational movement such as the Greens. Each of the various activities identified previously as components of Green strategy[10] can be embodied in their approach to sustainable-energy policy. The sustainable-energy program builds alternative institutions in such forms as municipal power cooperatives, neighborhood self-help initiatives, or cohousing developments. It emphasizes education of the energy activists themselves as well as their neighbors and elected leaders. The program may use direct action to impede the activity of polluters, slow the construction of nuclear plants, or dramatize its goals. Independent politics will be used to elect energy activists to office or to use initiatives and referenda to implement ecological energy policies. Finally, citizen activism will be emphasized in all areas, whether through the cooperation of neighbors in self-help efforts, through participation in municipal task forces, or through organized pressure on state and federal government. Such activism will take a prefigurative approach, developing the organizational forms today that will provide the cooperative, caring, and democratic foundation for building a truly ecological society.

In 1992, the Orange County Greens participated in the U.S. Greens' national action plan entitled "Solar Power through Community Power." The activities they engaged in expressed many of the elements of Green strategy. The Greens worked with a cooperative market to develop a day-long Sun Day festival. The event featured educational events, including a well-known speaker on acid rain, tours of solar homes in Orange County, information booths staffed by a number of organizations dealing with alternative energy, and demonstrations of various do-it-yourself energy techniques. At the Sun Day event, independent political action was encouraged as the Greens launched a petition campaign calling on the county government to make a commitment to energy efficiency and renewable resources in all new buildings. Just prior to Sun Day, the Greens also successfully petitioned the Chapel Hill Town Council to establish a citizens' task force on energy to look at town government and community energy use, thus legitimatizing citizen energy activism in the public arena. Other Green groups around the country included direct action components in their "Solar Power through Community Power" events, often holding demonstrations at nuclear power plants or proposed radioactive-waste sites.

In articulating a sustainable-energy strategy, the principles of wedding politics and ecology are clear. The strategy will reflect explicit values emphasizing ecological wisdom, social responsibility, and grassroots democracy. It will stress decentralized, cooperative organizing to support the unique needs of a particular locale. The municipal and community orientation will be supported by a transitional strategy to channel resources and power from the state and national government as well as from big business back to the grassroots. None of these factors are suffient independently to bring about an ecological society. Taken together, they provide the necessary building blocks, the tools, and the vision. Add to these the commitment and will of the people, and a great transformation can be achieved.

Those with sufficient political and material resources may readily embrace and succeed in such a strategy. It is not difficult to imagine communities applying this strategy to a variety of needs: water, food, health care, tranportation, and child care, to name a few. Unfortunately, many people around the planet lack the basic capacities required to implement change. Democratic government and civil rights are certainly a sine qua non of the strategy. I argued with a fellow Green activist once as to the most important key value. He maintained that it was ecological wisdom, without which the planet could become uninhabitable. I argued that it was grassroots democracy, without which we do not have the ability to actualize our concern for the other values or to protect the Earth. Of course, the values interconnect, and none is "most important." But many people, even under ostensibly democratic governments, lack the political power to effect change. While some nations require a complete change in government from authoritarian to democratic rule, others may need only an evolution toward more participatory forms and more power in the hands of the people.

For many around the world, implementing this transformational strategy will depend on the restructuring of national and even global systems. Third World peoples will need an end to development strategies that leave nations in debt, require cashcropping, and drive the people from the land. The industrial nations have robbed the developing nations of their material and human resources for several centuries, leaving a legacy of human misery and environmental degradation. Aid policies returning technical skills, training and materials, and cash must be geared toward self-reliant, sustainable development. Only then can the environmental destruction be curtailed.[11]

Similarly, impoverished communities in both the inner cities and rural areas of the industrial nations need capital, education, and political power so that they can serve, not as cogs in the expanding global economy, but as vibrant communities that celebrate their human and natural heritage. A movement committed to the rich vision of cooperation, self-reliance, participatory democracy, and the ecological society will embrace an ethic of justice to make that goal accessible to all people.

"If I Could Tell You, I Would Let You Know"

As we have seen, the environmental crisis cannot be blamed on the lifestyle choices of the contemporary consumer. Nor is it caused simply by his or her reproductive practices or use of technology. Rather, it is the result of a historic progression of economic and political change which has led to a loss of community, a narrowing of values, and a limiting of the opportunities for citizens to respond through a democratic process. In this light, one could look at the environmental situation and despair: it seems so complicated, where does one begin? Still, the solution can be expressed simply: ecology and politics are bound together. Therefore, it is not as consumers but as citizens that we will solve the environmental crisis. This simple change of perspective lies at the root of successful action. Environmental thinking and environmental action must be undertaken by citizens, with the full implication of citizenship as participation in a broader democratic process. In this way, we can begin to build the values, the communities, and the democratic practices that are desperately needed.

The task of building an ecological society is neither quick nor easy. The entire thrust of modern global culture is antithetical to such a society. Still, the building blocks are known. The values of a destructive, power-hungry society must be replaced with values that are life-enhancing, sustainable, and committed to the well-being of humanity and nature. Structures of cooperation and community, even as they prefigure a future society, are desirable and rewarding in their own right. Community, properly understood, will connect people not only to their neighbors but to nature as well, giving human society its place in the natural world. Participatory democracy will give people the power to create social forms that actualize the inherent human caring for the Earth. A bioregional orientation will base society on an understanding of place and scale that is essential for ecological living. Finally, organizing principles like those of the Green movement will simultaneously build a decentralized counterpower while directly addressing the antiecological concentration of power embodied in the nation-state and the transnational corporation. These organizing principles hold the potential for uniting widespread movements for ecology and justice in a common effort that empowers people at the grassroots while challenging the citadels of power. All of these elements will arise and connect in diverse and unique ways in a multiplicity of contexts around the planet.

A quarter century ago, describing a then-anticipated transformation of consciousness, the psychiatrist R. D. Laing declared that "If I could turn you on, if I could drive you out of your wretched mind, if I could tell you I would let you know."[12] Today, while identifying the necessity for and the elements of a social and political transformation, this sense of "if I could tell you I would let you know" remains relevant. I have presented the image of a fork in the road, one path leading down the familiar route of environmental and social destruction, the other leading toward the ecological society. In fact, the second path is many paths, each forged by those with the imagination and commitment to walk it. An ethic based on a simple choice between good and evil is an ancient one in our culture. It goes back at least to the Old Testament message that "I have set before you life and death, the blessing and the curse; therefore choose life."[13] To our modern ears, the choice of life or death sounds like a simple one, perhaps no more involved than Coke versus Pepsi. But remember that this message is preceded by many pages of commandments and precepts defining just what the choice of life entails. While an ecological society will certainly not be built on patriarchal commandments, it will depend on a recognition of the complexity of the natural world and the place of human society within it. The biblical message remains relevant, for just as the ancient Hebrews flourished or perished not as individuals but as a people, so our choices today must be made as a community, through cooperative, organized political endeavors. Another biblical motif is also relevant here. Remember that the Hebrews escaping from Egypt were not able to enter the Promised Land; only their children attained that goal. It may be that we today are so imbued with the material and instrumental values of our culture that the most we can accomplish is to set out on the path toward an ecological society, a destination that can be reached only by our descendants. Nonetheless, for our generation to embark upon that journey is now the most critical task.

Society today is beleaguered by crises. A familiar litany includes ozone depletion, species loss, acid rain, toxic wastes, AIDS, homelessness, and poverty. For the most part, those suffering from these crises struggle to resolve them within the available political structures. They are not oriented toward reenvisioning and reorganizing society to correct these many problems, properly understood not as the result of failed policy, but as the inevitable failure of a destructive social, political, and economic system. Social scientists addressing the issues usually attempt to influence elites and policymakers, offering prescriptions for improvements to society. By contrast, a book like this must engage the imagination and commitment of the grassroots citizenry. It can offer an analysis, a framework, and even a program, but the ecological perspective itself will assert the importance of a diversity of forms, even of political programs, arising from different lived experiences of place.

I have attempted, in a short work, to take a long voyage through the modern era, placing the story of its failures in the context of new opportunities for change. The Book of Proverbs warns that "where there is no vision, the people perish."[14] Offered here is a vision, one based on the premise that ecology and politics are always and in all ways bound together. Alone, this vision is not enough. Readers can take heart, however, in the possibilities for cooperation and community and for a renewed democratic culture that are embodied in this vision. Ultimately, the imagination and involvement of citizens will create the foundation of the ecological society. What is required is a renewed art of citizenship, an understanding that the fate of our communities lies in the collective participation and commitment of us all.

Finally, we must ask if the society envisioned here is utopian, in the pejorative sense of unattainable. Is a world of decentralized, bioregional communities—confederated with one another, each sensitive to its unique ecological and social milieu, respecting the diversity of humanity and of nature, democratic in form, cooperative in character—so different from the world we know today that it is hardly relevant? In *Back to Methuselah,* his retelling of the Genesis story, George Bernard Shaw portrays the serpent declaring to Eve, "You see things; and you say, 'Why?' But I dream things that never were; and I say, 'Why not?'"[15] Like Shaw's serpent, we dream things that have not yet been and ask, Why not?

One's political outlook, be it optimistic or pessimistic, or one's choice of political strategy depends in the last analysis on one's view of human nature. Can people genuinely care for one another and for the Earth? Can education and culture reinforce and develop the best aspects of human character? Can we make the choices, create the institutions, and imagine the way of life whereby that caring character can be actualized in the form of an ecological society? The idealistic ecologist will assert in word and deed that human ethics, human reason, human sentiment, and thus human society can be reconnected to the natural world in a way that is fulfilling to each individual, enriching to society, and sustaining to the planet that is our home.

AFTERWORD: URGENCY IN AN ORGANIC CONTEXT

A battle is now brewing between those who favor a hyper-efficient, technology-paced time world and those who advocate a new ecological time vision. —Jeremy Rifkin, Utne Reader, *September–October 1987*

If there is one message that has been consistent as environmental concern has grown, it is that there is not much time left. Since the start of the Decade of the Environment in 1990, the urgency surrounding the environmental crisis has been the rallying cry in a variety of battles and the sales pitch for numerous products. For example, Working Assets has promoted its long-distance phone service with a plea from the environmentalist Randy Hayes: "Half the species on Earth will die unless we act now."[1] The University of Arizona Press calls on us to buy its environmental titles "before it's too late."[2] The specter of time running out as humanity chokes on its own pollution, drowns under rising seas, and suffers from a host of environmentally caused cancers raises the fears and stirs the imaginations of schoolchildren, homemakers, activists, and politicians alike.

Of course, species *are* dying at a catastrophic rate; pollution and greenhouse gases *do* pose a dire threat; we must act *now*. The sense of urgency surrounding the environmental crisis leads a concerned but disempowered citizenry to look, not to the slow process of building an ecological society from the grassroots, but rather to a quick fix by the governmental and corporate powers that be. Unfortunately, these are the same forces that got us into this mess, and thus they are unlikely sources for the solutions. Their solutions, when forthcoming, often amount to little more than Band-Aids or appeasement. For example, the North Carolina legislature created a transit authority to develop mass transit for the Research Triangle Park area but initially neglected to fund it, meanwhile allocating nine billion dollars for new highways. For another example, the plastics industry, responding to the garbage crisis, offered biodegradable trash bags that in fact do not degrade and that provide little more than a "green" facade to an industry that is among the worst polluters.

The feeling of urgency is itself an expression of an understanding of time that arose with the modern world-view underlying the crises of our era. For most of history, time was little more than the changing of seasons, the sunrise and sunset, the biological, geological, and astronomical rhythms of life. Although knowledge of the changing seasons was important to determine the time for planting or for hunting migrating animals, hours, weeks, and even months were not known through most of human experience. Often, time was marked by the holders of esoteric knowledge, who used elaborate sundials, special pyramids, or megalithic constructions such as Stonehenge primarily to schedule rituals and ceremonies.[3] Before the industrial era, time was marked by the natural events that structured an organic way of life. For most of us, it is a nostalgic memory to think of farmers rising with the rooster's crow to milk the cows, called to lunch by the ringing of a bell, and trudging home from the fields at dusk.

The modern era brought with it a new awareness of time. In the Middle Ages, clocks were introduced and first used primarily by monks to organize their daily prayer schedule.[4] By the sixteenth century, clocks in town squares were used to announce public occasions and meetings. These early clocks had only an hour hand, were highly inaccurate, and needed to be reset regularly to match the more reliable sundials.

The clock became a guiding metaphor of the early modern

era. God was the cosmic clockmaker, creating a universe that worked with mechanical precision. What could be more natural than for human affairs to be held to the same mechanical standard? Beginning in the eighteenth century with the introduction of the pendulum and the minute hand, clocks could be used to regulate the work of the newly created urban proletariat. The rationalization and increasing mechanization of factory life required a disciplined work force that knew when to arrive, when to leave, and how to spend each hour of the day. The ability to measure work performance over time has been gradually refined to the point where today's computers can monitor the activity of workers down to the second. For the rising bourgeois class, the clock became a status symbol and was brought into all aspects of life. The clock and the growing awareness of the passing hours and minutes served to bring daily life within the framework of the mechanical world-view.

As labor power was transformed into a commodity, so too was time itself. Measuring their labor in hours against a proffered wage, workers developed a sense of their time as a scarce resource with a specific, limited value. This has led to a hierarchical time culture in which status is measured by the value of a person's time.[5] For example, long waits for an "appointment" with a doctor are today commonplace. The message: the doctor's time is valuable, the patient's is not.[6]

With the commodification of time, those who are impoverished in economic and political terms are also temporally poor. It is well known that the poor are hardest hit by environmental problems. Their communities are where dangerous waste dumps or polluting industries are placed. They have the least defense against environmental ills. Consumer choice is rarely an option for the poor. For them the crisis has the greatest urgency. They possess the least time.

The well-to-do, by contrast, are time rich and can live outside the polluted inner cities in cleaner suburbs, away from toxic wastes and emissions. As the environmental crises mount, they have more time: time as represented by their ability to keep threats away from their homes longer, time as represented by their ability to relocate to escape increasing pollution, and time as represented by their access to better products and the finest health care. Antinuclear activists challenge power-company executives, who claim that no radiation is released from nuclear power plants, to live near the plants. Of course, it is a plant's maintenance workers who are more likely to live in the immediate vicinity. Should a nuclear catastrophe occur, the executives will have more time.

Look around: if you live in a typical middle-class American household, insistent reminders of time surround you with the precision of digital display. The microwave oven tells the time, as do the VCR and the clocks in your bedroom and car and, of course, the watch on your wrist. Your entertainment is scheduled by the television. All this emphasis on time measured right down to the second conveys one essential message: there's not much of it. We yearn for more time, perhaps to get away to the beach or mountains, leaving the alarm clock, the microwave, and the television behind.

The scarcity of time is one of the great obstacles to achieving an ecological society. Building alternatives of cooperation, community, and direct democracy takes time, time that most of us do not have. Recall, for example, that a cohousing project can take two years of weekly planning meetings to be successful. It is a daunting prospect, but in fact it entails a process that, when complete, returns much of the participants' home life to a richer sense of time. In such projects, it is especially important for the "time rich" to make efforts to include the "time poor," not in a paternalistic manner that does the work for them but in a caring, empowering way that offers convenient meeting places and schedules, child care, and financial assistance.

In the ecological society, in the just society, time is what all people have in abundance. Recast in terms of the cycles of nature, time awareness is broadened beyond the changing seconds of digital time to the movement of the sun and the turning of the seasons.[7] Time is no longer associated with power and control but rather with sharing and care. The democratization of time can return time to its organic context, just as the democratization of politics and economics can do for society.[8]

Achieving this organic, democratic time awareness will not be easy, and it certainly will not be quick. An understanding of the nature of an ecological society leads to the conclusion that such a society must be built gradually. But the sense of urgency which justifiably surrounds our contemporary crises indicates that this gradual process must be begun and pursued speedily and with commitment.[9] For a gardener, if it is springtime, the seeds must now be sown. Inevitably, it will take the summer for the slow development of the anticipated harvest. Like the gardener, those seeking an ecological society must possess a respect for natural processes and rhythms. The seeds of that society take the form of the structures of cooperation, community, and democracy in the context of life-affirming values. It is to that steady and gradual process that we must ardently commit ourselves in word and deed. The seeds of the ecological society call urgently to be planted today and nurtured with patience and hard work so that a bountiful harvest can at last be celebrated.

NOTES

1. The Specter of Population Growth

1. Paul Ehrlich, *The Population Bomb* (New York: Ballantyne, 1968), 1.
2. *Economist* vol. 323, May 30, 1992.
3. Ehrlich writes that "the explosive growth of the human population is the most significant terrestrial event of the past million millennia. Three and one-half billion people now inhabit the Earth, and every year this number increases by 70 million. Armed with weapons as diverse as thermonuclear bombs and DDT, this mass of humanity now threatens to destroy most of the life on the planet. Mankind itself may stand on the brink of extinction; in its death throes it could take with it most of the other passengers on Spaceship Earth. No geological event in a billion years—not the emergence of mighty mountain ranges, nor the submergence of entire subcontinents, nor the occurrence of periodic glacial ages—has posed a threat to terrestrial life comparable to that of human overpopulation" (Paul Ehrlich and Anne H. Ehrlich, *Population Resources Environment* [San Francisco: W.H. Freeman, 1970], 1).
4. D. Meadows, et al., *The Limits to Growth* (London: Pan, 1974), 24.
5. *Time,* January 2, 1989, 26.
6. *Scientific American,* September 1989, 119.
7. Ehrlich has been a prominent voice on issues besides population, though they do tend to be of the doomsday variety. For example, in the early 1980s, he was outspoken on the catastrophic threat of nuclear winter (see *Coevolution Quarterly,* Fall 1984, 88-93). In 1991, he and Anne H. Ehrlich coauthored *Healing the Planet* (Reading, Mass.: Addison-Wesley), which reviewed a number of important environmental issues.
8. *Time,* January 2, 1989, 32.
9. *Time,* January 2, 1989, 48.
10. A study by the government of Indonesia "concluded that the amount the banks were lending for environmentally destructive activities . . . was 10 times greater than the amount of money that was going in for allegedly environmentally sound activities" (*Multinational Monitor,* June 1987, 15).

11. Eric Mann, "LA's Smogbusters," *Nation,* September 17, 1990, 268.

12. See Joseph A. McFalls, Jr., "Population: A Lively Introduction," *Population Bulletin,* October 1991, 32-37.

13. Germaine Greer, *Sex and Destiny* (New York: Harper & Row, 1984), 445.

14. Frances Moore Lappe writes, "For what the ecologists too often miss is that human reproductive decisions, in dramatic contrast to almost all other species, are not purely biological but are complicated by psychological, cultural, and social forces. Where society denies people (especially women) security, status, and opportunity, the family—and often the bigger the better—provides the only possibility for all three. . . . Increasingly robbed of their land, with few jobs in sight, having virtually no access to health care, education or old-age security, and with many of the traditional religious and communal forms no longer working to provide a framework of meaning, many Third World parents see in their children's labor and later incomes the only security they can hope for, and in their family life a compensation for the growing alienation they experience in the public sphere" (*Utne Reader,* May-June 1988, 81; this issue of *Utne Reader* provides a number of perspectives on population growth).

15. See Barry Commoner, *Making Peace with the Planet* (New York: Pantheon, 1990): "All of these problems have a common solution: the elimination of poverty. Poverty is the reason for the failure thus far of developing countries to stabilize their populations. Poverty is the reason why their peoples are malnourished, sick, and hungry. Poverty is the reason why they experience such difficulty in applying the remedy: ecologically sound economic development. Poverty engenders poverty, holding the efforts of developing countries to overcome its tragic effects in a tight nearly incapacitating embrace. . . . If the root cause of the world population crisis is poverty, then to end it we must abolish poverty" (166-168).

16. See, for example, Frances Moore Lappe and Joseph Collins, *Food First* (Boston: Houghton Mifflin, 1977): "Much of the destruction of the agricultural environment on examination turns out to be the result, not of the size of a country's population, but of other forces: land monopolizers who export food and luxury crops that force the majority of farmers to overuse marginal lands; colonial patterns of taxation and cash cropping that continue today; well-meant but unenlightened 'aid' and other forms of outside intervention in traditionally well-adapted systems; and irresponsible profit-seeking by both local and foreign elites." Lappe and Collins conclude that "cutting the world's population in half tomorrow would not stop any of these forces" (45-46).

17. This discussion draws from Greer, *Sex and Destiny.* Greer concludes that "when we come to study the population regulation systems of other countries we might remember the four hundred years or so when we achieved a satisfactory balance between population growth and predominantly agrarian economy without any intergalactic family planning agency to tell us how to do it" (101).

18. The following examples are also from *Sex and Destiny.* Almost two hundred cases of primitive societies limiting their populations are provided by

Alexander Carr-Saunders, *The Population Problem* (Oxford: Clarendon Press, 1922). A good summary of Carr-Saunders's work can be found in Richard G. Wilkinson, *Poverty and Progress* (New York: Praeger, 1973), chap. 3.

19. Greer, *Sex and Destiny,* 348.

20. The causes of population expansion are complex and subject to dispute even among historians and demographers. Suffice it to note that European population growth took off in the seventeenth century, Asian in the eighteenth, and American and African in the nineteenth (Colin McEvedy and Richard Jones, *Atlas of World Population History* [New York: Facts on File, 1978]).

21. On the negative side, in contemporary societies the slow evolution of these traditions can on occasion prolong stage 2 of the demographic transition discussed above. For example, certain tribal societies have in the past made a cultural adaptation to the need for high birthrates through a linking of male esteem to the number of offspring. In these societies, even though the women may today desire a lower birthrate, the men still insist on their cultural prerogatives. Such attitudes can stymie even the best-intentioned program for population control.

22. See Wilkinson, *Poverty and Progress,* chap. 3.

23. Wilkinson (p. 88) cites a study of one African tribe that proudly maintained a traditional system of herding even though overgrazing was threatening soil erosion, which would have ultimately destroyed their traditional culture. Although the local repercussions would be devastating, the global impact would be nil.

2. Does Technology Harm the Earth? Can Technology Save It?

1. Lewis Mumford, *The Pentagon of Power* (New York: Harcourt, Brace, 1970), pl. 23.

2. *Making Peace with the Planet,* 44-45. Also, *The Closing Circle* (New York: Alfred A. Knopf, 1971), 176.

3. *The Closing Circle,* 187.

4. *Making Peace with the Planet,* 211.

5. Robert A. Frosch and Nicholas E. Gallopoulos, "Strategies for Manufacturing," *Scientific American,* September 1989, 144.

6. Quoted in Commoner, *The Closing Circle,* 181.

7. *The Closing Circle,* 189.

8. Lewis Mumford writes that "technics has never till our own age dissociated itself from the larger cultural whole in which man, as man, has always functioned. The classic Greek term 'techne' characteristically makes no distinction between industrial production and 'fine' or 'symbolic' art. . . . Technics was related to the whole nature of man . . . was broadly life-centered" (*The Myth of the Machine* [New York: Harcourt, Brace, 1966] 9).

9. See Murray Bookchin, *The Ecology of Freedom* (Palo Alto: Cheshire Books, 1982), 223.

10. Bookchin writes, "Technics itself tended to follow an age-old tradition of nestling closely into a local ecosystem, of adapting itself sensitively to local

resources and their unique capacity to sustain life. Accordingly, it functioned as a highly specific catalyst between the people of an area and their environment. . . . This high sense of the hidden natural wealth of a habitat—a knowledge that has been so completely lost to modern humanity—kept the latent exploitative powers of technics well within the institutional, moral, and mutualistic boundaries of the local community. People did more than just live within the biotic potentialities of their ecosystem and remake it with an extraordinary sensitivity that fostered ecological diversity and fecundity. They also (often artistically) absorbed technically unique devices into this broad social matrix and brought them into the service of their locality" (*The Ecology of Freedom*, 260).

11. See the discussion in Wilkinson, *Poverty and Progress*. Marshall Sahlins cites an account of an African tribe of hunter-gatherers who, "although surrounded by cultivators, have until recently refused to take up agriculture themselves, 'mainly on the grounds that this would involve too much hard work" (*Stone Age Economics* [Chicago: Aldine-Atherton, 1972], 27).

12. *Stone Age Economics*, 253.

13. *Discourse on Method*, trans. F. E. Sutcliffe (Baltimore: Penguin, 1968), p. 78.

14. *The New Organum*, ed. Fulton H. Anderson (Indianapolis: Bobbs-Merrill, 1960), p. 70.

15. Described in Morris Berman, *The Reenchantment of the World* (New York: Bantam, 1981).

16. *The Structure of Scientific Revolutions* (Chicago: University of Chicago Press, 1970), 10-23.

17. Bookchin describes how these limitations on both technological and economic development are linked historically: "Once societal constraints based on ethics and communal institutions were demolished ideologically and physically, technics could be released to follow no dictates other than private self-interest, profit, accumulation, and the needs of a predatory market economy. The time-honored limits that had contained technics in a societal matrix disappeared, and for the first time in history technics was free to follow its own development without any goals except those dictated by the market" (*The Ecology of Freedom*, 254).

18. William Leiss considers that "the vision of human domination of nature becomes a fundamental ideology in a social system which consciously undertakes a radical break with the past . . . and which sets for itself as a primary task the development of productive forces for the satisfaction of material wants. The first social system in the history of civilization in which these tendencies are found is in Western capitalism" (*The Domination of Nature* [New York: Braziller, 1972], 179-180).

19. Mumford points out that "to understand the physical world, and ultimately man himself, who exists in this world, as merely a product of mass and motion, one must eliminate the living soul. At the center of the new world picture man himself did not exist, indeed he had no reason to exist" (*The Pentagon of Power*, 55).

A good discussion of the relationship between technology and social forms is found in Langdon Winner, *The Whale and the Reactor* (Chicago: University of Chicago Press, 1986), part 1. Winner asserts that the development of technology follows a political and social agenda. He believes that "crucial choices about the forms and limits of our regimes of instrumentality must be enforced at the founding, at the genesis of each new technology" (58).

20. Buckminster Fuller, *I Seem to Be a Verb* (New York: Bantam, 1970), 66b.

21. "Like wild chaotic nature, women needed to be subdued and kept in their place" (Carolyn Merchant, *The Death of Nature* [New York: Harper & Row, 1980], 132). "The old organic worldview, the vision that saw sacred presence in all of life" Starhawk, *Truth or Dare* [San Francisco: Harper & Row, 1987], 7).

22. Mumford, *The Pentagon of Power*, 186.

23. Mumford describes the creation of product demand: "We come to the great paradox of both early mechanization and its ultimate expression in automation: so far from being responses to a mass demand, the enterpriser had in fact to create it; and in order to justify the heavy capital investment necessary to create automatic machines and automatic factories that assembled these machines in larger working units, it was necessary to invade distant markets, to standardize tastes and buying habits, to destroy alternative choices, and to wipe out competition from smaller industrial competitors, more dependent upon intimate face-to-face relations and more flexible in meeting consumer demands" (*The Pentagon of Power*, 177).

24. "Reformers who would treat the campaign against environmental and human degradation solely in terms of improved technological facilities, like the reduction of gasoline exhaust in motor cars, see only a small part of the problem. Nothing less than a profound re-orientation of our vaunted technological 'way of life' will save this planet from becoming a lifeless desert" (Mumford, *The Pentagon of Power*, 413).

25. For Mumford, "It was this capitalistic devotion to repetitive order and mechanical discipline and financial rewards that helped to undermine the lively, diversified, but finely balanced polytechnics" (*The Pentagon of Power*, 146).

26. Mumford cautioned against discussing "the technological factors that are polluting and destroying the living environment, without reference to this immense pecuniary pressure constantly exerted in every technological area" (*The Pentagon of Power*, 169).

27. For Murray Bookchin, this entails "an ethical enterprise for rehumanizing the psyche and demystifying techne" whose precondition is "the rounded person in a rounded society, living a total life" (*The Ecology of Freedom*, 312).

28. *The Reenchantment of the World*, 189.

3. Consumer Choice: We're All to Blame

1. *Remaking Society* (Montreal: Black Rose Books, 1989), 9.
2. *Time*, January 2, 1989, 30.
3. *New Age Journal*, Special Issue, Spring 1990, 81.
4. *Whole Earth Review*, Fall 1986, 18.
5. *Whole Earth Review*, Fall 1986, 19-24.
6. Excerpted in *Utne Reader*, May-June 1990, 97.
7. This discussion draws on the ideas of Richard Grossman, *Wrenching Debate Gazette*, February 1989, 3.
8. Also discussed by Grossman.
9. *Raleigh News & Observer*, February 4, 1990, 17A.
10. *Time*, January 2, 1989, 26. The critique that follows owes much to Grossman.
11. See chapter 4 for discussion.
12. *E* magazine, September-October 1990, 15.

4. The Struggle for Democracy: Concentration of Power

1. The epigraph at the head of the chapter is from Alexis de Tocqueville, Democracy in America, trans. George Lawrence (Garden City, N.Y.: Doubleday, 1969), 238.
2. "All history affords but few instances of Men trusted with great Power without abusing it" (Thomas Gordon and John Trenchard, in *Cato's Letters*, quoted in Jackson Turner Main, *The Anti-Federalists* [New York: Norton, 1961], 9).
3. *The Anti-Federalists*, 9.
4. *The Anti-Federalists*, 19.
5. *The Anti-Federalists*, 104.
6. Charles Beard, *An Economic Interpretation of the Constitution of the United States* (New York: Free Press, 1935), 324.
7. Quoted in Jerry Fresia, *Toward an American Revolution* (Boston: South End Press), 32.
8. *The Federalist Papers* (New York: New American Library, 1961), 81.
9. *The Federalist Papers*, 84.
10. See *The Anti-Federalists*, especially 130-131.
11. *The Anti-Federalists*, 134.
12. Adrienne Koch, *Jefferson and Madison* (New York: Alfred A. Knopf, 1950), 39-40.
13. *The Anti-Federalists*, 248.
14. *The Anti-Federalists*, 250.
15. *The Anti-Federalists*, 251.
16. *The Anti-Federalists*, 184.
17. *The Anti-Federalists*, 133.
18. *Democracy in America*, 261.
19. *The Papers of Thomas Jefferson*, vol. 17 (Princeton: Princeton University Press, 1952), 195.
20. "Jefferson believes that men are sociable, reasonable creatures, who, with

the passage of time, and the aid of science, can return to the garden. Hamilton, in contrast views men as 'ambitious, vindictive, and rapacious,' who, given the opportunity, will turn Jefferson's garden into a pigsty" (Richard K. Matthews, *The Radical Politics of Thomas Jefferson* [Lawrence: University Press of Kansas, 1984], 116).

21. Jefferson writes that "whenever the people are well informed they can be trusted with their own government. . . . If we think them not enlightened enough to exercise their control with a wholesome discretion, the remedy is not to take it from them, but to inform their discretion by education" (*The Papers of Thomas Jefferson,* vol. 12 [Princeton: Princeton University Press, 1964], 163).

22. Koch, *Jefferson and Madison,* 66.

23. *The Papers of Thomas Jefferson,* vol. 1 (Princeton: Princeton University Press, 1950), 348, 362.

24. Letter to Samuel Kercheval, July 12, 1816, in *The Works of Thomas Jefferson,* vol. 12 (New York: Knickerbocker Press, 1904), 8-9.

25. "Where every man is a sharer in the direction of his ward-republic, or of some of the higher ones, and feels that he is a participator in the government of affairs, not merely at an election one day in the year, but every day; when there shall not be a man in the state who will not be a member of one of its councils, great or small, he will let the heart be torn out of his body sooner than his power be wrested from him by a Caesar or a Bonaparte" (letter to Joseph C. Cabell, February 2, 1816, quoted in Matthews, *The Radical Politics of Thomas Jefferson,* 27).

26. "The way to have a good and safe government is not to trust it all to one, but to divide it among the many, distributing to everyone exactly the functions he is competent to" (quoted in *The Anti-Federalists,* 82).

27. *The Radical Politics of Thomas Jefferson,* 83.

28. "I hold it that a little rebellion now and then is a good thing, & as necessary in the political world as storms in the physical. . . . It is a medicine necessary for the sound health of government" (letter to James Madison, January 20, 1787, in *The Writings of Thomas Jefferson* vol. 4 [New York: G. P. Putnam, 1894], 361-363).

29. This discussion is based primarily on the work of the preeminent historian of the Populist era, Lawrence Goodwyn, whose "short history of the Agrarian Revolt in America," *The Populist Moment* (New York: Oxford University Press, 1978), is important reading for anyone wishing to understand the democratic tradition in the United States.

30. *The Populist Moment,* 32 and 81.

31. Lawrence Goodwyn, "Populism and Powerlessness," in *The New Populism,* ed. Harry Boyle (Philadelphia: Temple University Press, 1986), 28-29.

32. "Alliance national presidents literally meant what they said when they spoke of 'centralized capital, allied to irresponsible corporate power' and pronounced it a 'menace to individual rights and popular government'" (Goodwyn, *The Populist Moment,* 114).

33. *The Populist Moment,* 80-87.

34. Goodwyn, *The Populist Moment,* 139.

35. "The forces of traditionalism were narrow in outlook, primitive in economic theory, and well protected by an enormous and passive constituency. Most importantly, [they] possessed all of the commanding heights in the culture—the nation's press, the universities, the banks, and the churches. Collectively they had power. The forces of reform, on the other hand, deployed several regiments of stump speakers, a thousand weekly newspaper editors, and a sizable constituency that carried strong but receding memories of the Alliance cooperative crusade. Collectively, they had hope. It was not a balanced contest" (Goodwyn, *The Populist Moment*, 212).

36. As Goodwyn says, "The third party movement in South Carolina became immobilized. . . . The leaders of the agrarian movement found themselves either outmaneuvered and cornered or forced to go along with Tillman—even as their organization lost its internal cohesion and political identity. . . . Tillman had co-opted the Alliance platform and, through effective demagoguery, had destroyed the coherence of the reform movement" (*The Populist Moment*, 196-197).

37. Gabriel Kolko, *The Triumph of Conservatism* (Chicago: Quadrangle, 1967), 283.

38. "Businessmen defined the limits of political intervention. . . . The basic fact of the Progressive Era was the large area of consensus and unity among key business leaders and most political factions" (*The Triumph of Conservatism*, 280).

39. *The Triumph of Conservatism*, 305.

40. Goodwyn sums up the power of corporate America: "Today, the values and the sheer power of corporate America pinch in the horizons of millions of obsequious corporate employees, tower over every American legislature, state and national, determine the modes and style of mass communications and mass education, fashion American foreign policy around the globe, and shape the rules of the American political process itself. Self-evidently, corporate values define modern American culture" (*The Populist Moment*, 322).

For a thorough and readable discussion of the extent of concentration of power in the United States today and resulting problems, see William Greider, *Who Will Tell the People?* (New York: Simon & Schuster, 1992).

41. Frances Moore Lappe, *Rediscovering America's Values* (New York: Ballantine, 1989), 203.

42. See Mumford, *The Pentagon of Power*, 238, which compares the structure of power in ancient Egypt under the pharaohs with that of the modern industrial nation-state. Mumford's ideas are echoed by Marilyn French in her feminist analysis of the history of power relations. French concludes that "the tendency of Western culture for hundreds of years has been toward centralization for good and ill" (*Beyond Power* [New York: Ballantine, 1985], 346). Perhaps alluding to the democratic sensibilities of the Populists, Ivan Illich writes that "the centralization of power which now seems normal could not have been imagined a century ago" (*Tools for Conviviality* [New York: Harper & Row, 1973], 70).

43. Quoted in Howard Zinn, *A People's History of the United States* (New York: Harper & Row, 1980), 254-255.

44. *From Max Weber,* ed. H. H. Gerth and C. Wright Mills (New York: Oxford University Press, 1958), 71.

45. *The Worldly Philosophers* (New York: Simon & Schuster, 1980), 303.

46. *Nation,* December 17, 1990, 771.

47. Reported by David Corn, "Beltway Bandits," *Nation,* January 6, 1992, 8.

48. French writes that "corporations are 'inherently undemocratic' in structure, and their policies of secrecy, collusion, and influence on government provide a shadow government that is unaccountable to the public. The form alone of giant corporations—centralized power, bureaucracy, hierarchy, lack of autonomy—provides a structural example for totalitarianism, and teaches us the qualities we need to submit to it: fear of responsibility, fear of making decisions, fear in general; obedience, subservience, and conformism. Corporations are not of course the only institutions built this way, only the most powerful and widest reaching" (*Beyond Power,* 431).

49. *The Pentagon of Power,* 168.

50. Like Mumford, Murray Bookchin has studied the history of power, in his case through the evolving forms of human domination. In *The Ecology of Freedom,* he reviews the development of priestly ruling castes, the subordination of women, and the rise of the state and the capitalist economy. He concludes that "under state capitalism . . . domination fulfills its destiny in the ubiquitous, all-pervasive State; its legacy [is] the dissolution, indeed, the complete disintegration, of a richly organic society into an inorganic one." Paralleling this social transformation is a transformation of the natural world, as much of the impact of capitalism has been to reduce biological diversity, replacing natural organic processes with mechanical, cybernetic, and artificial ones (see *The Ecology of Freedom,* 139).

5. The Narrowing of Values: "Grow or Die"

1. Adam Smith, *The Wealth of Nations* (New York: *Modern Library,* 1937), 423.

2. *An Introduction to Financial Management* (Glenview, Ill.: Scott, Foresman, 1980), 9.

3. It is exclusively concerned with "the value to the investors who supply the necessary capital funds" (*An Introduction to Financial Management,* 13).

4. *An Introduction to Financial Management,* 14.

5. *An Introduction to Financial Management,* 325.

6. "If we accept the false hypothesis, the result will be catastrophic. If we reject the true hypothesis, we will forgo marginal satisfactions and will have to learn to share, which, though difficult, might well be good for us. If we later discover that the hypothesis is true we could always resume growth. . . . It would seem prudent to reject the omnipotent technology hypothesis" (*Steady-State Economics* [San Francisco: W. H. Freeman, 1977], 115).

7. Barry Commoner offers the following statement from the Manufacturing Chemists' Association. It is a clear statement from industry of this connection between profit and technology. "The maintenance of above-average profit margins requires the continuous discovery of new products and specialties on

which high profit margins may be earned while the former products in that category evolve into commodity chemicals with lower margins" (*The Closing Circle*, 260).

8. In an important work, *America By Design* (New York: Alfred A. Knopf, 1977), David Noble describes how the engineering profession was created in the nineteenth century, placing the force of science and technology fully in the service of capitalism. Noble concludes that "the technical work of the engineer was little more than the scientific extension of capitalist enterprise; it was through his efforts that science was transformed into capital" (34).

9. Joseph Heller, *Catch 22* (New York: Simon & Schuster, 1955), 237.

10. Fred Hirsch writes that "the complex relationship seen by Smith has been summarized as follows: '[Men] could safely be trusted to pursue their own self-interest without undue harm to the community not only because of the restrictions imposed by the law, but also because they were subject to built-in restraint derived from morals, religion, custom, and education'" (*Social Limits to Growth* [Cambridge: Harvard University Press, 1976], 137).

11. For Hirsch "the pursuit of private and essentially individualistic economic goals . . . must be girded at key points by a strict social morality which the system erodes rather than sustains. The social morality that has served as an understructure for economic individualism has been the legacy of the precapitalist and preindustrial past. This legacy has diminished with time and with the corrosive contact of the active capitalist values [and] . . . thereby lost outside support that was previously taken for granted by the individual" (*Social Limits to Growth*, 117).

12. "So deeply rooted is the market economy in our minds that its grubby language has replaced our most hallowed moral and spiritual expressions. We now 'invest' in our children, marriages, and personal relationships, a term that is equated with words like 'love' and 'care.' We live in a world of 'trade-offs' and we ask for the 'bottom line' of any emotional 'transaction.' We use the language of contracts rather than that of loyalties and spiritual affinities" (*The Modern Crisis* [Philadelphia: New Society, 1986], 79).

13. "People could contrast the 'dog-eat-dog' attributes of the market place with the solidarity of a village-type neighborhood world and its rich supports in the extended family, whose older members formed living recollections of a more caring preindustrial society" (*The Modern Crisis*, 80–81).

14. Bookchin has consistently cautioned against a romantic view of precapitalist societies. See, for example, *Toward an Ecological Society* (Montreal: Black Rose Books, 1980): "There can be no return to these periods—either socially or technically. Their limits are only too clear to excuse an atavistic yearning for the past" (p. 122).

15. *New Options*, November 30, 1987, 2.

16. U.S. National Research Council, *Conserving Biodiversity* (Washington: National Academy Press, 1992), chap. 3.

17. Mumford, *The Pentagon of Power*, 334.

18. A good critique of the GNP is provided by Hazel Henderson: "The social costs of a polluted environment, disrupted communities, disrupted family life, and eroded primary relationships may be the only part of the GNP that is

growing. We are so confused that we add these societal costs into the GNP as if they were real, useful products" (*The Politics of the Solar Age* [New York: Doubleday, 1981], 12). The GNP has also been criticized by feminists, who point out that it devalues much of the work of women in the nonmonetary sector of the economy.

19. See, for example, Herman E. Daly and John B. Cobb, *For The Common Good* (Boston: Beacon Press, 1989), 401.

20. According to Mumford, the scientist "can defend the wholesale immediate use of pesticides, bactericides, and possibly equally dangerous pharmaceuticals, by saying that it would take ten years to test them sufficiently to certify their value and innocuousness and that *'industry cannot wait'*—it is obvious that his rational commitments to science are secondary to financial pressures, and that the safeguarding of human life is for industry not a matter of major concern" (*The Pentagon of Power*, 336).

21. Commoner writes that "inevitably by the time the effects are known, the damage is done and the inertia of the heavy investment in a new productive technology makes a retreat extraordinarily difficult. The very system of enhancing profit in this industry is precisely the cause of its intense detrimental impact on the environment" (*The Closing Circle*, 261).

22. Heller, *Catch 22*, 261.

23. *Catch 22*, 263.

24. For Daly, the present-value calculation has "an element of positive feedback that is destabilizing from the point of view of conservation. Financial prudence usually advises depleting now and investing short-term earnings in depleting some other resources. The presumption is infinite resources" (*Steady-State Economics*, 113).

25. Daly and Cobb, *For the Common Good*, 152.

26. For Commoner, "The irresponsible entrepreneur finds it profitable to kill the goose that lays the golden eggs so long as the goose lives long enough to provide him with sufficient eggs to pay for the purchase of a new goose. Ecological irresponsibility can pay—for the entrepreneur, but not for society as a whole" (*The Closing Circle*, 267).

27. According to the world-systems theory of Immanuel Wallerstein, the capitalist world economy had expanded to cover the globe by the end of the nineteenth century. This was the first time a single system had encompassed the entire planet. See Alvin Y. So, *Social Change and Development* (Newbury Park, Calif.: Sage Publications, 1990), 178, and Wallerstein's *Historical Capitalism* (London: Verso, 1983).

28. Lenin himself described socialism as "nothing but state-capitalist monopoly" (quoted in Bookchin, "Marxism as Bourgeois Sociology," in *Toward an Ecological Society*, 196). For Immanuel Wallerstein, "establishing a system of state-ownership in a capitalist world-economy does not mean establishing a socialist economy" (quoted in So, *Social Change and Development*, 186).

29. Bill Weinberg, *War on the Land* (London: Zed, 1991), chap. 12.

30. Daly, *Steady-State Economics*, 17. Daly is perhaps the premier advocate of steady-state or sustainable economics.

31. As Daly puts it, "Basic needs of the future should take precedence over

the luxuries of the present [along with the realization that] other species also deserve their place in the sun" (*New Options*, November 30, 1987, 6). The steady-state position was anticipated in the nineteenth century by John Stuart Mill, who wrote, "It is scarcely necessary to remark that a stationary condition of capital and population implies no stationary state of human improvement. There would be as much scope as ever for all kinds of mental culture and moral and social progress; as much room for improving the art of living and more likelihood of its being improved" (quoted in Paul Wachtel, *The Poverty of Affluence* [New York: Free Press, 1983], 107).

32. To Murray Bookchin, "We will either re-vision nature as a domain of fecundity and development or, in the marketplace mentality, conceive of it as a rank jungle to be savagely exploited as we exploit each other in the buyer-seller relationship. [A market economy and a moral economy] stand counterposed to each other in the way men and women envision themselves and the ideals they advance for human intercourse. . . . [They] raise fundamentally opposed notions of humanity's self-realization and sense of purpose, concepts which define the very meaning of material premises on which our development eventually depends" (*The Modern Crisis*, 97).

6. The Loss of Community: Land and Labor as Commodities

1. The historian Karl Polanyi points out that "land and labor are not other than the human beings themselves of which every society consists and the natural surroundings in which it exists. . . . Traditionally, land and labor are not separated; labor forms part of life, land remains part of nature, life and nature form an articulate whole. Land is thus tied up with the organizations of kinship, neighborhood, craft, and creed" (*The Great Transformation* [New York: Farrar & Rinehart, 1944], 178).

2. *The Worldly Philosophers*, 25.

3. Polanyi, *The Great Transformation*, 72.

4. "Labor is only another name for a human activity which goes with life itself. . . . Land is only another name for nature, which is not produced by man. . . . Land and labor are no other than the human beings themselves of which every society consists and the natural surroundings in which it exists. To include them in the market mechanism means to subordinate the substance of society itself to the laws of the market" (*The Great Transformation*, 71–72).

5. *The Worldly Philosophers*, 25.

6. To Polanyi, "Land [was] the pivotal element. . . . Whether its possession was transferable or not, and if so, to whom and under what restrictions; what the rights of property entailed; to what uses some types of land might be put—all these questions were removed from the organization of buying and selling, and subjected to an entirely different set of institutional regulations" (*The Great Transformation*, 69–70).

7. According to Ivan Illich, the commons were "that part of the environment which lay beyond their own thresholds and outside their own possessions, to which, however, they had recognized claims of usage, not to produce com-

modities but to provide for the subsistence of their households" (*Whole Earth Review*, Winter 1983, 7). In describing the commons, Illich gives the example that "an oak tree might be in the commons. Its shade, in summer, is reserved for the shepherd and his flock; its acorns are reserved for the pigs of the neighboring peasants; its dry branches serve as fuel for the widows of the village; some of its fresh twigs in springtime are cut as ornaments for the church—and at sunset it might be the place for the village assembly."

8. Karl Marx, *Capital*, trans. Ben Fowkes (New York: Random House, 1906), 797.

9. Heilbroner, *The Worldly Philosophers*, 30.

10. Marx described how the villagers "were systematically hunted and rooted out. All their villages were destroyed and burnt, all their fields turned into pasturage. British soldiers enforced this eviction, and came to blows with the inhabitants" (*Capital*, 802).

11. *The Worldly Philosophers*, 30.

12. *Capital*, 180.

13. *Capital*, 800.

14. Heilbroner describes the tragic fate faced by the peasant: "Deprived of the right to use the common land, he could no longer maintain himself as a 'farmer.' Since no factories were available, he could not—even if he had wanted to—metamorphose into a factory worker. Instead, he became that most miserable of all social classes, an agricultural proletarian, and where agricultural work was lacking, a beggar, sometimes a robber, usually a pauper" (*The Worldly Philosophers*, 30).

15. Marx describes how "the agricultural people [were] first forcibly expropriated from the soil, driven from their homes, turned into vagabonds, and then whipped, branded, tortured by laws grotesquely terrible, into the discipline necessary for the wage system" (*Capital*, 806–809).

16. Comparing the lives of industrial laborers to those of their forebears, Mumford reached the somber conclusion that the laborers had achieved the "freedom to abandon the medieval system of guild protection and social security and to be exploited by those who owned the costly new machinery of production." *The Pentagon of Power*, 133.

17. See the discussion in Fernand Braudel, *Civilization and Capitalism* (New York: Harper & Row, 1979), vol. 2, 51–54.

18. "What we call land is an element of nature inextricably interwoven with man's institutions. To isolate it and form a market out of it was perhaps the weirdest of all undertakings of our ancestors" (Mumford, *The Pentagon of Power*, 178).

19. *A Sand County Almanac* (New York: Ballantine, 1966), xix.

20. As Daly and Cobb put it, "[For] hunting and gathering peoples, the land is the giver of life and the source of all good. . . . The people belong to the land and reverence it. . . . They are related through it to their ancestors and descendants. There is no concept of ownership of land" (*For the Common good*, 100). They go on to quote John Stuart Mill, who, in language that would make his nineteenth-century contemporary Chief Seattle proud, wrote that "no man made the land. It is the original inheritance of the whole

species. Its appropriation is wholly a question of general expediency" (105).

21. Rousseau, *The Basic Political Writings,* trans. Donald Acress (Indianapolis: Hackett Publishing, 1987), 60.

22. *Whole Earth Review,* Winter 1983, 7.

23. Harry Boyte writes that Reagan's "brand of conservatism functioned as a kind of 'enclosure movement' that threatened basic public goods, from our natural resources to government science programs" (*Commonwealth* [New York: Free Press, 1989], 15).

24. See the discussion in Ivan Illich, *Gender* (New York: Pantheon, 1982).

25. *Gender,* 48.

26. Illich writes that "of everything that economics measures, women get less" (*Gender,* 4).

27. Katha Pollitt writes that "so-called surrogacy agreements are so unprecedented that the resulting human arrangements bear no resemblance to adoption, illegitimacy, custody after divorce, or any other relationship involving parents and children, yet, at the same time, bear an uncanny resemblance to the all-sales-final style of a used-car lot" ("The Strange Case of Baby M," Nation, June 23, 1987, 682.

7. Values: The Pillars of Effective Activism

1. Benjamin Barber, *Strong Democracy* (Berkeley: University of California Press, 1984), 139.

2. *A Sand County Almanac,* 240.

3. In Lovelock's view, "The entire range of living matter on Earth . . . could be regarded as constituting a single living entity, capable of manipulating the Earth's atmosphere to suit its overall needs" (*Gaia* [Oxford: Oxford University Press, 1982], 9).

4. For the philosopher Lorne Neil Evernden, this fragmentation is the source of our concept of environment itself: "The environment exists because it was made visible by the act of making it separate. It exists because we have excised it from the context of our lives" (*The Natural Alien: Humankind and Environment* [Toronto: University of Toronto Press, 1985], 125–126). Evernden concludes that "we are not *in* an environmental crisis, but *are* the environmental crisis" (134).

5. *Remaking Society,* 39.

6. *Conserving Biodiversity,* 94–96.

7. Bioregionalism will be discussed in detail in chapter 8.

8. As Herbert Marcuse put it, "The widespread concentration of power and control in the nation-wide political and military Establishment necessitates the shift to decentralized forms of organization, less susceptible to destruction by the engines of repression" (quoted in George Katsiaficas, *The Imagination of the New Left* [Boston: South End Press, 1987], 206).

9. Ynestra King, letter to *Nation,* December 12, 1987, 731. It is important to note that ecofeminism as a body of thought is diverse and often contradictory. Janet Biehl describes and criticizes its various trends in *Rethinking Ecofeminist Politics* (Boston: South End Press, 1991). Biehl feels that the overall thrust of

ecofeminism is counter to that of social ecology. My brief discussion, by contrast, selects those tendencies in ecofeminist thought that are consistent with social ecology and with Green politics.

10. Irene Diamond and Gloria Feman Orenstein, *Reweaving the World* (San Francisco: Sierra Club Books, 1990), 120–121.

11. Carol Gilligan, *In a Different Voice* (Cambridge: Harvard University Press, 1982), 144.

12. *Everyone's Backyard,* January–February 1990, 2.

13. Mumford describes the importance of individual change to challenging what he terms the power system: "Though no immediate and complete escape from the ongoing power system is possible, least of all through mass violence, the changes that will restore autonomy and initiative to the human person all lie within the province of each individual soul, once it is aroused. Nothing could be more damaging to the myth of the machine, and to the dehumanized social order it has brought into existence, than a steady withdrawal of interest, a slowing down of tempo, a stoppage of senseless routines and mindless acts" (*The Pentagon of Power,* 433).

14. "On Strategic Nonviolence," *Green Perspectives,* November 1988, 6–7.

15. As Frances Moore Lappe puts it, in her own examination of the question of values, "It is also the dynamic of the common life itself, in which citizenship means joining in public dialogue to uncover and give shape to our common values and to decide how to act upon them. Citizenship, understood this way, sees democracy as a value, not just because it protects the individual's well-being, but because it promotes a public arena of deliberation over common concerns, an interchange that is itself morally transformative, inseparable from our individual moral development" (*Rediscovering America's Values,* 63).

8. Cooperation and Community

1. Harry Boyte describes community this way: "It means relearning how to talk to each other. It means discovering how to share spaces. It involves recovering memories, in this most forgetful of societies. It requires the repair of our capacity to solve problems and to discern the common values in different heritages and traditions" (*Community Is Possible* [New York: Harper & Row, 1984], 11; see also 137).

2. For example, consider these views presented in essays printed in the anthology *Home! A Bioregional Reader,* ed. M. Van Andrus et al. (Philadelphia: New Society, 1990). Helen Forsey writes that "community living is life-affirming and nonviolent. . . . It is an affirmation that better ways do exist" (76–77). Wilfred Pelletier and Ted Poole write that "a community is invisible from the outside—just a collection of people. But from the inside it is a living organism that manages itself. A community has no institutions . . . only a way of life, and . . . a kind of trust that people outside that community can hardly imagine and which people inside the community cannot name" (84).

3. M. Scott Peck, *The Different Drum* (New York: Simon and Schuster, 1987), 61–68.

4. *The Different Drum,* 317.

5. *The Different Drum,* 272.

6. "Community Building," *Peacetalks,* April 1988, 12–15.

7. *The Art of Loving* (New York: Bantam, 1956), 22–26.

8. As Murray Bookchin has written, it is "only within a locally oriented political community that the uniqueness of the natural environment can be fully experienced in all its intimacy" (*The Rise of Urbanization and the Decline of Citizenship* [San Francisco: Sierra Club Books, 1987], 266).

9. The bioregionalist Kirkpatrick Sale writes that "if there is any scale at which ecological consciousness can be developed, at which citizens can see themselves as being the *cause* for the environmental *effect,* it is at the regional level; there all ecological questions are taken out of the realm of the philosophical and the moral and are dealt with as immediate and personal" (*Dwellers in the Land* [San Francisco: Sierra Club Books, 1985], 54).

10. *The Once and Future King* (New York: Berkeley, 1958), 170.

11. Peter Berg, one of the founders of the bioregional movement, has described living in place to mean "following the necessities and pleasures of life as they are uniquely presented by a particular site, and evolving ways to ensure long-term occupancy of that site" (*Home! A Bioregional Reader,* 32).

12. Berg writes that "people must be firmly rooted before they will fight destruction that comes from beyond their boundaries. Community is the beginning and end of bioregionalism" (*Home! A Bioregional Reader,* 86).

13. "When the people who live there have to look after the particular affairs of a district, the same people are always meeting, and they are forced, in a manner, to know and adapt themselves to one another. It is difficult to force a man out of himself and get him to take an interest in the affairs of the whole state, for he has little understanding of the way in which the fate of the state can influence his own lot. But if it is a question of taking a road past his property, he sees at once that this small public matter has a bearing on his greatest private interests, and there is no need to point out to him the close connection between his private profit and the general interest" (*Democracy in America,* p. 511).

14. Quoted in Sale, *Dwellers in the Land,* 142.

15. "We must create in every region people who will be accustomed, from school onward, to humanist attitudes, co-operative methods, rational controls. These people will know in detail where they live and how they lived: they will be united by a common feeling for their landscape, their literature and language, their local ways, and out of their own self-respect they will have a sympathetic understanding with other regions and different local peculiarities" (*The Culture of Cities* [New York: Harcourt, 1938], 386).

16. Peter Berg, Beryl Magilavy, and Seth Zuckerman, *A Green City Program* (San Francisco: Planet Drum Books, 1989), xvi.

17. "There needs to be a profound shift in the fundamental premises and activities of city living. Urban people have to adopt conserver values and carry out more responsible practices in wide areas of daily life. Municipal governments need to restructure their priorities so that long-term sustainability can become a feasible goal. . . . Cities need to become 'green.' They must be

transformed into places that are life-enhancing and regenerative" (*A Green City Program,* xiii).

18. Ironically, even the 1980 Republican party platform raised the call for community self-help and cooperation ("[government must be] committed to nurturing the spirit of self-help and cooperation through which so many neighborhoods have revitalized themselves"), indicating the deep resonance that these concepts have with the American people. Of course, hidden behind the Republicans' pseudopopulist call for neighborhood self-help is the institution of "self-help" and cooperation on a mammoth scale between large corporations and the central government. As federal policies enrich and empower the already rich and powerful, neighborhoods are left in dire need of help, whether self-help or otherwise. As much as the Republicans (or Democrats, for that matter) are likely to praise cooperation, they are unlikely to see that this praise implies a criticism of one of the sacrosanct foundations of the modern economy: competition. They are certainly not going to develop programs based on an understanding of the interweaving of competition and concentration of power at the root of our contemporary environmental and social ills.

19. An extreme albeit humorous example of this appeared in a "Far Side" cartoon. A woman looks through her living room window at a missile launcher in her neighbor's yard. She says to her husband, "Wouldn't you know it! Now the Hendersons have the bomb." Her own missile looms in the foreground. Gary Larson in a single stroke satirizes both the arms race and keeping up with the Joneses, two aspects of the same competitive mind-set (*The Far Side Gallery* [Kansas City: Andrews, McMeel, Parker, 1980]).

20. Susan Meeker-Lowry's book *Economics As If the Earth Really Mattered* (Philadelphia: New Society, 1988) examines many of the aspects of economic life discussed here. Meeker-Lowry explores those alternatives that will encourage cooperation, self-reliance, and living harmoniously with the planet.

21. *The Modern Crisis,* 92.

22. Paul Elkins, ed., *The Living Economy* (London: Routledge & Kegan Paul, 1986), 266.

23. Braudel, *Civilization and Capitalism,* vol. 1, 439.

24. This account of Mondragon draws primarily from Roy Morrison, *We Build the Road As We Travel* (Philadelphia: New Society, 1991) and a short essay in C. George Benello, *From the Ground Up* (Boston: South End Press, 1992), chap. 8. Morrison's book, a study of the history and nature of the Mondragon experience, is an excellent, more detailed and nuanced companion to the discussion of cooperatives here.

25. Quoted in *We Build the Road As We Travel,* 12.

26. The discussion that follows draws primarily from Kathryn McCamant and Charles Durrett, *Cohousing* (Berkeley: Ten Speed Press, 1989), a study of the Danish cohousing movement.

27. *Cohousing,* 153.

28. Roberta Wilson, in the newsletter of Santa Monica Friends Meeting, January 1991.

9. Participatory, Grassroots Democracy

1. Robert N. Bellah et al., *Habits of the Heart* (New York: Harper & Row, 1985), 200-201.

2. Marge Piercy, *Woman on the Edge of Time* (New York: Alfred A. Knopf, 1976), 277.

3. Benjamin Barber writes that "democracy rests on the idea of a self-governing community of citizens who are united less by homogeneous interests than by civic education and who are made capable of common purpose and mutual action by virtue of their civic attitudes and participatory institutions rather than their altruism or their good nature" (*Strong Democracy*, 117).

4. Murray Bookchin describes the citizen of Athens as "a knowledgeable, civically dedicated, active, and above all *self-governing* being, who . . . made the welfare of his community—its general interest—his primary interest, to the exclusion of his own self-interest" (*Remaking Society*, 179).

5. Barber concludes that "what is required is nothing more than a faith in the democratizing effects that political participation has on men, a faith not in what men are but in what democracy makes them" (*Strong Democracy*, 237).

6. Harry Boyte describes how the process of democratic participation awakens the sense of citizenship in people: "In *democratic* populist movements, as people are moved to activism in *defense* of their rights, traditions, and institutions, they change. They discover in themselves and their traditions new resources, potentials, resonances. They repair capacities to work together for collective problem solving." Boyte sees contemporary citizens' movements as ultimately entailing a change "from understanding politics merely as a protest against threat to coming to see the need for a struggle for new conceptions of rights and participation and power" (*Community Is Possible*, 32).

7. This discussion of Swiss democracy is based on Benjamin Barber, *The Death of Communal Liberty* (Princeton: Princeton University Press, 1974). Here, 16.

8. *The Death of Communal Liberty,* 190.

9. *The Death of Communal Liberty,* 193.

10. "In political affairs the individual [Swiss] was remarkably well informed. He grew up in politics, listening to his father and neighbors distilling political wisdom from the chaos of European affairs. . . . No referendum question was too complicated, no jurisdictional quarrel too entangled for him to comprehend. . . . As the citizen's political education permitted him an active and prudent participation, his regular participation augmented his civic wisdom" (*The Death of Communal Liberty*, 200).

The Swiss referendum is by no means ideal. The political scientist Jurg Steiner describes referenda that outlawed kosher butchering and that failed to provide for conscientious objection to military service. He points out that referenda outcomes, like any public vote, can be influenced by propaganda and that voter turnout for referenda has been declining since the 1950s (*European Democracies* [New York: Longmans, 1991], 173-177).

11. *The Death of Communal Liberty,* 271.

12. Barber sees the automobile as a particularly pernicious case, as it "takes

citizens and makes of them individuals . . . takes communards and sets them loose in a homeless society where independence means loneliness and liberation conveys only the sad sense of solitude" (*The Death of Communal Liberty,* 249).

13. Barber also notes that it was not until the twentieth century that the Swiss tradition of maintaining common grazing lands began to fall prey to the fencing-off required for modern agriculture. Thus, as the Swiss have joined the twentieth century, "From traditional communal man comes modern economic man, uprooted from his community, turned in upon himself, alienated from his labor, and ready for a solitary life of affluence in the jungle of cities" (*The Death of Communal Liberty,* 272).

14. Barber himself draws a more optimistic conclusion, albeit one that calls into question the values on which modern society is based. He concludes *The Death of Communal Liberty* with the hopeful remark that the Swiss experience "suggests that freedom need not be incompatible with communal collectivism; that autonomy for the individual can be won through political participation in self-governing communities; that politics need not always be defined by self-interest but can instead itself define public interest; and that citizenship can help give meaning and purpose to human life. . . . [If the modern world] is inhospitable to such values, it may be a world that even at its very best requires radical remaking" (274).

15. For example, according to Renew America, in 1984 the U.S. government subsidized nuclear power in the amount of $15 billion for an output of 1.5 quadrillion btus. Renewable energy received a $1.7-billion subsidy for an output of 2.5 quadrillion btus. These figures reduce to fifteen times as much electricity from renewables as from nuclear energy on the basis of dollars of federal support. If the subsidies were reversed and the $15 billion were devoted to renewables, those technologies would develop quickly, and we could soon be free of both nuclear and fossil-fuel dependency.

16. Jane J. Mansbridge describes adversary democracy as the system familiar to "every American schoolchild," in which "you elect representatives . . . [and] when you do not agree, you take a vote and the majority rules" (*Beyond Adversary Democracy* [Chicago: University of Chicago Press, 1983], 3).

17. *Beyond Adversary Democracy,* 15.

18. Mansbridge writes, "The mechanical aggregation of conflicting selfish desires is the very core of an adversary system. But this idea verges on moral bankruptcy. . . . Adversary democracy is the democracy of a cynical society. It replaces common interest with self-interest, the dignity of equal status with the baser motives of self-protection, and the communal moments of a face-to-face council with the isolation of a voting machine" (*Beyond Adversary Democracy,* p. 18).

19. *Beyond Adversary Democracy,* 17.

20. Barber quotes Theodore Roosevelt to the effect that "the majority of the plain people will day in and day out make fewer mistakes in governing themselves than any smaller body of men will make in trying to govern them" (*Strong Democracy,* 151).

21. Some of the processes advocated by Barber, such as town meetings televised by "civic communications cooperatives," civic videotext services, and

electronic balloting, are in fact contrary to the kind of citizenship sought by strong democracy. Just as environmental responsibility depends on the development of a lived relationship to the Earth, so ecological community requires a participatory democracy in a face-to-face context. Frank Bryan and John McClaughry criticize Barber for falling "prey to the urge to use technology to democratize the whole rather than its parts" (*The Vermont Papers* [Chelsea, Vt.: Chelsea Green, 1989], 78).

22. This idea is conveyed by the political scientist Chantal Mouffe, who writes that "the common good can never be actualized; it must remain as a kind of vanishing point to which we should constantly refer. . . . This challenge should lead different groups . . . to realize that they have a common concern, that is, the establishment of a common political identity as 'radical democratic citizens'" ("Radical or Liberal Democracy," *Socialist Review*, April-June 1990, 63-64).

23. *Woman on the Edge of Time*, 153.

24. *Strong Democracy*, 238-239.

25. *Strong Democracy*, 266. Murray Bookchin disagrees about the importance of democratic action as the expression of democratic talk, insisting that policy formulation must be done in a participatory manner but that administration and implementation can be delegated. Ironically, while Barber gives the example of everyone pitching in to build a bridge to demonstrate the Swiss connection of policy-making and implementation, Bookchin discusses road building to differentiate policy formulation from administration. He maintains that not everyone must know how to build a road, which is an administrative responsibility: There is "a serious confusion between the formulation of policy and its administration. For a community to decide in a participatory manner what course of action it should take in dealing with a problem does not oblige all its citizens to execute that policy. . . . The decision to build a road, for example, does not mean that everyone must know how to design and construct one. . . . [That] is a strictly administrative responsibility. To debate and decide the need for road . . . is a political process" (*The Rise of Urbanization and the Decline of Citizenship*, 247.) A clarification of terms may help resolve this difference. It is important to distinguish self-reliance, in which a community seeks to do what it can for itself, from self-sufficiency, in which a community attempts to remove all dependency on its neighbors. While obviously not everyone must know how to construct a road, a self-reliant community will, in fact, execute policies itself to the extent that it is able to do so. Those things that it cannot do by itself may be obtained from other communities, preferably nearby but perhaps distant. Certainly, it makes sense for citizens to contribute to the execution of public policy primarily in areas where their skills are best developed. On the other hand, some activities, such as scientific research or artistic creation, might require a regional level of support to allow for the proper facilities and equipment.

26. For a discussion of the impact of the market on democracy, see Samuel Bowles and Herbert Gintes, *Democracy and Capitalism* (New York: Basic Books, 1987), 133-135.

27. *Democracy and Capitalism,* 67.

28. An excellent presentation of a variety of aspects of economic democracy is found in Martin Carnoy and Derek Shearer's *Economic Democracy* (White Plains, N.Y.: M. E. Sharpe, 1980). Particularly relevant to issues raised here are their elaborate discussions of worker ownership and democratic control of technology. Carnoy and Shearer see economic democracy as a potential unifying force for a broad progressive coalition to transform American political, social, and economic policy. Unfortunately, their treatment by and large omits the issues of scale and place that are essential to an ecologically wise economy. In fact, Carnoy and Shearer do not discuss the relationship of the structure of the economy to the environment at all. They also fail to fully come to grips with the structures of power that would oppose a movement for economic democracy. For example, they propose a strategy of reform via the two-party system based on such "significant gains" as Upton Sinclair's near winning of the California governorship in 1934, the experience of the Minnesota Democratic Farmer-Labor party, and a four-year period of reform in the 1920s in North Dakota (32). Unfortunately, these close failures and short-lived successes highlight not so much the potential for reform from within the two parties as the awesome obstacles to success in that arena. Nonetheless, when Carnoy and Shearer stick to their knitting—that is, to analytic and programmatic aspects of economic democracy—they provide a thorough and compelling work.

29. *Utne Reader,* January–February 1990, 120–121.

30. This history is told in some detail by Richard Rudolph and Scott Ridley in *Power Struggle* (New York: Harper & Row, 1986).

31. Deborah Sliz, "Bond Limits, Rate Relief among Legislative Challenges," *Public Power,* January–February 1988, 10–11.

32. While communities should in most cases produce for themselves what they can, as Bookchin notes, "Self-sustaining communities cannot produce all the things they need—unless it involves a return to a back-breaking way of village life" (*Green Perspectives,* November 1990). The concept of confederal municipalism, as presented here, is derived form Bookchin's social ecology (see *The Rise of Urbanization and the Decline of Citizenship*).

33. *Woman on the Edge of Time,* 152.

34. In *The Rise of Urbanization and the Decline of Citizenship,* Bookchin describes a process whereby, prior to the institution of official town meetings, citizens would hold unofficial meetings to debate and establish policy. As these grew in popularity, they would bring the political force of public opinion and the moral force of citizen action to bear on the elected government. In the process, the citizenry would grow to appreciate the nature of participation and likely seek authority to hold official, policy-making town meetings.

35. *The Rise of Urbanization and the Decline of Citizenship,* 251.

10. From Participation to Power: Green Politics

1. The preamble to the German Green Party Program describes these components: "We are the alternative to the traditional parties. . . . We see ourselves as linked to all those working together in the new democratic movement: groups for the protection of life, nature, and environment, citizens' initiatives, the workers' movement, Christian initiatives, peace, human rights, women's and Third World movements" (*Programme of the German Green Party* [London: Heretic Books, 1983], 6).

2. The political scientist Carl Boggs describes the Green movement as arising from "an emphasis on nonviolent forms of direct action; a struggle to recover community that had been destroyed by rampant urbanization; revulsion against the worst manifestations of economic modernization and consumer society; hostility toward the party system and interest-group bargaining; and a skepticism toward conventional ideologies of whatever sort" (*Social Movements and Political Power* [Philadelphia: Temple University Press, 1986], 174).

3. Quoted in Jeremy Brecher and Tim Costello, "Labor Goes Global," *Z*, March 1991, 90.

4. Elements of the program of the Maquiladora Coalition include "internal market-based development, increasing employment and incomes of the poor, government support for cooperatives, environmental sustainability, and a lowered priority for payments on international debt" ("Labor Goes Global," 93).

5. George Katsiaficas writes that "like parliamentary and trade-union struggles, direct actions may create a deeper understanding of the nature of the system—its limits and flexibility, violence and rewards—and they may even create major crises as they mount in intensity. But the complete redefinition of the 'rules of the game' depends on the prior reorganization of power relationships and the emergence of a socially legitimate alternative to the existing system" (*The Imagination of the New Left*, 204).

6. A good discussion of the direct-action movements is found in Barbara Epstein's *Political Protest and Cultural Revolution* (Berkeley: University of California Press, 1991), which includes a concise synopsis of the political movements of the 1960s and trends in radical politics in the late twentieth century.

7. Greens protesting the utility's plans were surprised to find that their march crossed paths with a rally awaiting the Bill Clinton–Al Gore campaign bus tour. Ironically, President Clinton appointed Northern States Power executive Hazel O'Leary to head the Department of Energy.

8. Germany's system of proportional representation guarantees seats in the Bundestag and federal financial support to any party receiving at least 5 percent of the vote.

9. "We once said that the Green party had a 'standing leg'—its center of gravity—outside parliament, and that this leg was more important than the 'playing leg' inside parliament. But the leg in parliament became the 'standing leg' and the movement leg was being cut off" (*Green Perspectives*, December 1990, 3).

10. The former German Green party leader Thomas Ebermann commented

that "it became so important to us to look at concrete electoral results, to win a certain number of votes, and from that to calculate a certain percentage number that it alone was capable of making us either satisfied or dissatisfied" (*Green Perspectives,* December 1990, 5).

11. In Petra Kelly's opinion, "It was not so much the radicalism of our agenda that failed as it was the divisive way in which we practiced our internal politics" ("The Future of The German Greens," *Green Letter,* Spring 1991, 27).

12. The relevance of recall in this context is discussed by Ed Jahn in "The Problem with Elections," *Regeneration: A Magazine of Left Green Thought,* Fall 1992, 7.

13. Boggs sees Green electoral strategy as stressing local autonomous forces, which must be combined with a social democratic strategy that "seeks to expand and further democratize the liberal-pluralist tradition." This synthesis provides the basis for a truly radical strategy that "entails the broadening of representative institutions, processes, and norms rather than their abolition. At the same time, it allows for the dynamic contribution of popular movements that (ideally) give rise to local forms of authority such as factory and neighborhood committees, which permit a remaking of the national state on foundations of self-management. The goal is a socialized political system relatively free of corporate and bureaucratic control." In Boggs's view, the Greens "have undertaken perhaps the first realistic and sustained challenge to the old organizational premises" (*Social Movements and Political Power,* 238).

14. Murray Bookchin sees this effort of prefigurative organizations to resemble the society they seek to develop as entailing an "enormous responsibility [that] can tolerate no disjunction between ends and means." Bookchin describes several of the components of such organizing: "Direct action, so integral to the management of a future society, has its parallel in the use of direct action to change society. Communal forms, so integral to the structure of a future society, have their parallel in the use of communal forms—collectives, affinity groups, and the like—to change society. The ecological ethics, confederal relationships, and decentralized structures we would expect to find in a future society are fostered by the values and networks we try to use in achieving an ecological society" (*The Ecology of Freedom,* 346–347).

15. Katsiaficas analyzes the global crisis of 1968 and compares it to similar global upheavals in 1848 and 1905. He seeks to understand the source of these leaps, which activate "whole strata of previously passive spectators, the millions of people who decide to participate in the conscious re-creation of their economic and political institutions and social life" (*The Imagination of the New Left,* 10).

16. "Missoula Greens Take Lead in Anti-War Organizing," *Green Letter,* Spring 1991, 34.

11. From Principles to Practice: Energy Strategy

1. Michael Totten, *Energywise Options for State and Local Governments* (Washington: Center for Policy Alternatives, 1990), 17. Totten's book is a great source of ideas for state and local energy initiatives.

2. Described in David Morris, *Self-reliant Cities* (San Francisco: Sierra Club Books, 1982), 184.

3. "Achieving Energy Self-reliance in Springfield, Illinois," *Connections,* February 1985, p. 1.

4. Craig Canine, "The Second Coming of Energy Conservation," *Utne Reader,* January–February 1990, 114–121.

5. "Austin's Conservation Power Plant," *Energy Conservation Bulletin,* January-February 1986, p. 2.

6. *Community Efficiency Now: Ten Steps,* (Washington: U.S. Department of Energy, 1980).

7. A strategy based on transitional use of natural gas and eventual use of solar-hydrogen power is described in *The State of the World 1992,* ed. Linda Starke (New York: Norton, 1992), chap. 3.

8. See the discussion of municipal power in chap. 9 above.

9. Described in McCamant and Durrett, *Cohousing,* chap. 4.

10. Described in chap. 10.

11. For a discussion of sustainable energy strategies for developing nations, see Nicholas Lensser, "Providing Energy in Developing Countries" in *The State of the World 1993,* ed. Linda Starke (New York: Norton, 1993), 101–119.

12. R. D. Laing, *The Politics of Experience* (New York: Ballantine, 1967), 190.

13. Deuteronomy 30:19.

14. Proverbs 29:18.

15. Shaw, *Selected Plays* (New York: Dodd, Mead, 1949), 7.

Afterword: Urgency in an Organic Context

1. Working Assets ad, *Utne Reader,* May–June 1990, 31.

2. *E* magazine, September 1990, 62.

3. Edward T. Hall, *The Dance of Life* (New York: Doubleday, 1983), 118.

4. Much of this discussion is drawn from Jeremy Rifkin, *Time Wars* (New York: Holt, 1987).

5. "The time-poor are made to wait, while the temporally privileged are waited upon" (*Time Wars,* 196).

6. I am of course describing changes in the Western perception of time. Different cultures are believed by anthropologists to understand time differently. Much of the impact of colonialism as well as much international misunderstanding can be attributed to different time systems (see *The Dance of Life,* part 1).

7. Rifkin points out that those holding to an ecological vision "believe that social and economic tempos must be reintegrated with the natural tempos of

the environment if the ecosystem is to heal itself and become a vibrant, living organism once again" (*Time Wars*, 200).

8. Rifkin calls for a "democratization of time," establishing what he terms "emphathetic time," in which the "emphasis is on reestablishing a temporal communion with the natural biological and physical rhythms and on coexisting in harmony with the cycles, seasons, and periodicities of the larger earth organism" (*Time Wars*, 199).

9. Kirkpatrick Sale writes that "the bioregional vision . . . has the virtue of *gradualism*. It suggests that the processes of change—first of organizing, educating, activating a constituency, and then of reimagining, reshaping, and recreating a continent—are slow, steady, continuous, and methodical, not revolutionary or cataclysmic. . . . [We must] begin the gradual process, since we know it has to be gradual, with all due speed and commitment" (*Dwellers in the Land*, 176-177).

INDEX

ABOUT THE AUTHOR

Daniel A. Coleman founded the North Carolina affiliate of the Green movement and worked on the Greens' national platform. In Chapel Hill he has done grassroots organizing and participated in election campaigns on behalf of local Green candidates and environmental initiatives. He was a founding editor of *The Prism,* a grassroots newspaper in Chapel Hill. This is his first book.